THE RELUCTANT
LEADER

Own Your Responsibility with Courage

Cherie,
Thank you for using me
as a resource on how to
be a great Leader.
   Enjoy Jocelyn's Story.

Author **Ron Rael**

Ron Rael

2018

Acknowledgments

In any major endeavor, there are contributors who commit to the cause and add value. I give a shout out to the High Road™ Institute team of Darcy Juarez and Michelle Cash who take care of those vital details so that I can write, travel, and speak.

I commend Wilene Dunn for inspiring me to retain my vison for this book and dispensed pep talks whenever I needed them.

I thank my CEO Mastermind Team all who offered encouragement, acknowledgement, and advice. Bravo to Dino Guzzetti, Dan Faulkner, Nate Bean, Debbie Rosemont, Abby Durr, Matt Baker, Pia Cohen Larson, and Samira Badshaw.

I appreciate the selected panel of peers who provided insight and crucial comments on the first draft. You all helped make this product better. Thank you Ann Amati, Scott Auer, Dr. Carrie Babcox, Tom Brasberger, Michael Buschmohle, Bonnie Cox, Robert Fox, Karen Jett, Lynn LaSof, Jim Lindell, Art Pulis, Ken Tysiac, Hayden Williams, Peggy Wolff, and Eric Wukitsch.

This book would not have been possible without the love and support of my book writers Mastermind Team of Fran Fisher, Toolie Gardner, and Emiko Hori.

Most of all, I owe a debt of gratitude to the one person of infinite patience who provides me with loving support each day. Here's to you Ann!

Dedication

This book is dedicated to each Reluctant Leader© whom I have met on my journey.

CONTENTS:

Introduction

This Book Is about You and for You

Even if you do not currently define yourself as a leader, your interest in this book tells me you desire to make a difference, something that all true leaders aspire to do. Every individual has the capacity to lead. This book is designed to rekindle your desire to make a difference as well as empower you into growing from a Reluctant Leader into a competent and courageous one. It will encourage you to become someone of note who owns the obligation to fill the world with competent influencers for today and tomorrow.

For the purposes of this book I use the term *High Road* to define the highest ideals and characteristics for the sort of individual I would be proud to follow. A High Road[1] Leader is a person worth following and is described as:

- A person of great integrity
- A lifelong learner
- Able to create a vision
- Accountable
- Competent
- Consistent
- Credible
- Enthusiastic
- Ethical
- Focused
- Honest
- Inspiring
- Results-driven
- Self-driven
- Tirelessly persistent

---

[1] High Road is a registered trademark of Ron Rael and The High Road Institute

These traits, when combined, produce an outstanding and true High Road Leader, yet *no single person has all these traits.*

The Impact of Leadership

In a group and organizational setting, leadership has an impact. When a group accomplishes a great milestone or victory, the catalyst for this success can be traced to the leadership. Conversely, when a company goes bankrupt, and shareholders, employees, and suppliers get financially harmed, the causes can be traced to its leadership. The reason behind this reality serves as the first lesson about your impact and responsibility, and is the **1st Natural Law of Leadership.**

> **The success and failure of any nation, state, organization, and/or team is dependent on the quality of its leadership.**

The Cost of Neglecting Leadership

In business, government, education, healthcare, religion, and elsewhere—even in our families—are many people who hold a 'leadership position' but are, in reality, pretending to be leaders and are wreaking havoc on the things and people they manage. You can never assume that the person with a leader-like title or position is the genuine article. Most, if not all, widespread challenges are caused by poor leadership. Pick your choice of any lingering, intractable, and costly issue we face today, such as:

- The ever-rising costs of healthcare and education, which are producing less-than-optimal outcomes as they approach a tipping point where the cost will far exceed any benefit
- The insatiable demand for higher profits and stock valuation that leads to fraud, exorbitant CEO salaries, outsourcing of high-paying jobs, and lingering unemployment

- The poverty and famine that lead to war conditions, and the billions spent on weapons of war
- The *us vs. them, I win-you lose* mentality of politics that creates constant fights over taxes, spending, and benefits for our elderly, the poor, and our children
- The big brother-like monitoring of all personal communication as an excuse to protect the nation from terrorists
- The ever-rising cost of around-the-clock care of aging, disabled parents that seems to be out of reach for most middle-class families
- The neglect of this nation's children in the areas of adequate education, nutrition, or safety
- Business executives who are awarded with a bonus, while the company is laying off employees

All of these are caused by people currently holding leadership positions but who are not behaving as a true leader would. These situations and others are why many leadership experts believe we have a crisis in leadership.

The primary cause of the shortage of courageous, caring, ethical, and compassionate leaders is this: *Many people who hold a position of leadership fail to see themselves as leaders.* Because of this, they do not know how to behave and serve when leading a group of people. I would confidently estimate that as much as 70 percent of individuals who, as an aspect of their job duties, meet the traditional definition of 'leader' do not define themselves as one. They lack the full understanding of the vast expectations placed upon them to lead.

Despite their title or position, these individuals do not act as and thus don't serve as true leaders. To me what is most alarming is that these individuals (maybe it's you) could have significantly greater impact on their realm of influence if they (you) chose to redefine themselves as a true leader.

Before introducing a solution that will enable you to have a positive impact as a leader within your team and company, I

will lay a foundation so you have a greater understanding of why leading others is important to your own success as a person and a professional.

Leadership Defined

Leadership is about having followers.[2] Leadership is an influencing process and occurs *between* people. Successful leadership depends on the *perception of the follower* more than on the leader's skills and abilities. Leadership is a dual relationship, a special trust between you and your followers.

Leading others successfully is both an art and a science. Imagine that I just hired you to head up a newly formed department. I give you a leadership title, authorize a budget to you, and assign a team to work for you. I send you to our internal leadership training program and suggest books to study. My providing those elements—and assuming you follow through—fulfills the science of leading. Ultimately, your ability to inspire the people you supervise and to obtain profitable and personable results with them and through them depends on your ability to master the art of leading.

Understanding this obligation leads to our next truism, the **2nd Natural Law of Leadership.**

> **Leadership is much more about the people you lead than it is about you. If you do not know how to lead, you will be unable to bring forth the full potential of your followers.**

Does your job require that you get things accomplished using other people's talents?

Do you want people to follow you to a specific destination even though the way there is unclear?

---

[2] Definition of Leadership developed by Ron Rael and High Road Institute

Do you aspire to bring out the best in the people you work with?

If you answered 'yes' to at least one of those questions, you are a leader, even if you do not apply that label to yourself. A 'yes' answer also means you need to master the intangible, softer side of taking charge, which is the art of leading. This expansive knowledge is acquired by doing the work and, of course, learning from your successes and inevitable mistakes.

Look at Me!

A mistake I made in my first position as a leader was when I made it all about *me*. I was now the one *in control and in charge*. I acted like a peacock, strutting around, silently saying, "Pay attention to me! Follow the leader!" I could not figure out why my team didn't care about the things I wanted and needed them to pay attention to. It was like I was herding cats and babysitting infants at the same time. Then, on my ninetieth day as 'leader,' after getting a miserable performance review from my boss (who did know how to lead well), a light bulb went off in my head: Being a leader is about focusing solely on the individuals on my team. My job and sole responsibility were to be there for them so that they could do their jobs successfully. I recall the catalyst was a sheet of paper my boss handed me. On it was a quotation by Tom Peters: "The job of the leader is to get the silly BS out of the way and let the troops get on with the job."

In that moment of introspection I discovered the meaning of this 2nd law, which reminds you (as it did me) that the quality of your leadership is not defined by you; it is defined by the people who follow your example. True leadership is the impact that *you have* on your followers, which creates their perception, if you are capable of leading them. You can claim "I am a leader!" yet the true test of whether you are or are not rests in the opinions of those you impact through your intentions, actions, and words. That is why leading successfully depends on the perceptions others have about you. To convert their perceptions or judgments that you can lead into fact is when you consistently respond as a true leader should and you take your leadership responsibilities seriously.

A Leader's Overall Responsibilities

The person who becomes a leader has a desire to make things happen with other people. The effective leader develops the habit of doing things that others don't like to do. Every leader must lead with his or her heart, mind, and soul. Using a balance of caring and power, everyone who has a leadership role can and must be the catalyst for positive change. Because a leader is the main and most visible communicator of values and morals in his or her organization and team, a leader needs to be highly self-aware of his or her limitations, influence, and message.

Organizational leaders, through their attitudes, behaviors, and beliefs, have the ability to make or break the fortunes of the investors, employees, and business partners. Because of this influence, leaders must understand their power and wield it wisely. The best leaders are those who know they personally do not have all of the answers and thus rely on coaches, mentors, and synergy to create something beneficial.

To be successful today, leaders must have integrity. With integrity, their brand is enhanced, employees trust them, and customers return to buy more. Without integrity, the leader loses all credibility and becomes an empty shell spouting meaningless slogans. To be powerful and influential, leaders must view their decisions and actions within the context of the employees' desires, the stockholders' needs, the customers' concerns, and society's demands. Without this *inside-out vision* and the ability to execute their plans, a leader becomes a mere bureaucrat.

Leaders impact the lives of others and the world as a whole, so they must be vigilant to their role, talents, and influence. If the leader opts out of this obligation, he or she cannot wield the most powerful tools available: *presence and example*. This is why mastering the art of leadership is critical to your success.

An organization is successful when all of its existing and emerging leaders use the organization's mission as their guide. This overarching purpose inspires the employees, who manage the resources. The resources become the foundation for a viable business, which generates profits, which in turn sustain the business. Without all of these necessary elements in place, the business or organization will never live up to its full potential.

Since change is constant, every one of the elements of organizational success (ideas, employees, resources) will degenerate into chaos without sufficient attention. This creates the need for today's leader to be a frontline agent of positive change. A leader's role is to engage and inspire his or her team and those around them to offer novel ideas and implement creative solutions. Therefore, the cultivation of leadership talent is necessary to leapfrog the competition and survive the ups and downs caused by today's dynamic, interconnected world. Knowing what to change and what to leave alone is the art of leading.

Yikes! Leadership is all that and more! Perhaps this is why there are so many people today who are reluctant to lead or take charge.

The Reluctant Leader[3]

What is a reluctant leader?

The Reluctant Leader© can best be defined by understanding how most people end up in a leadership role.

How Leaders Become Leaders

"Mommy, I am going to be a fireman!"

"When I grow up I want to teach."

"My high school counselor told me the aptitude test predicts I would make either a good minister or musician."

"When I graduate from college, I plan to build things."

"I want to be a doctor."

Do you remember making statements such as these whenever an adult asked that funny and hard-to-answer question: *What do you want to be when you grow up?*

Do you recall the many careers or roles that you thought you might have as an adult? Do you remember ever saying this: *When I grow up, I want to be a leader?*

As children, none of us said that we wanted to become a leader. Yet in pursuing our dreams (or a paycheck) we became leaders anyway, not necessarily because we wanted to, but as a direct and natural result of a synergy between our efforts to realize our dreams and the intrinsic qualities of leadership within ourselves.

How does the typical person get into a leadership role? They enter through the leadership door.

---

[3] The Reluctant Leader is copyright of Ron Rael and The High Road Institute

Leadership Door[©]

I use the Leadership Door[4] as an image and symbol to explain how you advance from being a follower to a leader. Assume there's a room you need to enter and the door to it is shut. *How do you get into that room?* Simply open the door and walk across the threshold, right? Not always.

Option A – Being Pushed

Universally, this is how a majority of people become a leader. You selected a field that appealed to you or looked lucrative. You pursued a career in it and accomplished a lot. The people around you saw that you had a special 'star' quality that others lacked. Then, you were invited or instructed that you could *or would* be a leader.

Option B – Walking In

A smaller number of us did not wait for someone else to recognize this drive or desire. If you are like me, you saw what it took to be a leader and you invited yourself through the leadership door. You became a leader because you saw a door as an opportunity and proceeded to walk through one.

---

[4] Leadership Door is copyright of Ron Rael and The High Road Institute

LEADERSHIP DOOR

Many were pushed through this door and became leaders out of necessity because of an emergency, a boss's maternity leave, rapid and unexpected business growth, or another reason, such as your track record of accomplishments in your chosen field. Many stumbled through that door, not knowing what to expect and, even worse, not understanding what was expected of them.

This leadership door is available to everyone and opens constantly. Throughout your life you will be in situations where you need to serve as a leader for an hour, a day, a month, a year, or a career. This book is designed to give you the confidence to lead others whenever the leadership door opens for you.

Anyone Can Fill a Leadership Void

Everyone will find themselves in a position of guiding others at least once in their lifetime. This opportunity (or curse, to some) often arises when there is a void in leadership. The opportunity could occur because of:

- A promotion
- An early departure of a boss
- A temporary or pressing need
- A committee or team membership
- A crisis
- A death
- Someone's inability to be effective
- Other people's unwillingness to take charge
- Your track record of accomplishments
- You are the smartest person in the room
- You raised your hand at the wrong time!

Even though most individuals have the potential to be a leader under the right conditions, an employer cannot always find someone to step up and serve as a true leader. Whether you were shoved or invited through that leadership door, you were likely ill-equipped to lead others, which then begets disastrous and embarrassing situations. Others see you falling on your face and think, "You won't catch me volunteering to take charge of anything." Word spreads that people are unhappy with your leadership 'style' and so they refuse to support and cooperate with you. You believe you're a failure and want to give up this leadership thing because it's "too hard." You get fired for not "sufficiently motivating your people." No wonder you and your coworkers sit on your hands whenever someone in management comes around and announces, "I need someone to..."

The questions that employers frequently ask are: *Why are my employees NOT stepping up as leaders, even when the need is obvious?* Notice that these are really complaints rather than questions. Notice the cause-and-effect pattern:

Causes = promotion without training and support, and sink-or-swim conditions; Effects = inability to lead well, and no more volunteers

The Challenges Ahead for Convincing Employees to Lead

In 2014, the Center for Creative Leadership (CCL) issued a report titled *Future Trends in Leadership Development*.[5] The CCL researcher, Nick Petrie, used a year-long sabbatical from Harvard to research the current approaches for developing leaders and determining what the future holds for this vital endeavor.

Based on his team's research and numerous interviews of leadership experts, Petrie identified four trends which will impact your organization as you attempt to turn reluctant leaders into inspiring ones.

Trend #1 – The development of both new and seasoned leaders is moving from a 'horizontal' development method which focuses solely on competencies, to a 'vertical' development where leaders develop in stages. Vertical leader development is a process where the individual who wishes to improve must earn what he/she needs, whereas horizontal leader development relies on an expert to explain how to lead.

Trend #2 – To have great leaders tomorrow, the existing leadership body must find new ways to move the employees "out of the passenger seat and into the driver's seat" of their own leadership development. Companies will no longer rely on one department—i.e., Human Resources—to provide the development experiences needed by tomorrow's leaders.

Trend #3 – The focus of leadership training and development will not be directed toward those who are already leading, but

---

[5] *Future Trends in Leadership Development Whitepaper* ©2014 Center for Creative Leadership

instead will be designed as a collective process spread throughout networks of people. The question of leader development moves from answering "Who are our leaders?" to answering "What can we do for leadership to flourish in the network and expand the system's capability to develop even more leaders?"

Trend #4 – Businesses and other arenas that require good leaders are moving into an era of rapid innovation. Therefore, organizations must experiment with new approaches which collect and combine diverse ideas in new ways, and they must quickly share those within the leadership collective.

You Will Survive Falling Down

No leader is perfect because all leaders are human and because the quality of leading is in the minds and hearts of a leader's followers. Every leader has his or her own flaws and less-than-flattering characteristics, which by nature would render the person less effective. However, research has proven repeatedly that the individuals whom we honor with the title of 'great leader' use their positive traits in positive ways and work hard at not letting their flaws or detriments undermine their ability to take people to a better place.

The hallmark of a High Road Leader is that *you have a positive influence on people even when you are not in the room.*

Leadership is a broad topic; therefore, to narrow down why this book is written about you and for you, we explore the 3rd **Natural Law of Leadership.**

Leadership always occurs within a specific context.

Context is the framework describing why a topic and/or issue exist. The meaning of this third truism is that leadership is defined by the conditions and surroundings in which it occurs. Each context defines the form of leadership required, and every context or situation requires a different form of leadership.

Context for Your Leadership Role

There is always a purpose or role behind the reason you either will become or already have become a leader. If you find this confusing, use the following analogy: You desire a family and find a suitable mate. Then you desire children and you become a parent with this mate. One day you wake up to discover that you have become a leader in a family unit.

The context surrounding leadership is that you are or will be fulfilling a role that is vital to your organization's success and longevity (e.g., CEO, VP, manager, supervisor, director, shift lead, team leader, and entrepreneur). You wake up to discover that you have become a leader. You entered through the leadership door. The people around you expect you to lead them, which is scary because this was probably NOT your primary objective or at least NOT what you were trained to do. You either define yourself, or others see you, as a Reluctant Leader.

Since leadership occurs within a particular context, I define six of them, which are the focus of this book.

- You are a leader
- You wish to become a leader
- You will soon be a leader, whether or not by choice
- You would like to enhance both your skills and talent as a leader
- You are a professional and want to make a difference
- You recognize the importance of quality leadership in your company and profession

The Drama of Business[6]

If it was not for the Drama of Business©, there would be no need for MBAs, or consultants who dispense advice on how to successfully manage, lead, and run a business. No matter what your organization sells or delivers, it would not exist without people. People thrive on drama. People are unpredictable. People do the unexpected. People do and say things that foster needless drama.

Leading an organization means that you must not allow the drama of business to interfere with your drive for success.

The true leader knows you don't get rid of the drama; rather, you manage it and use this human energy for positive purposes. This is another example of the art of leading.

Leaders Who Are Not Leading

Nearly every day I observe and work with people who have a leadership title or a leader position on an organization chart, but they are not a 'true leader.' This individual has yet to understand the full spectrum of leading. I stated already that as many as 70 percent of people in a leadership position or role do not own the role and its responsibilities. While this number cannot be measured by nose count, it can be measured by the problems these reluctant, inexperienced, and clueless leaders create.

To help you see the path that allows you to walk through the leadership door and lead boldly, I created a fable about Joslyn, the Reluctant Leader. Joslyn is a composite of numerous reluctant leaders whom I have coached since 1984. Her situation is quite common. The fact that she holds the position as CEO of a major company does not ensure that she a) knows how to lead well, or b) is effective in her role as a leader. People who hold a leadership position and do not act as a leader often harm their own careers, their organizations, and the people they work with.

---

[6] The Drama of Business is copyright of Ron Rael and The High Road Institute

Why is there a lack of people committed to mastering and practicing the art of leadership? From my experiences as a leadership coach, I share two of the primary reasons.

Holistic View of Results

The first reason has to do with the total package of results that a leader is judged on. In Joslyn's case, she produces profits and growth, but to the detriment of the employees, the company culture, and the organization. Many leaders in all walks of life are like Joslyn: They are promoted to a position of leadership because of a singular talent and ability, and then they are evaluated solely on those results, as Joslyn was prior to her boss's intervention. However, once you step back and take a holistic view of the entire impact that the leader has, you will clearly see evidence that he or she is a Reluctant Leader.

I suggest ways to holistically evaluate a leader's effectiveness in the final chapter of this book.

Cause and Effect

There's a truism about life: *you get what you ask for.* A related expression is *you get what you pay for.* Because we have not paid ample attention to or devoted resources to developing resourceful, courageous, and ethical leaders, we now have a situation in the United States and indeed throughout the world where quality leadership is severely lacking.

Of all the individuals whose characteristics I used to create this book's main protagonist, Joslyn, none of them had any leadership training. Yet they held positions as executive director, president, senior executive, VP of marketing, CEO, CFO, manager, and even chairman of the board.

Not long ago, organizations took time to develop and invest in their future leaders, instilling them with values that led to high integrity, ethical results, and win-win outcomes. For a number of reasons we now undermine ourselves when it comes to high-quality leadership. One very evident cause is our obsessive focus on short-term profits, leading to constant cost-cutting, inadequate training, over-reliance on technology, and a focus on processes instead of people. A second cause is that we allow affiliations like political parties, nationalities, and religious designations to create divisions and separations that lead to self-righteous goals.

This last cause is extremely wasteful of resources and energy because of the **4th Natural Law of Leadership.**

> **When people fight amongst themselves**
> **they cannot think and act strategically**
> **or globally. When people fail to share**
> **the same mission, they waste resources**
> **and become overly self-focused.**

It's a simple case of cause and effect.

A True Fable

The fable about Joslyn is unique because I delve into the drama of business and the art of leadership. As you read it, you might not be able to anticipate what comes next, because that is how real life operates. I hope you notice how the coach uses Joslyn's self-created drama to help her transform herself from reluctant to inspirational.

Nearly every person who has written about leadership has their own descriptor to define the absolute best leader. Adjectives used to describe this honorable and worthy person range from the Extraordinary Leader to the Level 5 Leader, from the Influential Leader to the Principled Leader, from the Heroic Leader to the Resonant Leader, and from the Contrarian Leader to the Positive Leader. These labels, applied to leading with excellence, describe an ideal for the individual who leads people, teams, and organizations.

My intention in sharing this tale based on true events is to let you see yourself through Joslyn's eyes. You will walk in her shoes (varied and quite expensive!) as you read her story and will soon be engaged in your own learning as Joslyn begins to master the art of true leadership.

Our Experiences Matter

You might wonder why I am qualified to offer advice on how to be a better, less-reluctant leader. I started my journey to understand leadership when I entered the dynamic business world as an entry-level employee in 1968 and worked my way up the ladder to become CEO. I held positions of leadership—formal and informal—working for others and for myself. I experienced the hurt and damage caused by untrained and unqualified leaders. Since 1988, I have had the honor of meeting with, observing, and listening to more than 10,000 US and Canadian mid-level managers and senior executives who shared their stories, victories, and disasters.

During this period of hands-on empirical research, I authored 17 books and more than 50 workshops on the skills leaders need to be successful and effective.

As to my own leadership development strategy, it was not planned or organized. My development was vertical (experiential) rather than horizontal (competency-based). However, if you ask my friends and colleagues to describe how I learned to be a leader, they would say, "He's self-taught and self-motivated." I attribute this label to the fact that most of my important lessons came from leading the wrong ways, making mistakes, and recovering from them.

These experiences and milestones are simply fuel to the passion in my heart to help every leader improve and be successful. I want to improve the world of commerce and trade, and I know that the only way to do this is by developing better leaders. Two people keep my vision and passion alive: my grandchildren, who will soon inherit the world we are in charge of. I am very dissatisfied with the messes we leave to the next generations. Therefore, each day I do my part to leave them a better legacy.

Who knows? Maybe one day one or both of them will choose to walk through that leadership door.

Act Now!

By reading this book, you are committing to having an impact and making a positive shift. I encourage you to use this book to develop a *Personal Leadership Action Plan*. This plan or roadmap will help you uncover opportunities to walk through the leadership door so that you practice the art of leading. Internalize the lessons Joslyn has to learn. Think about how you too can transform yourself as you learn how she travels quickly from a person with a leadership title and a natural reluctance to lead toward being a confident and capable High Road leader.

Thank you for being a part of the solution that will eventually overcome our growing crisis in leadership.

Namaste.

Ron

Chapter 1
The Need or Desire to Lead

*"Why should I care about leadership? I have a
business to run and a board to satisfy!"*

She threw this defensive question at me the moment I entered her office. As I strode toward her, I noticed the sunlight streaming in the west-facing window and the sweet aroma of fresh-cut flowers on the oversized maple desk where she sat, staring at me. I took in a well-dressed professional clad in a powder-blue wool suit, a lilac silk blouse, and flawlessly coifed blond hair, sitting with three cups of cold coffee in front of her.

Joslyn stood but nearly refused to shake my hand. I did earn a forced smile and curt hand. I could feel tension radiating in her body through her arm. Since she was obviously upset about something, I stifled the temptation to deliver a flippant answer: *You just answered your own question.*

"Thanks for seeing me on such short notice," she said tersely, as we sat across from one another. The huge yellow roses took up half the table between us. The seating arrangement sent me a strong message: *This is my territory, and you are the interloper.* She wanted me to know who was in charge.

"I know you are very busy and I promise not to take too much of your *valuable* time," she said, not bothering to disguise the sarcastic tone.

"We have as much time as you need. It's a pleasure to finally meet you, Joslyn. Stephen speaks highly of you. Just start at the beginning. Please tell me what's on your mind."

"I don't know how much Stephen, our board chair, told you, but I think I've lost my credibility somehow. I am sensing that I am about to be canned, yet I can't imagine WHY. I took *their* company from a struggling also-ran to a $7 billion market leader in less than three years. I sense the board or maybe some influential shareholders don't have confidence in me anymore. Stephen, the one person I can confide in, strongly urged me to see you. He must think I am a poor leader to suggest being coached by you."

I could feel the deep ache in her pride as she admitted this. Her lightly rouged cheeks turned bright red as she looked down at the table. Then she turned to her laptop, ignoring me.

An Initial Evaluation of Joslyn

I recalled the bio and CV Stephen had sent me the previous week. Joslyn was highly intelligent, earning her MBA from Stanford, where she graduated in the top five percent. She had an enviable track record of success, starting from a run-of-the-mill sales clerk, then a sales management position, next rising to Vice President of Marketing, and then to Chief Operating Officer. Just by looking at her work summaries, I could see the history of larger team sizes and bigger budgets, along with specific accomplishments. In her twelve years in the industry, each successive job took on greater challenges. She claimed to always accomplish what she set out to do.

Yet I spotted a problem. I would have expected more promotions, but after just a few years at each job, she "left for a better position" or "resigned for personal reasons." I sensed these were subtle clues that she was asked to leave, the kind of thing that a résumé does its best to hide. Stephen told me that in the sales area, she was a risk-taker and a big thinker. *Maybe she took too many risks?*

Sitting across from me was a highly motivated problem-solver who could get things done quickly and effectively. However, it was the way Joslyn went about getting results that was most likely her personal challenge. I would need to determine her leadership Achilles heel quickly. Stephen told me that he thought highly of Joslyn but she was "like a human tornado—

causing havoc wherever she lands." In her four years at Neoteric, he said, Joslyn "went through personal assistants like a person with a runny nose uses tissues." Two talented, tenured Vice Presidents had recently resigned rather than work for her any longer.

The Issue

Stephen is a good friend and a High Road Institute client. He, too, is someone you can count on to deliver bottom-line results, the reason why he was named chairman after only four years with Neoteric Products. When asked to select his replacement as CEO, he chose Joslyn, someone who had proven herself by producing continuous sales growth. However, as Stephen put it, "Joslyn has a hard side. The diplomacy that she showed us in the beginning seemed to evaporate the moment she was promoted to CEO. Maybe I made an error in judgment appointing her." I sensed a bit of regret in his voice.

Stephen then related his concern. "Just when we all should be celebrating because of our meteoric rise from the ashes of near bankruptcy, morale is at an all-time low. A few board members are pressuring me to terminate Joslyn's contract, but I am not willing to give up on her. Can you help us?"

Because he needed a face-saving solution, I promised Stephen that I would meet with Joslyn within the next few days. Normally, we wait for the leader who desires or needs coaching to approach us, but Stephen's concern was real and urgent. Michelle, one of my very tactful assistants, arranged this meeting with her. While I prefer to meet at my office or another neutral location, I thought that visiting Joslyn's office would ease the sting to her pride and provide me with valuable insights about her by observing her in her comfort zone, where she might let me see aspects of her personality she kept hidden.

Joslyn tuned me out for about five minutes, staring at the laptop screen. I couldn't tell if she was being rude or had something on her mind. Impatient on the inside, I sat calmly and waited.

"I see here on your website that you have a different angle on leadership," she said. "I have never seen one quite like this before." *She's checking out my company's website.*

Here is a brief summary of what she saw on our home page:

> *The High Road Institute believes that when people bond over a common purpose, they pull together, but when people fail to have one purpose, they fight each other. This is an example of leading from the High Road, a path that is of vital importance to your firm's success.*

She pointed to the laptop's screen, as if I could see what she was referring to. Then she read aloud, "Common purpose! The High Road! A true leader focuses on the greater good!" I could tell that she was picking out elements of our philosophy regarding today's leaders. She glared at me without speaking.

I hypothesized that she was angry because the content had hit a nerve.

"Are you a preacher? What is this greater good you mention? To me that means nothing! I am supposed to make a difference? *I need to grow sales. Generating profits is what I am good at.*" She noticed her three untouched coffees, paused to sip one, and regained her composure.

She's too busy or too distracted to even drink her coffee. Hmm.

Refusing to be baited into her fight, I sat smiling in response to her scowl. The awkward silence was broken when her mobile phone chirped. She frowned at the screen, pushed the phone a few inches to the side, and then looked back at me. There was a fire blazing behind her eyes.

Joslyn's Resistance

"You seem upset, Joslyn. Even the phone seems to displease you. What is going on? Am I your enemy?"

She breathed deeply, sighing as her shoulders caved in a bit. "I am worried. Angry and upset, actually. The call was from Angela, the Vice Chair of our board. I promised her a report today which I assigned last week to Lauren, my assistant. Then, the *idiot* quit Friday without any notice, and I don't know what she did or didn't accomplish. On top of that, I am in the middle of several fiascos created by my Sales and Marketing team. Lately, all my time goes to fixing problems and picking up the ball that someone else dropped; I've been here since 4:00 a.m. But I will be damned if I tell Angela I don't have the report done. She'll just have to wait in line."

"Joslyn, can we move away from this desk and over to that table? I have a couple of things to show you, and it will be easier if I have space to spread my materials out." Actually this was a tactic to physically move her away from her defensive position so that we could become allies. She then intentionally moved her chair so the sunlight, which streamed through the window behind her, blinded me. *She really likes to make power moves*, I noted. As we arranged ourselves at her side table, I scooted my chair toward her and noticed she leaned to her left, away from me. *I am still the enemy.*

Value of Leadership Coaching

"Many leaders and CEOs like you have engaged me as their coach for two specific reasons. First, they want an honest assessment about who they are or how they are perceived. The second reason is because I always protect their interests in all the work we do together. My goal is to help you feel successful. Would an honest reflection about you be of value? Do you want to know how others see you?" I was entering an area where she would feel threatened and the sooner we got there, the quicker Joslyn would benefit.

She leaned in toward me and whispered, "Yes." It sounded like a question so I didn't react. She repeated it, this time with a little more conviction. "Yes, I do. Or I guess I need to."

"Are you sure you want me to be honest about the person you saw in the mirror this morning?"

She paused then said loudly, "Go ahead!" Like a petulant child, she sat back in her chair and crossed her arms.

"Joslyn, you are a leader. You lead a company, a team, and as a result of your past accomplishments, you lead an industry. However," I said, slowly and deliberately "you do not act like a leader."

Seeing her recoil in her chair, you would have thought I electrocuted her. Knowing she would object, I put my hand out with the universal wait sign. "We have been together for 17 minutes and this is what I have noticed:

- "As CEO you are the human logo of your company. The image I see is surly, abrasive, and very angry. This implies to me that, as a potential customer, Neoteric Products must not want my business.
- "You were curt and dismissive with Brian as he ushered me into your office. According to Stephen, you have gone through three assistants so far this year, and maybe this is why.
- "You work for the entire board, yet when Angela the Vice Chair tries to reach you, she gets ignored. How would you feel if one of your VPs purposely ignored you? You would call him on the carpet, right?"

She nodded noncommittally as she made a sound like "Hmm." I added one more thing to the list.

- "The arrangement you placed us in at your desk conveys to anyone who sits across from you that you are the master, and they are your servant."

"You noticed all that in 17 minutes?" She actually laughed for the first time. It was pleasant, not forced. "What you are saying is that *I am not qualified* to be a CEO!" Joslyn instantly assumed her warrior persona again.

"Your business card and position on Neoteric's organizational chart say you are the CEO, but your behaviors, which are created by your attitude, say otherwise. This may be why the board might be looking to send you packing. They are at this moment wondering if you are the right person for the job. Yes, profits are great and continued sales growth hides many CEO mistakes. However, as the most visible leader you set the tone. The high turnover rate within your team, your employees' lack of accountability, the fact that the VPs don't support you— all these behaviors begin and end with the person assigned to that desk over there." I pointed right at the maple marvel. "You are not serving as a true leader!"

I paused purposely to look out the window as Joslyn needed some time to absorb my words. I could tell my assessment had its intended effect because her reply was given in a shaky voice. "I don't know what to say."

I continued gently. "Unless you can prove from this day forward to the entire board that you are a real leader, then it will be moot as to how much sales growth or profits you deliver. They will use any excuse to look for a CEO who is genuine, someone who by her or his actions—not words or title—proves they have the ability to lead and inspire others."

Joslyn rose swiftly and began to pace. "I guess maybe I do need *some* coaching. Maybe Stephen does have my back, since I haven't heard a word of this before. What do I do?" She stood still, but with tension radiating through her body.

"Can we take a break?" I offered. "Show me where I can get a drink of water, and if you have time could you give me a tour? Then let's return here so I can share with you some information about leadership that will help you immediately."

As Joslyn showed me around Neoteric's main production facility, followed by their sales and administrative offices, I noticed people either ignored her or were extremely deferential to her, seemingly out of fear. I do not think she noticed how employees reacted to her presence. Once back in her lair, she invited me to sit at her side of the work table in a position out of the sun's glare and set our newly refreshed coffees down. It was time to start teaching her what leadership is about. The room was still very warm. For the first time, I heard the faint sound of opera music coming through her wall.

The Need or Desire to Lead

I said, "One aspect of leadership is about skills, such as being a good communicator, knowing how to delegate, and being able to empower people. Another aspect of leadership is about the inner traits that produce visible outcomes." She looked puzzled. I pulled an iPad out of my well-traveled black briefcase. "May I show you a visual of what I mean by your inner leader traits producing visible outcomes?"

She nodded despite appearing somewhat annoyed.

Finding the videos I needed, I positioned the device so she could see it, and hit play. The first video showed a small room filled with Ping-Pong balls on the floor. Each ball rested on a mousetrap. A bright orange Ping-Pong ball was tossed into the room and it landed on one ball which triggered the  trap. The affected ball popped up and landed on another. Instantaneously the whole room was filled with hundreds of balls going everywhere. She was laughing and so was I.

I now had her interest, and to retain it I showed her another video. I pressed play again of a video showing a vintage pinball machine. A hand slowly pulled the plunger backward and released it, setting in motion a

silver ball. The camera followed the ball as it caromed all over the place. As we watched different lights light up and heard accompanying pleasant dings, I asked, "Have you ever played pinball?"

"Yes, as a child I did. Daddy had one in the garage. I think it was a baseball game, and he let us play as a reward for finishing our chores. It was fun, and I got very good at it."

I saw the wistful look in her eyes as she reminisced. *This is good.*

"Now keep those two videos in your mind as I describe one more concept, one less pleasant but it will complete the image I want you to hold onto. An atomic bomb, despite its destructive nature, is really a simple device. A power trigger sets off an explosion which produces neutrons which are fired directly at a closely packed mass of atoms. This collision sets off a chain reaction which produces a tremendous amount of energy." I laughed. "By now you are somewhat confused by these three images but in a second it'll all make sense. I promise."

She silently withheld her judgment.

"These images and analogies are what we are going to cover in this coaching program. As a leader you have some characteristics, which I will refer to as inner traits. These leadership traits, when triggered, will produce outcomes. However, without a beneficial triggering event, your inner traits won't be set in motion. In this coaching program I will take you on a journey that covers multiple character traits of leadership. The first one we will cover today is the triggering device, which is your need or desire to lead. This trigger is like the orange ball that was thrown into the room and impacts the second Ping-Pong ball, which is your leadership energy. This is an important component of your inner leader.

"Once triggered, your energy activates three more Ping-Pong balls or internal characteristics into motion. These are the other three inner leader traits: fostering unity, displaying courage, and having self-awareness. As each of these four internal traits gets activated, just like those Ping-Pong balls, they produce reactions in four more Ping-Pong balls. This second set of four are aspects of your external leader: practicing good stewardship, living your convictions, demonstrating caring and compassion, and experiencing serenity."

She nodded, though I doubted she fully grasped all this at the beginning of her learning curve.

"As your coach, my role is to help you spark and tap into the first four inner traits, which in turn will enable the four external traits to easily show up. Before we can even start, we must help you find your trigger. Stephen provided that when he said to you indirectly *you need to become a better leader.*"

Her face was relaxed so she was keeping up.

"I am sure that you have questions about this, so fire away."

With some hesitance, she asked, "You said I have some inner characteristics. What if I don't have any?"

"I will help you understand that you already have access to them. You would not have gotten this far in business and sales management if you lacked them. Coaching assists you to connect the dots by going from what you have accomplished already to what is required so that you are a more effective executive."

"Okay. I think I understand. Now how do these Ping-Pong balls fit together? How do I say this...do they fit into some sort of pattern? Are they related...connected?"

"Over the next few months," I answered, "as we explore all eight traits, you will grow to understand the various relationships they have with each other. Their relationships are not complicated, but rather like the funny chaos produced by the Ping-Pong balls. Even in slow motion we could not track which ball triggered the other ones. It is simply the act of setting the first one in motion that triggers and becomes a catalyst for the rest, increasing your ability to lead. Nearly every person has an inborn ability to lead, within the right circumstances."

I could tell that she wasn't completely satisfied but Joslyn didn't push it, which let me know that she wanted to trust me. That WAS a good sign. It was time to test if she was ready to improve.

"Do you want to retain your job?"

She nodded without much passion.

"Are you willing to do the work to keep your job?"

She perked up and responded with a quiet "Yes."

"Then do you believe that you must become a better leader if you want to remain the CEO?"

Joslyn took a deep breath, and said very slowly, "Yes. It is painfully clear."

Commitments Required

I took a deep breath to center myself and then said, "Coaching is designed to support you in becoming a good leader. By understanding how to enhance and leverage the eight traits, you will quickly be viewed as a true leader. If you choose to engage me, we will meet every two weeks, and when you reach certain milestones, we can meet less frequently. I will assign specific actions for you to work on, which will accomplish two things: 1) test your ability to apply the skill or trait properly; and 2) spark your own ideas on how to improve."

"Are you trying to change me?" Joslyn inquired skeptically.

"I cannot change or transform anyone. Consider this: In both your role as the CEO and my role as a coach, we can only activate and incentivize change in someone. The person we direct our attention to must want to change and do the work required to be different and better. Do you agree?"

Shrugging her shoulders, she responded, "I guess so. I've tried to get my people to change, without any success."

"Working with someone who says she wants to be better is hard work for both parties. For now, all I ask is that you take this program seriously, commit to doing the work, and commit to applying the lessons you learn. These actions will get you better results and, in the process, you transform. Remember, any and all change must come from within you. Once that occurs, the ways that people react to you will begin to transform also." I paused for effect. "Do you want to improve as a leader, Joslyn?"

I stayed silent as she absorbed the question. This repetition of the question was to test her resolve.

"I guess I had better, because the board will fire me if I don't."

"That answer does not apply to the question I asked. I will rephrase my question: *Do you*, as a CEO, want to improve your ability to lead others? Will it benefit you to improve how and why you lead?"

With a small smile she responded, "Yes, and yes."

"Then I must ask you to commit to working with me for a minimum of twelve months."

She started to object but I put my hand out to get her to stop. "This commitment is required for you to make an emotional investment. It will be easy to backslide into old patterns and habits. Assume that we work together for just a few months. You are fighting against poor leader-like behaviors developed over many years and will naturally succumb to the patterns

PAGE | 32

with which you are comfortable. To help you to get past the urge to return to what is not working, while enhancing the desire to travel a new road as you shift away from outdated mindsets, we need 12 months. At the 10- to 11-month mark you will be able to assess the appropriate level of support necessary so that you do not backslide."

"I guess I can commit to that...that is, assuming I have a job at that point," her voice trailing off.

"Joslyn, even if you do get replaced, I would still work with you on becoming a better leader. Why would I do that? Because even though you have a track record of success in certain areas, you may not get another opportunity to sit in the CEO's chair. Tell me, are you willing to take a lower-level position?"

"No! I like being a CEO, and hope one day to serve in that capacity for a larger public company or, if I stay here, move into Stephen's chair."

"Then you need to commit to working with me for a while. Also, it would be better that you hire a coach out of your own volition rather than having the board select one for you. As of today, I think hiring a coach is a suggestion instead of a mandate."

Again I paused to let her absorb this. "What do you think about this arrangement and our work so far?"

"I *think* I can make the time for it, as long as it doesn't interfere with doing MY DAMN JOB."

We have a ways to go, I thought. *I hope I'm up to the task.*

I chose to ignore this refusal to own her contribution to the problem Stephen outlined, which was: Even though Joslyn is the CEO, she will never be very effective until she becomes a real leader. She is causing harm when she should be helping.

She will face the painful ramifications of her inability to lead and inspire soon enough. In her present state, Joslyn is a Reluctant Leader, one whose title is that of a leader, yet her people are reluctant and unwilling to follow, and she is reluctant and unwilling to lead.

I inquired, "What questions could I answer for you? What concerns do you have?"

The High Road Leader

Waiting a beat, she then asked, "What is *your* definition of a good leader?"

I could tell it was a challenge rather than a question, yet I delivered the line that has become my mantra:

> *A leader who travels the high road is a sincere, multi-layered, complex individual who wants or needs to make a difference as he or she serves the greater good.*

I continued after pausing for effect. "Joslyn, are you ready to become a leader like the one I just described?"

"Honestly, if you had asked me that question in the first half of this meeting, I would have said *Go to hell!* But now, with all that you explained, I believe I have a different answer, which is 'Yes, I am willing to.'"

"I assure you that as we go through this coaching process, you will likely get mad at me and dislike the image you see in the feedback mirror I ask you to 'look into.' The only way for you to kindle the desire to be different is for you to be unhappy with the status quo. I have thick skin and I do not mind being perceived as the bad guy. All I ask is that you remember **The First Rule of Being Human**: The thing you most dislike about the other person is a direct result of how you feel about yourself."

> **The behavior, trait, or characteristic that you intensely dislike in another person is a direct result of how you feel about yourself. Once you determine a better way to embrace that aspect of yourself, this trait will no longer bother you.**

I studied the ceiling for a moment. "Whenever you get upset with me for telling you the truth about you, you are really upset at yourself, because somewhere inside, you already know that you are not being the person you are capable of being. The leader inside of you is trying to get out."

Joslyn's First Assignment

I explained that between coaching sessions she was required to work on assignments or application activities, which were actions that allowed her to apply the assignments and to grow. They would be crafted based on what she was working on, experiences she had, and on sticking points. I warned that she was accountable to me and herself for doing this work. While I would not force her to do the assignments or activities, she would have to pay the cost. The three penalties for not taking the assignments seriously are that I would be disappointed, her improvements would take longer, and Stephen would know she was not improving.

I could tell that she was upset but I knew her anger was about the accountability and not the 'homework.'

Joslyn's first application step was to write about two topics regarding what leadership meant to her. The first assignment was to elaborate on this phrase: *As a leader, I intend to…*

The second assignment was to answer this: *My philosophy of leadership can best be defined as…*

This introspection would assist Joslyn once she got into the hard work of reframing how she defines herself and starts getting in touch with the eight leadership traits. Far too many people in leadership positions never do this self-analysis. They dwell on the perks, the power, or the duties. Because leadership is a calling and not a job title, the person serving as a true leader will benefit by understanding the impact they have on their people and their organization.

The High Cost of Neglecting Leadership

Before we ended this session I thought it vital that Joslyn understand the significant impact that her poor leadership was having on her organization, but I went about explaining this indirectly.

Waiting until she finished taking notes about her assignment, I asked, "What happens if leadership is missing? Have you ever been in a situation where there was not any leadership?"

After a time she replied, "Do you recall several years ago when Seattle had more than fifty days of rain?" I nodded that I did. "My family lives in a community near a small lake which, due to the rains, overflowed its banks. The two creeks that feed it overflowed, too. Soon a channel of water threatened to flood our entire neighborhood. I called the City. They claimed *It's not our problem* and to call the County. I did. Same response, *Not our problem*. I wasn't the only resident panicking and seeking help. No matter whom we contacted, no one wanted to help us. We thought for sure we would have to evacuate. Luckily, the rain stopped and someone thankfully placed sandbags in the low spots. Disaster was averted... yet a lot of money was wasted needlessly and there were several costly lawsuits filed over it. I can imagine how much better things would have been for our community if someone had simply taken charge."

"I understand. Assume that your neighborhood was a business, say Neoteric, in crisis and the leadership was missing in action. No one wants to take charge of quickly finding reasonable solutions, claiming 'It's not my problem!' Do you think that same kind of confusion might exist?"

I believe she anticipated where I was going with this. With tight lips she agreed, and I saw her flinch slightly for what was coming.

"Right now some employees are thinking leadership here at Neoteric is *missing in action*."

She started to protest but I intentionally cut her off.

"You may not think so, but I can tell by observing how employees treat you and act around you. I've experienced many situations like this one. I guarantee that many employees and even members of your own management team are concerned. Some are thinking, *When will a real CEO show up to lead us?*"

"I don't agree with you." She was angry. I had challenged her as far as she was willing to go, and our time was up.

Before we said our goodbyes I asked, "Would you like to be the sort of leader who, 15 years from now, employees say, *Joslyn was exactly the sort of leader we needed to get us where we are today*?"

She thought for a moment. "The obvious answer is yes, but I'll bet this is a test. You are really asking if I want to be remembered as a leader who had a positive impact throughout the organization and not just on profits. Right?"

"You are right on the money. I know that by working together we can help you rapidly improve as a leader because you are a quick study. Please remember to do those application steps. You are accountable for the results you want from coaching."

I was exhausted and wanted to get out of that hot and hostile environment but I stayed cool as I placed my materials into the briefcase and finished off my water. I shook her damp hand and said, "I am looking forward to our first coaching session in two weeks."

Ron's Initial Assessment of Joslyn's Situation

Upon returning to my office I entered the following information into Joslyn's client file.

Joslyn is the archetype of a reluctant leader who does not know how to engage in self-care. She uses her tremendous energy to enhance a 'me' focus instead of an 'us' or 'we' focus. She produces results that are mostly harmful and detrimental to her team and organization. She has the capacity for self-care but doesn't know how to practice it or is afraid of doing it. Either way, she misuses her tremendous energy. My intention in this coaching program is to show her how to convert the positives of her inner self to change the perceived or outer self.

In her coaching program we will follow this formula:

Beliefs → Intentions → Results

By changing her beliefs, Joslyn will alter her intentions so that she is more altruistic and a better outward leader. As a better leader she will produce better results that are focused on inclusion, accountability, and compassion, thus producing greater loyalty and trust in her as a leader.

I will provide her with large doses of feedback so that she can begin to see what she is currently oblivious to. As a leader, she needs to be perceived as a safe haven so that if (when?) employees warm up to her way of leading, they can feel comfortable being honest and sharing their concerns. The beliefs of her inner leader need to be positive and uplifting for the traits of the outer leader to produce positive and uplifting results.

Joslyn is clearly a reluctant leader whom no one wants to follow because she does not know she cannot lead.

Before I put her file away I studied Neoteric's Organization Chart to understand all the players in this unfolding drama.

*****

The Bottom Line of Leadership

Poor leadership costs the average company 7 percent of its annual revenue, so they cannot afford to ignore this. The harm produced by pseudo-leaders includes higher-than-average employee turnover, loss of customers, and deteriorating productivity.[7] Neglecting the quality of leadership hurts profits in three areas:

Employee Turnover: Poor leadership is the reason given by up to 30 percent of people leaving their organizations, according to exit interviews conducted by The Saratoga Institute.

Customer/Client Turnover: Poor leadership negatively impacts employee satisfaction, which in turn negatively impacts customer satisfaction and retention. Research published in *Harvard Business Review* calculated that every 5-point change in employee satisfaction scores caused a 1.3-point change in customer satisfaction scores.

Employee Productivity: Poor leadership leads to poor employee productivity. Research from Ken Blanchard's organization shows that direct report productivity can be improved 5 to 12 percent through better management practices.

Most senior executives instinctively know that leadership impacts their company's bottom line, but they don't place value on the right metrics. Whenever you see high employee and customer turnover or low productivity, you need to observe the ways that your leaders are fostering these expensive problems. However, look in the mirror first to see if you are the seed that has grown into a weed.

---

[7] *Making the Business Case for Leadership Development: The 7% Differential,* The Ken Blanchard Companies, 2011
http://www.kenblanchard.com/img/pub/pdf_Making_the_Business_Case.pdf

NEOTERIC'S ORGANIZATIONAL CHART

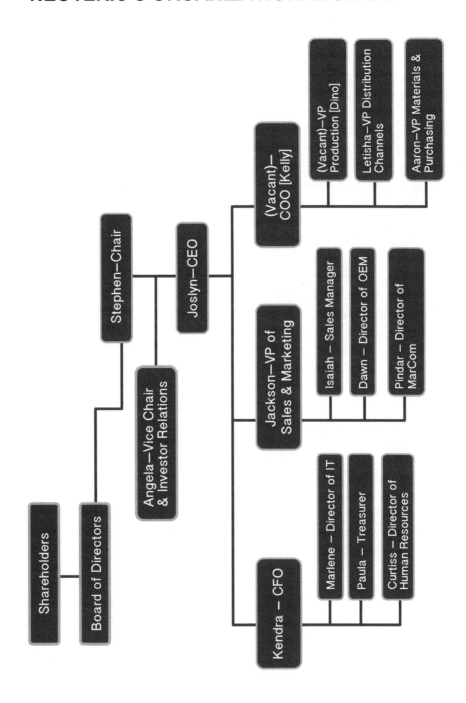

Chapter 2
Leadership Energy

"My intention is to create a great organization."

"Ron…I have been thinking since our first meeting, and…," Joslyn said hesitantly, "I am not sure that I need to change what I am doing. Most likely, I just hired some incompetent employees and if I do a better job of finding the people who will support me, the board won't need to be concerned. Will you help me in selecting them? On the other hand, maybe I should just tell the board to take a hike and let someone else deal with this mess!" Her words came out in a rush.

Two weeks had passed since we first met and when I called to confirm our first session, this is what Joslyn hit me with. I was not going to let her off the hook. My primary intention with Joslyn was clear. In order to assist her in finding her inner leader, I would need to take her through the five stages of grief. She was now going to fight me at every turn because she believed that her ineffective leadership was not the issue and she was not the cause of employee turnover and disloyalty. My intuition told me that the Peter Principle was in play and that Joslyn had fallen into that trap the moment she was promoted to CEO.

Like everyone who faces the need to step up their leadership game, Joslyn would be experiencing what she perceived as arrows in her pride, specifically a loss of face, paint on her prestige, and conflicts in her carefully crafted image. Her pride would tell her she was perfect and that those on the lower rungs of the corporate ladder needed fixing. Her ego would convince her that the people who worked for her were to blame.

Innate Refusal to See the Problem

People in a leadership position usually rise to that stature because of their competence and through their motivators or inner drivers of accomplishment, contribution, challenge, competency, influence, and power. Satisfying each of these motivators requires the person to have a high sense of self-worth, self-esteem, or ego. Having an above-average level of self-opinion is noble and valuable; however, a person in a leadership position often lets their ego blind them to truth and reality. In Joslyn's case, she had reached the point in her career where her abilities at managing and leading people were insufficient to the task. Yet she had a self-imposed blindness and resisted anyone telling her that she had a problem, similar to an addict denying they have an abuse problem.

As Joslyn begins to truly accept the reality of her situation and realizes she does not know how to lead an organization, she will begin to grow as a leader. She will become stronger and her denial will slowly fade away. However, as I move forward with Joslyn, all the frustrations she has been stuffing inside for some time will surface.

Peter Principle

The Peter Principle is the belief that a person who excels at their position is often rewarded with a higher position, eventually one that exceeds the employee's field of expertise. This phenomenon is an observation put forth in the late 1960s by Dr. Laurence J. Peter, a psychologist and professor of education. Dr. Peter wrote, "In a hierarchically structured administration, people tend to be promoted up to their level of incompetence," or, as he went on to explain in simpler terms, "The cream rises until it sours." The study of this yet-to-be proven hypothesis has even found its way into Masters of Business Administration curriculum.

Some "leaders" who are not the genuine article are promoted to a leadership slot because of an expertise, accomplishment, or tenure. However, this common business practice lends credence to the belief that almost anyone in management can rise to a level beyond their competence. This is a primary reason that true leaders know that they do not have all the answers, rely on other's wisdom, and commit to life-long learning.

First Coaching Session

Being an action-oriented person, Joslyn needed to be in motion. Because we would be addressing her emotional state today, I believed that a meeting in an open environment where she would not feel constrained was best. We met at an urban park with a walking path and numerous benches. It was 72 degrees and sunny when I arrived to stake out a bench for us. The smell of freshly cut grass filled the air as birds chirped and sang.

As she approached the bench, I noticed that Joslyn was dressed in black from head to foot, as if in mourning. The slacks matched her blouse and sweater; even her shoes were black. With her long blonde hair in a ponytail, she could be mistaken for a college student. Greeting me warily, Joslyn sat carefully on the bench and stared out at the 50-foot pines in the park's center. "This looks like a nice place for a private meeting." With her eyes hidden behind sunglasses, I couldn't tell if she was telling the truth or being ironic. We sat in silence while I took in a measurement of her mood.

"How are you today, Joslyn? Are you ready to work?"

She dropped her expensive-looking black attaché on the bench as she asked, "Why are we doing this? I think I am doing a good job as the CEO and a part of me doesn't care what the board thinks. I work for the shareholders and they are happy. Our stock's resale price is now at an all-time high."

She is definitely in denial, I thought as I readied my response. "Joslyn, can you tell me what these CEOs have in common: Leo Apotheker of Hewlett Packard, Bill Perez of Nike, and Jeff Kindler of Pfizer?"

"Other than being the CEO of a public company, I cannot think of a connection. Did they all graduate from the same university?"

Smiling I said, "Each of these accomplished senior executives was terminated for the same reason. Despite proving that they could boost profits, all of them were shown the door because they were not being the leaders they needed to be. Leo, described as visionary, was a poor communicator and was unable to carry out his good ideas. Bill, despite contributing to S.C. Johnson's growth in his prior job, was unable to fit into Nike's culture where employees are trusted and empowered to 'Just Do It' without asking for permission. Jeff, described as a bright man with fresh ideas, acted like a dictator, belittling his subordinates, being constantly confrontational, and worse, not trusting his employees." I noticed that she flinched when I mentioned these behaviors, because she was guilty of them, too. "Their track records of accomplishment allowed their boards to overlook the bad behavior, but eventually it became apparent that they were unfit for the job."

"Are you trying to tell me something, Ron?" she said in a sarcastic tone.

"Up until recently, CEOs and other senior executives were given a free pass on unprofessional behaviors and confrontational attitudes as long as they made their companies profitable. Today, however, both senior and junior leaders who exhibit traits that are overly aggressive, dictatorial, and that create tension and turmoil are losing their jobs. Boards are saying, through these terminations, that these behaviors are not acceptable. Today's leader is expected to bring people together to work interdependently for a common purpose. By creating a desirable work environment, the organization automatically becomes profitable and financially viable."

I noticed several young boys kicking a soccer ball in the park. "In other words," I said, "Today's leader must have and use skills that build people up, not tear them down." I paused to let this sink in. "What does this have to do with your situation? More specifically, you asked me *why should I care about leadership.* How would you answer your own question?"

She stood up and started to pace.

"Let's walk and talk," I suggested, as this would allow her to think clearly. We walked about 100 yards before she spoke.

"I believe you are suggesting that I need to be less bottom-line oriented."

"That's a start, but it goes deeper than that."

"The board, according to your examples, wants me to be more people-friendly?" She turned her frowning face to the sun and stood still.

"No, that's not it. I sense that you are guessing. Please think about why these CEOs were given the axe. Not only is a CEO termination a major embarrassment to the CEO, it's also a black eye to a major public company because of the negative press, shareholder concern, and regulatory paperwork involved. What message is the board sending to the unemployed CEO?"

Walking again and picking up her pace, Joslyn stared at the cinder path. "If I were the board, I am sending this message: 'Mr. CEO, you are not living up to our expectations.'"

"What are those expectations?" I probed.

"That is what I cannot figure out." She sighed loudly and headed back to our bench.

"Let's go over your assignment, and I believe you will soon know what they expect. I asked you to write out your leadership intention." Joslyn leaned over to reach into her case and pulled out a black notebook. I was surprised and pleased that she had done the homework.

Reading from her notes, she recited in a monotone voice, "This is what I wrote: *My leadership intention is to make this company profitable and do whatever it takes to grow sales.*"

"Is there anything else?" I did my best to hide the disappointment I felt.

In a flat voice, Joslyn again read from the notebook:

> *My business intention is to have a company where people want to work and are willing to work to get the job done, satisfying and doing our best for our customers as well as being profitable. I hope or dream that it would be a fun place for people to work and as a result, they want to stay and contribute. As for me, my intention is to have a job that I am good at, as I push the company to reach its full potential.*

"That's all I thought of. Wasn't this what you wanted?"

"Yes and no. There is a café at the west edge of this park; let's head over there as I explain what a leader's intention is about and why yours needs expanding."

Inner Leader Trait – Intention Energy

"Do you recall the video I showed of the Ping-Pong balls and how the orange one started the release of the rest by hitting only one white ball?"

"Yes."

I handed her an orange ball with the number **1** written on it. She examined it casually.

"Today, we will explore that first ball, which is an inner trait. No one but you can experience it, yet it is so powerful that it will generate energy within your organization and all its employees. This first leadership trait is important to your success as a leader and vital as the CEO.

We begin your understanding with the **5th Natural Law of Leadership**."

> **When we have a common enemy,**
> **we unite to fight that enemy.**
> **When we fail to have a common enemy**
> **to fight, we fight amongst ourselves.**

"What this principle means is that a leader must get everyone focused on a visible and specific goal. When the people you lead are aligned toward a common purpose (i.e., battling a common enemy) you will see how quickly and effectively they work together. A primary responsibility of leadership is to create both the common purpose and the focus. You accomplish this by leading through your inner energy."

"Okay?" Her doubtfulness was normal.

"A good leader is a self-starter and self-generator and will always find a way to sustain themselves, especially in times of turmoil, opposition, lack of support, and even insurmountable obstacles. This inner trait, which I will refer to as energy, comes from your core, your essence. This is the primary reason you must get in touch with your inner leader, because knowing yourself is vital to being the type of leader people are want to follow."

I looked at the sky, then back at her. "As a U.S. citizen you have a responsibility to follow laws and pledge allegiance to the country. Leaders have a similar responsibility of allegiance to the organization they lead, and they fulfill it by enabling the firm to carry out its purpose. Before that can be accomplished, you must 'pledge allegiance' to your leadership ideals, which I assume are lofty and uplifting."

Her eyes followed a man jogging by us, but I could tell she was listening attentively.

"However, if you have not thought of or identified what those are, you will be unable to act and think strategically. This is the reason why emerging and inexperienced leaders—whom I refer to as reluctant—spend much of their time in the weeds and details instead of strategic and long-term goals. Despite being in two senior leadership positions for more than five years, you have yet to recognize this responsibility."

"I don't spend time in the weeds!"

"That's not what Stephen says. According to him, he has asked for your long-range plans several times, and you've failed to deliver them."

"Well...that's because I have to spend time on the minutiae since my employees FAIL to deal with petty issues!"

"Is dealing with low-level issues a good use of your valuable time?"

"I want to say yes because we can't let customers down...but I know that...my time is more valuable elsewhere."

To curtail more self-justification, I proceeded with my point. "As the CEO, it is vital you spend most of your day being strategic. Your team takes care of the smaller issues so you can focus on the big ones."

I knew what was coming next. *She's going to play her No Time and No Energy cards.*

"But I don't have the time. By the end of the day, I am exhausted." At that moment she looked tired, at least physically; I still couldn't read her eyes.

"If I could show you how you can have more time and energy, would you be willing to spend more time being strategic?"

"I guess I would." I understood better why Stephen was exasperated with her performance.

"You were awarded an MBA from Stanford and took courses from some of the world's greatest business thinkers." She nodded. "What tools does the CEO use to remain strategic and steer the ship of her company in the right direction?" Since teachers believe in their own lessons, I wanted her to take the lead and teach me something.

CEOs' Tools for Strategic Leading

In a slightly monotone voice she said, "A mission statement expresses a corporate vision for the company, while the business model is a reflection of how the firm's leadership will fulfill that mission. Then, the strategies selected to fulfill the mission are a definition of how each individual leader will carry out his or her part of the business plan." I nodded with encouragement, so she continued.

"A mission or purpose clarifies the value that we provide to our target customer, while describing the product or service aimed at our target market. It is oriented toward taking action in the present moment, and determines the opportunities we pursue. In summary, the mission is our envisioned future." I noticed she had put herself into the lesson.

By now her voice carried energy and passion. "Our company values statement clarifies the principles that will guide the behavior and decision-making of all employees. Values are basic, intrinsic qualities that we covet and that eventually become the code of conduct for fulfilling the mission. Values tend to be motives by which employees act and react. Values inspire people. It is the CEO's responsibility to instill these values by setting standards, and living by them. For an organization to be successful it must possess strong shared values, and these must be owned and practiced by every employee, not just a select few. The values typically reflect those of its most senior leader or its founders. You can determine whether your purpose is in alignment when you notice that everyone within your team and firm is united toward the same purpose."

She does know how to think strategically.

"Next are the specific goals and objectives a leadership team establishes, the level of achievement we hope to reach. They also clarify our measurements for success. Our strategic goals are high-level and recurring actions mandatory to fulfill the mission. The tactics that flow from our high-level plans for success work to clarify the approach and specific methods we will take for achieving the stated goals and objectives. Strategy is the what, while tactics are the how." She exhaled as if she were just finishing a race.

I applauded lightly and smiled.

"Will I need to take a final exam?" She laughed and relaxed. I pulled two bottles from my briefcase and handed one to her. We sat outside the café, sipping water and soaking up the sun.

I said, "That was well stated. May I show how to use this to get your employees more engaged?"

She nodded for me to proceed.

"Neoteric's mission and vision are invaluable leadership tools that foster a type of exciting energy in every employee. Yet it can be difficult for anyone who has not been involved in planning at a high level to understand all of the various components."

Shooting for the Stars Analogy

From my worn briefcase, I removed a document which I handed to her. It contained a graphic that illustrates the way these leadership tools fit together and how the various components connect. "You can show this to employees each time you ask them to reach for the stars, in the form of increasing profits and other measures of success."

SHOOTING FOR THE STARS

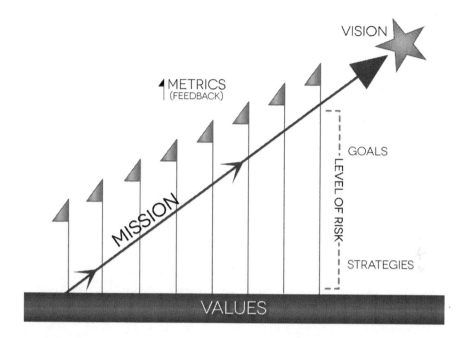

"Let's say that you are trying to reach for the stars in the way NASA does. Imagine that you have a powerful rocket ship that you intend to launch into space toward a particular star you want to explore. You need a launching pad and a specific trajectory that will get you to where you want to go. As you can see in the drawing, your strategic planning process provides this avenue. Notice the various elements required to get you to this destination. Something wonderful occurs when a leadership team engages in strategic planning. As you reach for the star, the supporting structure, the launching pad,

reinforces itself. In the diagram you can see core elements to strategic planning, such as:

- The values, which are the foundation that you build your plan upon
- The mission, which serves as your trajectory
- The strategies, which are your supporting structure
- The goals, which reinforce and exemplify the strategies

- The various metrics, represented as flags, which provide you valuable feedback
- The level of risk you face, which grows the higher and farther you travel
- The star, which serves as your ultimate overriding purpose

"Because you are their CEO, employees look to you to guide them through goal-setting and prioritization efforts about where to invest their time, energy, and resources. Therefore, you must take every opportunity available to remind others about the basic principles on which this organization was founded. That is where their combined energies are put to good use—channeled toward reaching for the stars. They know how it should look because of your plan."

She studied the diagram for a bit and could tell it matched what she had just told me. "I like the way you present it so visually."

"Thanks. Now let's talk about your leader energy, which is the catalyst for employees' combined energy."

"I'm ready."

"Your inner energy comes from what you intend to accomplish as a leader of this organization, but it's not your goals. I can explain with an analogy. Assume your family wants to have a great vacation. How would you define great?"

"It would mean I come back relaxed and I have the sense that we—meaning my husband, Harold, my daughter, Jayna, and I—all reconnected. We made memories. Each of us had the time to engage in our own version of fun. Mine is doing active things, while Harold's is hours of undisturbed reading."

"Sounds like a great vacation to me, too. Now assume you plan a 3-week stay in Australia and everything is ready. Then, just before you leave, travel to Australia is cut off because a nearby volcano is spewing ash. You quickly alter your plans and go to the Bahamas, return refreshed and everyone had their fun. You spent a little more than planned and engaged in different activities than planned, yet it still ended up as a great vacation."

"Got it. What's your point?"

"A great vacation is an intention, while the destination, activities, budget, and lodging are the goals designed to produce a great vacation. Even though the goals had to change, your intention did not and it was carried out successfully. The change in your plans did not diminish the energy you put into it and got out of it because of the overriding intention. Does this make sense?"

She nodded, "Right. Right."

"A leader's intention is what they plan on achieving in a global sense. For example, in the early days, Bill Gates of Microsoft had an intention of being the first to exploit this new thing called computers. Steve Jobs had the intention of being different from any other computer-maker. William Hewlett and Dave Packard, who started HP, had the intention of making accurate tools that engineers could rely on. They each formed a company, which adopted a mission built around the founder's intention. However, it wasn't the mission statement that filled Gates, Jobs, Hewlett, and Packard with the energy to accomplish all they did; it was their personal intention. They knew in their hearts they had to take the bull by the horns to *get 'er done*." I tried to sound like Larry the Cable Guy.

"I think I understand. Before the mission was ever written, these people conceived something no one else did and said *I intend to do this*. It probably grew into their company vision."

"By Jove, I think she's got it!" My fake British accent was equally terrible. She groaned.

"I promise. No more accents. Where was I? It is not just CEOs who need to identify their leadership intention. Because it is the primary source of their energy to do the work of leading others, every leader at every level needs to have an intention in order to reenergize themselves whenever needed. For example, even before I launched HRI, my intention has been to make a great leader out of anyone who wants or need to lead. It's like a fire in my belly that burns in a good way." She laughed as I stuck my stomach out and patted it.

We had to get serious again. "Your second assignment was to write out what your philosophy of leading is, or what you think it might be. I am ready to hear it."

"I didn't do it." She was clearly embarrassed, yet not apologetic. I had another clue to Stephen's concerns.

"We will do it right now." As we sat across the table from one another, I asked her to complete that part of the assignment. I was unconcerned with her obvious discomfort because she needed a reminder to be accountable to her commitments. It took a while. I noted her frustration, but to her credit she kept at it like a high school student completing her last final. When completed, I asked her to read it aloud.

> *My philosophy of leadership is to get things done through people. I lead the people who work for me, accomplishing MY goals and the company's goals.*

I nodded my approval, but she was nervous and needed to move so she got up to buy a round of beverages. *We really need to spend more time on this issue because she has yet to define herself as a leader.* Upon her return I voiced my thanks and let her enjoy an iced coffee while I told stories of my experiences.

Energy Applied in a New Organization

In 1998, I moved into a brand new condominium development. Because of my professional background, the developer asked me to form and serve on the initial board for the homeowners' association. I was green to this sort of living arrangement and owner self-management. I heard numerous horror stories about what could go wrong. My intention as the leader was to put into place something that would head off the various lawsuits, disputes, and problems that occur when people try to live side-by-side as co-owners.

With this mutually conceived intention in mind, that first board created a mission statement which read as follows:

Highland Park Homeowners' Association exists to create a safe, relaxed, and high-quality living environment where:

- *We create a sense of community to share our common interests and celebrate our diversity.*

- *We build a sense of privacy while living close to one another.*

- *We protect the value of our homes and the community.*

Our purpose was to create an environment among the 162 homeowners, many from Asia, Africa, and Europe, that would give us a focal point when we needed to come together for agreement or to settle our differences. We presented it to the homeowners at the first annual meeting, and I explained what we were attempting to accomplish. The homeowners agreed with the intent; they also wanted a community spirit without interfering with their ability to live as they saw fit, while simultaneously protecting the value of their homes, a major investment. It paid off and to this day still does.

In this association's many years of existence, we avoided the lawsuits and acrimony that most condo associations experience on a regular basis. In fact, through this intention and purpose, we were able to reach a win-win agreement with the builder and *developer that enabled us to resolve several major construction warranty problems, worth $3 million, without the use of an attorney or mediator.*

"I hope my story explains how leadership intention can get people working together for a common high-road purpose. However, when a group lacks that purpose, the opposite is true. The following is a situation where employees' selfish intentions undermined their leader's good intentions." I took a sip of iced tea.

Energy Misapplied in a Stale Organization

One of our clients, a government agency, had a visionary leader who introduced a new and novel purpose intended to change the stodgy, slow-paced organization and infuse it with a new can-do attitude. He was a Navy captain and his role was akin to a CEO's. On his arrival, he informed all employees, "We must think like a business organization and then act like one." His reasons were valid. Their culture was one of silos, us vs. them attitudes, and an unwillingness to change. Despite his best efforts, he was unable to get his people to shift their attitudes. His roadblock was altering the intention of those who worked in his organization, whose overriding intention was to preserve their jobs while retaining the influence and power they had amassed over their years of government service. Not all of them acted this way, but I estimate 80 percent did.

Employees of this organization could not see any value or benefit from cooperating with each other, ending the silos, becoming more customer service-oriented, thinking creatively, and saving money. This went against the norm for these tenured employees who averaged 25 years on the job. They knew that this Navy captain would be their leader for only three years, so they could afford to wait out his 'strange' leadership intention through passive resistance. Their indifference paid off. Despite the small amounts of productivity and efficiency improvements he introduced with our help, when he retired, there was more to do. However, a new captain took command with his own intended improvements and he tried to make changes without any outside assistance. In the end, those employees resisted his improvement intention also. Both captains' leadership energy was wasted.

Leadership Lesson

"What was your take-away from these two stories, Joslyn?"

She sat back in her seat. "I'll take a stab at this. While it is the CEO's job to define a purpose or intention, she needs to get others to buy into it. Like in your second example, the leader had a fire in his belly to make the organization better, but he was unable to convince his employees of its value. They seemed to have their own agenda that went against his. Now that I think about it, some of my employees have their own agenda. Oh, one more thing. I guess I really have not presented a clear vision for this company's future because I don't have one. The board may have its own, but I don't."

"You don't have one *yet*, but soon you will."

"Okay, I don't have a clear vision to sell...yet." She attempted a smile.

Demands on CEOs' Energy

Enjoying the refreshing sunshine, I said, "Another point I want you to take to heart is that too many current CEOs focus on their compensation, public image, and the perks of the job. They lack a primary intention. Today's leader must understand that he or she is setting the tone for everyone on their team and in the organization through this intention. Boards and employees want a CEO who is fair, approachable, open, communicative, and, finally, a bridge builder.

"Each time a CEO gets terminated there is a high cost to the organization in terms of disruption to operations, management philosophy, and culture. In addition, employees, partners, and shareholders grow concerned over the vacant corner office. Then, there is tremendous pressure on the new person sitting in the CEO's chair to produce success quickly and live up to expectations of the shareholders and directors.

"Before we figure out ways to better apply your energies, I assign myself the task of sitting down with Stephen and board members of Neoteric to get a better understanding of their expectations of you. My guess is they have not clearly articulated them to you because you stated earlier that you are not sure what they want from you beyond profits and growth. I believe we will spend most of our next session coming up with a plan to deal with their expectations by turning them into specific goals for you and your team."

"I cannot wait to hear what they are," she said flatly. Her enthusiasm was gone. *I will need to regularly rekindle her passion to be both a CEO and a leader.*

Joslyn asked, "What if a leader doesn't have a philosophy? Since before today I did not know I needed one, I suspect that many do not have one." She stared, waiting for a response.

"Your suspicions are correct. The best leaders have one, though not always written, and the rest do not. For those leaders we advise who lack one, we start by sharing the one we developed for the Institute. By studying ours, he or she can usually get a jump start on articulating their own."

Infusing Employees with Energy

"Joslyn, once you have become more aware of and understand your leadership intention, which infuses you with energy and sustains it, you then create a story that you use to inspire employees so they are more energized. I will use my company as an example. Recall that I said, *My intention is to make a great leader out of anyone who wants or needs to lead.* Therefore, in order to surround myself with people willing to help and support me in this endeavor, I wrote out a story that inspires them, at least I hope it does."

Leaders all over the world need our help and support. Our primary goal is to find opportunities to share our knowledge with them so that their jobs become easier. Your role, as an employee of The High Road Institute, is to allow leaders at all levels to devote their time and attention to making their part of the world better.

We had only about 20 minutes left. We sat in silence for a while. I sensed she wanted to know more but wasn't sure where to start, so I suggested that we return to the park. During our walk, I answered several questions.

Joslyn's New Intention

"I just rethought the intention that I presented earlier," Joslyn said when we arrived back at the park. "Can I try out my new one for you?" We arrived at the bench where we started. I sat as she paced, brainstorming out loud, looking up at the blue sky. This is what she settled on.

As the CEO, my intention is to create a great organization. We will be great by being profitable, capturing growth opportunities, retaining good employees, and working together under a long-term vision.

She looked at me like a child who wanted her parent's approval. "What grade do I get?"

"I couldn't rate this because it is a work in progress. There are some elements that need improving but..." I had to stop and pay attention because Joslyn's face fell. I forgot how vulnerable she was feeling.

"It was great for your first attempt! You just completed something that more than 70 percent of leaders never do." I smiled broadly so that she would brighten up. "I will estimate that it's more than halfway to where it could be. So please be kind to yourself and celebrate what you accomplished today. I see great progress already."

Joslyn dwelled on this and relaxed. "I had a thought. I've never asked Stephen about his leadership philosophy, which I believe you refer to as intention. Would it be appropriate for me to ask him?"

"Yes. It is a great idea. May I suggest that after he shares his, tell him yours and see what you learn from each other. Are you willing to do this?" I could tell she had not thought of disclosing hers, and this frightened her. *This trepidation is something she needs to work out on her own.*

Joslyn's Assignment

She listened attentively as we discussed her goals for our next session and what her next application homework would be.

"I suggest your first application step will be to complete what you started today, which is to define your leadership philosophy.

"Your second application could be to develop a list of low-value tasks you are currently doing that could or should be accomplished by someone else and then follow through on delegating each thing on this list. I suggest you do your best to carve out at least two hours of your day to spend on strategic issues, but do it without working longer days."

Reluctantly she said, "I'll try."

"Finally, your third assignment could be to follow through on your idea of meeting with Stephen to discuss leadership philosophies. Do you accept these assignments?" *This will be a test of the trust I've been building and of her commitment.*

Her quiet response was, "I will."

"Will you email me tomorrow with the date you plan to meet with Stephen?" I added this bit of tough love because I sensed she would not follow through on this important meeting without that support.

Joslyn was clearly fatigued. Before we parted to find our cars, she said, "This is a lot to remember; I feel myself getting numb."

"I understand. Much of this is new to you and, when combined with your other worries, it will feel overwhelming at first. I believe in sound bites because people can recall them easily. Whenever I can, I'll present you with the sound-bite version of what you worked on. If you commit to memorizing it and refreshing your memory of the lesson, you will be surprised at how much you retain. As for today's session, just remember this self-fulfilling prophecy of purpose and a related natural law of leadership.

The Self-fulfilling Prophecy of Purpose

> **Your purpose creates intention,**
> **which drives your strategy,**
> **which determines your tactics,**
> **which requires your execution**
> **to carry out your purpose.**

The 6th Natural Law of Leadership

> **A leader's intention is the reason she**
> **chooses to lead others.**

*****

Joslyn's Assessment of Her Progress

On my drive back to the office, I found myself muttering.

I feel like I am drowning in a sea of confusion without anything to float on or someone to save me! Ron refers to people like me as Reluctant Leaders. I'm not reluctant! Hell, I always charge ahead even when I don't know what I'm doing. Before he came into my life, I knew what I was doing!

Or maybe I didn't, if I pay attention to what Stephen said about me. I don't know anymore.

I drove, doing my best to not think and failing at it.

I feel sick to my stomach.

Ron keeps giving me things to do when I don't have enough time. Maybe I'll see things differently tomorrow. Maybe…I'll win the lottery and sail off to the Bahamas…so I don't have to think about leadership.

*****

The Bottom Line of Leadership

Organizations successful in competing, gaining market share, retaining customers, and, of course, remaining profitable, are focused. This concerted effort to win is created and then sustained by the company's primary cheerleader, its CEO.

The organization that loses its identity and momentum in constant meetings and endless debates about its goals, wasting time and scarce resources, is not very successful or profitable. Lasting success starts with the leader's intention.

Employees who are not "with the program" cost American and European businesses millions of dollars each year. These disengaged employees cost you money by being unfocused, absent, or unproductive. The factor that contributes most to employee disengagement is *the people who lead these employees*. In our consulting work we have found a common thread: Employees in any organization adopt the attitudes of those they work for. So if employees are unfocused and not carrying out their employer's mission, their leaders are doing the same thing, as found by studies conducted by The Gallup Organization and Watson Wyatt.

The experts at Gallup Research estimate that employees who are disengaged—i.e., not enthusiastic and committed to their work and who fail to contribute to their organization in a positive manner—cause between four hundred and fifty to five hundred billion dollars in lost productivity each year.[8]

If your organization suffers and loses money because of employees who are simply asleep at the wheel, doing the bare minimum, or showing up only for a paycheck, then you need to examine why the leadership group is leading without intention.

---

[8] *The State of the American Workplace: Employee Engagement Insights for U.S. Business Leaders*, findings from Gallup's ongoing study of the American workplace from 2010 through 2012

Chapter 3
Desire for Unity

*"You hold my career in your hands
even though none of this is my fault!"*

A Looming Deadline – from Joslyn's Viewpoint

The rain beat a steady rhythm against the window panes. The Seattle sky was filled with dense clouds. The place smelled of wet grass, probably due to all of the overly optimistic morning golfers who now seek shelter from the intense downpour. The Club is a membership place designed for ambitious professionals like me. I sense the targeting from the overwhelming amount of modern art and futuristic sculptures, the abundant pastel colors, and the background Muzak of 1990-era rock bands.

I ignored all this, impatiently waiting for Ron. *I should be at work instead of here.* I halfheartedly shook his hand when he walked to me. Rain dripped heavily off his navy coat as he draped it over his arm. Bypassing the line waiting for tables, I inserted myself in the front, grabbed the greeter's arm and said, "I want a table for two in the quiet spot by that window." I ignored the stares and snide comments meant for me.

I barely acknowledged Ron's presence even after being seated. I imagined that my silence and indifference were probably palpable. The server lost his practiced smile as he took our orders.

Stephen's Concerns

After placing the napkin on my lap I said to Ron, perhaps a little too loudly, "Tell me all about your meeting with Stephen. Don't hold anything back or sugarcoat it!" To myself I thought, *I don't want to hear what you have to say, yet I know in my heart I can't run from this problem any longer.*

After taking a sip of coffee he looked at me with concern and said, "I would describe Stephen as cautiously optimistic when he informed me, 'I am facing increasing pressure from certain board members to do something about *the Joslyn problem.*'"

Despite my tremendous self-control, I gasped. *They call ME a problem.*

Calmly and slowly he said, "Keep in mind that I am your advocate and that is the reason I strongly urged Stephen to allow you adequate time to make a shift toward being a real leader. I convinced him that you need six more months to prove that you can be the leader Neoteric needs you to be." Smiling at me, Ron added, "We debated the situation and came to an agreement. He and I do not believe you will undermine the board's goals for this year because there are capable people supporting you. The worst that could happen, though, is for any more of your team to leave; therefore, I suggested that the board take away your authority to terminate employees for a while. I know it is unusual for a CEO to lack this authority, but I think it is necessary. Stephen and I believe this action will impress upon you the seriousness of everyone's concerns about your performance."

At this I felt a stabbing feeling in my head and ache in my stomach. It was all I could do to keep from vomiting. I remained quiet.

Ron said, "I described your progress without disclosing specifics due the confidential nature of our work. After further discussion, Stephen agreed with my recommendation that we increase your coaching sessions to once a week. I took this to mean that Stephen was doubling down on his 'investment' in you, a good sign that he had not given up on you. I am telling you this to help you understand that you must avoid jeopardizing his support."

Just then our meals arrived. Despite my nausea, I ate small bites of the omelet and sipped the fresh orange juice slowly. Sadly, I didn't enjoy the food as much as he did. I tried to clear my mind but blurted out, "You hold my career in your hands even though none of this is my fault! And you're to blame for this stripping of my authority!"

I was taking my frustration out on him even though I already knew about Stephen's decision because of our inevitable and voraciously fast grapevine.

I Am Not to Blame!

Placing his fork down, Ron said calmly, "You may think that I made this happen, and I accept that. *You hold your career in your hands.*"

We lapsed into an awkward silence. He was probably waiting until I was ready before he started the coaching. I shook my head and sighed, "Let's get this party started."

Ron said, "At a prior session we talked about the difference between the internal and external aspects of leadership, and why the coaching you are experiencing is designed to help you understand and be effective in both areas but the fact..."

That's when it suddenly hit me. "Six months is all I have left? Why don't I just quit now?" I wanted to throw something.

In a calm manner he continued, "You could, but you would just be running away from your problem, and I guarantee it will crop up in your next job. If you use the time Stephen granted to do the work, you could become the leader Neoteric needs you to be. I see room for improvement simply because *you have been blaming everyone else for your problems.* Right now you are blaming me."

I scowled. I couldn't help myself.

"I believe in you," he said. "I convinced Stephen that you could prove *in less than 180 days* you are a capable leader.

However, in reality, the concerns that board members have regarding your leadership start with you. You are not to blame, and the fault lies with you."

"Hmm?" *That sounded odd.* "What did you say?"

With extreme patience he repeated, "You are not to blame for your leadership weakness, and yet you are the cause of it. I know that sounds strange, although it a basic paradigm of leadership. Let me break it down for you." My confusion intensified and, not paying attention, I gulped my coffee and burned my tongue in the process.

The No-Win Blame Game

In his patient coaching persona, Ron informed me, "In every organization, people need someone to lead them, so they look to the CEO and the management team for guidance. However, when the leader points the finger of blame on someone, it will eventually tear the team and company apart by creating disunity."

I sipped my cold juice to ease the burn.

He continued, "Placing blame creates lose-lose outcomes. Once you point the finger of blame at someone [he pointed at me], you initiate a predictable sequence that quickly spirals downward and fosters negativity for these reasons.

- The accuser feels superior, above the situation, and hands the onus for solving the problem onto someone else, the person who allegedly messed up.
- The scapegoat gets defensive and puts up a fight to defend his or her reputation and dignity.
- The issue or problem gets ignored due to the interplay between the blamed and the blamer. Any cooperation that existed is harmed and trust is trashed.
- All the energy of those involved gets diverted from creating solutions.

- The atmosphere within the group is negative and filled with angry emotion. Tactful honesty disappears.

"Now, let us turn this process around:

- The leader (a.k.a. blamer) states, 'It is my fault. I contributed to this by...'
- This ownership invites the other party (a.k.a. blamed) to own up to their culpability. 'I too contributed to this by...' or 'I should have...'

"When it is acknowledged openly that everyone contributed to the situation, this atmosphere allows the people involved to find a solution much faster because the energy stays positive. They can work together to get past the stalemate.

"The dialogue will always be somewhat guarded until each party realizes the finger of blame will not be forthcoming. Trust and cooperation among all parties are still possible."

There was a pause in the conversation so we could eat. I nibbled some more on my omelet while he dug into French toast.

When finished he said, "I will turn the spotlight on you, Joslyn. Since we first met, you have pointed the finger of blame at Stephen, Angela, the entire board, Jackson, Latisha, and Curtiss, as well as Neoteric's employees and me. You recently faulted Lauren, Kelly, and Dino, none of whom work for you anymore."

I felt my cheeks redden and pulse quicken, causing my perfume to intensify. He stayed silent until I admitted reluctantly, "Yes, I guess I did, though I don't recall specifically doing it."

After writing something, he said in his annoyingly calm way, "I made a note of that and we will turn it into one of your application steps. I will ask you to pay close attention, and each time you start pointing the finger of blame, catch yourself and find a more constructive way to deal with the issue."

I responded with a sigh. "If I really think about it...I can see how much I, to use your term, point the finger of blame." I pointed my freshly manicured index finger at him and, despite how I was feeling, I grinned a little.

"Don't point that at me. It could go off!" His hearty laugh helped me throttle back on my intensity.

Turning serious, he continued, "I am glad you recognize it, even though you don't always when you are engaging in this time-wasting behavior. In our work together, do I have your permission to point it out each time that you do?"

"Yes, I suppose I need to know when I do it." *But I don't blame.*

He said, "Stephen and I agreed that the main issue that the board wants addressed and improved is weak or ineffective leadership at Neoteric Products."

I wasn't ready for what came next.

He launched us into a rapid-fire exchange by asking, "Who is the person in charge of everything that goes on in Neoteric?"

"Me."

"And who is responsible for the day-to-day leadership that is demonstrated by the management team?"

Riddled with embarrassment, I stared down at the table as I replied, "I am."

"Who then is accountable for improving the weak leadership demonstrated by this group?"

"I am."

"Who do you think the group blames for poor leadership at Neoteric?"

"They blame me."

"And how does it feel to be the one whom everyone blames?" This question rattled me.

"It feels uncomfortable, even embarrassing." My cheeks reddened again. *Why am I so hot?*

Slowing the pace, he said, "Yes, it does feel uncomfortable and humiliating. Each time that Jackson, Curtiss, and the rest of the executives experience you pointing the finger of blame at them, how do you think they feel?"

"Like I do right now." My eyes filled with tears; not wanting him to see this I turned quickly to my right and stared at the painting on the far wall. My head throbbed again.

He gracefully paused to let his terrible question sink in.

"It is not my intention to be hurtful," he said. "If you are going to be the leader Neoteric needs you to be, your heart has to commit to the transformation, with you at the center of the changes. An intellectual commitment to becoming a better leader is like planting flower seeds on rocky, arid ground. You may see short-term action, but nothing will take root for the future."

Our server returned to see if we required anything else. Grateful for the interruption, I smiled at him. He flinched, I guess because I was rude to him earlier. I handed him my plate.

After our drinks were refreshed Ron returned to teaching mode.

"I'd like to explain the **7th Natural Law of Leadership**."

> **When you place blame on someone,
> you do it to take the focus off your own faults, not
> because of the other person's faults or behaviors.**

After a brief pause, he said, "What this truism means is that as humans, we find fault quite easily and then use others as scapegoats for our screw-ups. Yet each time you blame, meaning you point the finger at another person, you are giving yourself a free pass on your culpability."

He then surprised me when he said, "Please use your right hand and point to me," which I did.

"As a child, I was taught this adage. 'Each time you point your finger at someone, look at your hand. There is one finger pointing out and three fingers point back at you.' Study your hand to see if this is true."

I saw what he meant but said nothing.

"This piece of advice reminds us that in everything that goes wrong, we had a hand in it. In everything that goes wrong in your life, you have some culpability, and the same is true for me. It's okay if you disagree with me."

How did he know I did?

"But not believing this truth does not make it go away." His eyes seemed to probe me.

"As leader, your visible role and accountability make it hard to hide your culpability whenever things go wrong. Let's say Dawn, your Director of OEM accounts, makes a decision that hurts profits. Each time you publicly blame Dawn for her mistakes, people around you could likely wonder: *Maybe Dawn did that, but where was Joslyn when that happened?*

Why didn't Joslyn stop her? Why didn't Joslyn train her better?"

I nodded my agreement with his example because I anticipated where he was going with this.

"Who hired and empowered Dawn?"

"I did."

Nodding, he said, "That is why the High Road leader avoids the blame game and immediately focuses on how to get past the finger-pointing and shaming so that you can more quickly find ways to prevent the problem from happening again. Do you believe in taking the high road?"

I nodded that I did. I needed to relax and pay better attention, so I picked up a pen to take notes.

Inner Leader Trait - the Desire to Unify People

Ron continued the coaching lesson once I was ready. First, he pulled a white Ping-Pong ball out of his briefcase and laid it on the table. It had **2** written on it. Pointing to the ball he said, "The second inner leader characteristic is the desire to bring about unity. What can happen when a group  leader brings about dissension and infighting? Have you experienced that?"

It didn't take long to think of a response. "I have. I know that condition very well. In my first job in sales, we had a manager who tried to pit us against one another. At first I thought it was a good thing because I love competition. Participating in sports all through my teen years and into college, I thought that competition was exciting. However, soon I witnessed all sorts of problems. Some employees tried to steal sales opportunities away. I saw examples of lying and even cheating to make our mandated quota. Worst of all, many sales employees paid more attention to achieving the highest number of sales than to servicing our customers. It was awful, and I didn't last long in that environment."

He nodded. "What could happen to a company if the CEO did that? He or she produces an environment where each department gets pitted against the others?"

"I…the person would be the cause of a lot of needless drama and employee turnover." This insight hit me like a slap on the face. *Have my actions created an environment of needless drama and tension*?

I hoped he didn't notice my discomfort.

Defending myself, I asserted, "I would never do that. I always stress that I want my sales team to work together and support each other!" I said this with a lot more intensity than intended.

He let my storm pass and said next, "But what about the rest of your company? Does Human Resources always cooperate with the Production group? Do Accounting personnel always support Sales as they should?" He paused for effect. "If you do not know how to get people to sincerely rally around you and support you, you will not become a true leader."

My silence and stare let him know he was right. I had to change the subject because hearing this was painful. "What's the meaning of the Ping-Pong ball?" I touched it but left it on the table.

At that moment the server came by to clear off our table, asking if we wanted anything else. I snapped, "No!" He seemed to shrink as he plopped the check in front of me and walked away quickly. *More chaos and drama?*

I could almost read Ron's mind. He was not going to let my character flaw go, and I was certain he would bring it up again. *He's tenacious.*

Takers vs. Givers

"You asked about this ball." He held it so that I had to take it from him. "From my observations of you, I categorize your leadership style as a Taker instead of a Giver. As a Taker the contention you foster among the team produces behaviors designed to undermine and even humiliate you."

That I didn't need to hear.

I refilled my coffee cup from the carafe. "I have heard of this concept. Can you explain more?" *I'm surprised he describes me this way. It isn't a good label.*

Slipping back into his coach voice, he said, "The Taker is the individual who puts her own interests first. Takers avoid doing unpleasant tasks and fail to respond to requests for help. She tends to make demands on others and use information as a currency to get what she wants. The workplace has changed drastically, however, and being the Taker is no longer an acceptable way to exist in an organization. Today, more than half of US and European companies organize employees into teams. The rise of matrix structures requires employees to coordinate with a wider range of direct reports. The advent of project-based work means that employees collaborate with an expanded network of colleagues. High-speed communication and transportation technologies connect people across the globe who would have been strangers.[9] In this environment of collaboration, the Taker sticks out like a sore thumb. Today, the Taker is far less likely to climb up the corporate ladder."

I remembered to thank the server quietly when he returned to refill our water and juice again and took my credit card. *See, no drama.*

Without missing a beat, Ron continued. "The Giver is the member of the team who volunteers for unpopular projects,

---

[9] Grant, Adam, *Turning the Tables on Success.* Strategy + Business, summer 2013. http://www.strategy-business.com/article/00175?pg=all

shares knowledge and skills, and helps out in any way they can. This person helps to solve problems and manages a heavy workload. Employees with the highest rates of promotion into supervisory and leadership roles exhibit the characteristics of the Giver. Givers gain a reputation for being generous and group-oriented. Givers are motivated to punish Takers and reward fellow Givers."

I asked him to pause so that I could mentally review each member of my team. I realized that those who might be Givers were those who reluctantly supported me or had quit (Dino and Kelly). Those who might be Takers seemed to be the same ones who fight me no matter what I do (Isaiah, Curtiss, Aaron). I couldn't decide how to classify the rest. *Should I tell him?*

Without saying what I was thinking, I informed him I was ready to continue.

He said, "Today's interdependent work requires that employees be evaluated and promoted not only on the basis of their individual results, but also on the level of their contributions to others. This focus reduces the ability for the Taker to exploit Givers, and instead encourages the Taker to focus on advancing the team's goals. Having more team-based performance evaluations and bonuses forces Takers to engage in fewer manipulative acts, thus reducing the risks taken by Givers.

"When a Giver becomes the leader of a group or company, the group is quickly better off. Research shows that employees work harder and are more effective when their leader puts other people's interests first. Research on Takers and Givers found going the extra mile for the group, making personal sacrifices, or taking personal risks on behalf of the group inspired group members to give back to the leader and contribute to the group's self-interest. [10] A thorough analysis of

---

[10] Grant, Adam, Turning the Tables on Success. Strategy + Business, summer 2013. http://www.strategy-business.com/article/00175?pg=all

3,600 business units across numerous industries shows that the more frequent employees give help and share knowledge, the higher their units' profits grow. In addition, under these conditions, productivity, customer satisfaction, and employee retention went up significantly.[11]

"The single strongest predictor of leadership is the amount of compassion a particular employee expresses toward others' needs. A compassionate person is not only viewed as caring, she is also perceived as more knowledgeable and intelligent. By expressing concern for others, the Giver sends a message that she has the resources and capabilities to help others. Two of the defining qualities of today's great leaders are: the ability to make others look better, and the willingness to put the group's interests first. Givers increase the group's value in two areas: by increasing the team's ability to engage in interdependent work, and by better fulfilling the leader's role."

He allowed me to catch up in note-taking. Then he handed me a sheet of paper and pointed out a specific statistic: 40 percent of employees believe that they work for a bad boss.

"That's a high number," I said.

He said, "It is. One characteristic of a bad boss is his or her use of the blame game[12]. Approximately 23 percent of the respondents in that study stated that their supervisor blamed them or other workers to cover up for their personal mistakes[13]. However, this statistic hides the real cost of the frequently played blame game: A leader must earn the trust of their employees to be effective, but playing the blame game trashes trust."

This caught me by surprise so I laughed, saying, "I see you circled back to why the blame game can be destructive."

---

[11] Houston Chronicle website, article by Samantha Hanly
http://smallbusiness.chron.com/effects-bad-management-employees-13378.html
[12] Gayle L. Gifford, *How are We Doing?: A 1-hour Guide to Evaluating Your Performance as a NonProfit Board*, Emerson & Church, 2005
[13] National study conducted by Dale Carnegie Training and Forbes Magazine

He smiled too. "I'm glad you recognized this, Joslyn. Recall in the game of Ping-Pong how disheartening the slam is to the player on the receiving end. Working for a leader who is perceived as bad, who points the finger of blame frequently, and who is a Taker is akin to playing against someone who tries to slam the ball at you with every play. You get discouraged quickly and stop playing. I'll bet much of the tension you feel coming from other executives is that they don't like playing against you."

I agreed that was true and suddenly decided—why I don't know—to share with him my quick assessment of who on my team might be the Givers and the Takers.

"That makes sense," was his only comment.

The Harmful Blame Game

The Club's dining area was nearly empty. It was so quiet that I could hear the squeak of athletic shoes coming from the squash courts.

Out of nowhere Ron asked, "Do you play squash?"

"No. I'm a runner and usually just use the facilities here to keep my legs in shape and retain my stamina. The Club has some really good fitness instructors."

"I am a runner also."

I didn't know that. I then realized I didn't know anything personal about him.

Before I could comment he continued, "Allow me to relate an experience I had being on the receiving end of the finger of blame."

Early in my career I worked for a management team consisting of four men who disliked confrontation, which meant they avoided giving bad news or holding employees to task. During the meeting with the firm's CEO where we agreed to employment terms, I asked for a waiver on the requirement that employees had to be at their desk by 8:00 a.m. because twice a week I dropped my children off at school. I explained that for security reasons, children were not allowed to be on campus prior to 8:00 a.m. and this meant that I could not be at work before 8:15 a.m. He said, "That will not be a problem, Ron. I trust you'll put in the hours."

Six months later, at my first performance review with my supervisor (one of the four), I was informed that my professionalism was lacking because I was continually late to work. I explained that I had been given approval for this slight schedule deviation and asked, "Why didn't you say anything to me about this before?" His face-saving response was, "I never noticed if you were late, but a few of your coworkers complained to me about your tardiness." I concluded that this executive (doing my review) did not want to confront this problem so he procrastinated on saying anything until my evaluation. I also realized he was uninformed about the special arrangements. When I protested this black mark against my professionalism, he claimed, "It's your responsibility to inform me whenever you will be late!" I insisted that the CEO be included in this discussion regarding my alleged tardiness. When he joined us, I inquired why he had not communicated this arrangement to the other executives. He pointed his blame finger at me and said, "It's not my fault. I left it up to you to inform everyone." To my ears, that statement was a flat-out lie, and after that I knew I could not trust him.

After letting his story sink in, he then asked the question I was beginning to hate: "What do you take away from my story?"

Leadership Lesson

I ventured with my first thought. "The bond of trust you had with the men you worked for was shattered. Was it hard to work there after that?"

"It was and got to the point where I dreaded coming to work each day. So I began a job search to find a leader and boss I could trust, someone who was not a taker or blamer."

I nodded.

He continued in his gentle manner. "Joslyn, I suspect that because of your wanting to blame others for what goes wrong, the men and women on your team do not trust you, and this is the reason why this management group does not act cohesively. You say that you want Neoteric's non-management employees to look up to their leaders, but when they look at the team and its members, what do they see? Adults acting like children—bickering, complaining, and blaming."

"Oh! I never saw it that way." I wanted to say more but held back.

"A major contributor to the inspirational leader's effectiveness is when she strives to be an instigator of unity in all things involving people. Allow me to explain what I mean by that term."

We both glanced over at a nearby table where the wait staff began to gather for a meeting. *Is it almost time to leave? Please let this session be over!*

I turned my attention back to Ron when he said, "The leader is the one who must bring people together. Leading is a daily challenge and takes hard work, so whenever the leader's team members are fighting one another, it's nearly impossible to lead. That does not mean the team must agree on everything or be best buddies. Instead, a quality leader hones her skills on facilitating cooperation and instilling mutual commitment to a common cause.

"At The High Road Institute, we use the term *unity instigator* because of its two dimensions: unity builder and instigator. When people work together toward a common purpose and agree to support one another, they foster unity. Lasting cooperation and togetherness would be nice, but in reality, people in any situation will fall into many forms of disunity. The leader's job and duty are to notice these events and get people united again.

"The facilitator description is vital because a good facilitator has a bag of tricks that are designed to bring people together, to create partnerships, and to instigate forward progress. When one tool doesn't work, she uses another, and if that one is ineffective, she has another to rely on. A facilitator is also a neutral observer and momentum catalyst. So the leader must always stay aware of the mood of her team and use this skill to get everyone on the same page whenever the cats begin to stray. A good facilitator is a person who instigates change toward something better."

A very fit woman in yoga wear headed toward our table and waved to me; I had attended her yoga class once. I politely waved back even though I didn't know her. *I wish I looked that fit, but I don't have the time.*

Blame Wastes Valuable Time

Noticing that I was off somewhere else, Ron tapped my hand. "Joslyn, you mentioned that a lot of your staff meeting time is spent blaming one another for the company's problems. What would you estimate is the time wasted in each meeting as your employees argue over who is at fault or attempt to make themselves blameless?"

"Uhmm. At least an hour or even more." *I almost can't believe this...but it's true. We do.*

"How else could your team use this valuable time? In other words, if your weekly meeting ended an hour earlier, how could this time be used?"

Is he reading my thoughts?

I wanted to say, *I might have time for exercise* but instead I answered with, "I could probably use that time to meet with those who need my help or are struggling. However, based on what you previously said, I could spend time being more strategic."

"What else would improve if the team trusted each other and didn't waste time playing the blame game?"

I saw his point immediately and nodded rather than reply.

He continued the lesson. "The intense high-level coaching you are currently experiencing is more than just improving your leadership abilities. It is designed to get you to own up to your accountability for what you have done in the past and to own the solutions you could create to improve the future of the company, the employees, and yourself, in that order. I will repeat what I said earlier to make sure you understand what it means: 'You are not to blame, and the fault lies with you.' Tell me what this means to you."

He's making me work. Just when I thought we were done!

I had to concentrate on his question so I stood up and paced a bit. It probably looked odd because he was sitting at the table talking to me while I paced around it. I didn't care. *I think better and faster on my feet.*

His eyes followed me for a bit and then Ron suggested, "Let's try something. When I pose an introspective question like that one, simply walk around and voice your thoughts. Some people are able to process information better on the fly, and you strike me as someone who does that. Just tell me what's on your mind as you think of it. You are not striving for a perfect or complete answer."

Maybe he knows me better than I give him credit for! "You really don't want to know what goes on inside my head!"

He took a deep breath and said, "For the first time today, you smiled. You have a great smile, and I wish you did it more often."

My cheeks flushed at his compliment. I'm not used to people giving them.

Wearing a big grin, he said, "Yes, I do want to know what you are thinking. As I explained before, I do my best work when I know the real YOU."

It was then that I noticed my headache was gone and so was my churning stomach. I couldn't tell if he was teasing but I felt an urge to trust or at least believe.

Pacing to and fro I said, "That statement at first seems like a contradiction. I am not to blame...means don't point a finger at me. It also implies that there are conditions or circumstances that create...that lead to my being ineffective."

He nodded and contemplated my face.

Ignoring him, I continued. "The fault lies with me at first feels like blaming, but...Is there a difference between being blamed and being at fault?"

He stayed perfectly still, like he was waiting to exhale.

I was on a roll. "Based on the downward spiral you just explained, blaming someone demonstrates that I am looking for a scapegoat. Right?"

"Go on."

"Being at fault...that means that the person...me...this means that I contributed to the problem. It's my fault I am not being the leader they want me to be."

I realized at that moment that I, too, was holding my breath. This might be a breakthrough moment for me. My brain was buzzing.

He hand-signaled for me to continue so I said, "Maybe it is and maybe it isn't my fault."

"You are so close. Keep going."

Nothing came out of my mouth, so he asked, "Assume for a second that you are *partially* culpable. What aspects of Neoteric's leadership problems did you contribute to?"

I felt my cheeks burn.

I said, "This is a little embarrassing to say…but I don't like dealing with people issues I cannot control! When I was in sales and a customer had an objection, I had all the information to assist them. Even if they didn't buy, I found a way to both control the discussion and get my selling points across. Even if they didn't buy right away, my tenacity paid off with a sale soon after that. When I led a sales team and an employee had a problem, again I could find a way to satisfy both our needs. We spoke a common language so I didn't need to explain something ten different ways. Plus we all focused on one mission: Sell!"

Taking a deep breath and an embarrassingly audible intake of water, I continued. "As CEO, the problems people present to me are not so easy to solve. Take the situation where Jackson called me a liar. I've never had an experience like that. My teenage daughter yells at me, which I expect. However, I do not expect the person I hired and whom I once considered an ally to yell at me. He shouts at me in front of my employees! I didn't know how to handle that situation." I laughed at myself. "I can't take it when my daughter yells at me. Yet she does it nearly every day!"

Smiling he said, "Will you concede that your discomfort with people not behaving like you expect them to is your fault? Could your culpability be that you lack certain skills to deal with those intractable and messy people problems, like insubordination or disengagement?"

"So what you are suggesting is that I lack certain skills to deal with situations like that?"

"Do you?" He waited for my response.

I hate people who answer a question with a question!

"Yes. I will admit that I do... at times."

"Aha! Joslyn you may have just experienced a shift in your thinking. Well done."

His broad grin and sudden enthusiasm surprised me, warming me up inside. Yet I still felt tremendous tension in my stomach.

He then instructed, "Joslyn, let's make a list of those areas where you think you have contributed to the leadership problem. We will start with the premise that the board's belief of weak or ineffective leadership at Neoteric is true. What aspect of that is your fault, meaning that you contributed to it in some way? You talk and I'll write."

I took my seat at the table and finished off the rest of my lukewarm orange juice.

We spent nearly an hour on this task. There were times when Ron needed to get me refocused because, as he describes it, the closer I seem to get the truth, the harder it is for me to own up to it.

When I exhausted my thoughts, Ron pointed out four major themes emerging from my brain dump.

- I am uncomfortable dealing with unhappy, unpleasant, or disagreeable people.
- When someone does not conform to my expectations, I act like a drill sergeant ordering a private to get back in line.
- I get so wrapped up in what I love—working with customers, selling, and making deals—that I neglect other aspects of my CEO duties.

- I want my direct reports to be strategic, yet when I work with them I tend to focus on the details rather than the big picture.

He allowed me time to think about what I'd told him, but all I could think to say was, "Oh, sh...! That sounds like me. I hate it that you are right." This was an attempt at humor but it sounded bad, even to my ears.

He laughed for a minute and I felt much of my pent-up tension release because he was jubilant that I had "owned up to these issues," as he put it. He cautioned, "I suspect there would be many more, yet so far we have accomplished a minor alteration in your thinking. You are slowly getting past your denial or self-induced blindness, AND we have specific areas to work on, now that we know the thoughts that contribute to your beliefs regarding leadership which contribute to your reluctance to lead."

I started to protest that I wasn't denying anything but held back because the little voice in my head said, *The proof of your denial is there on paper!*

Calmly he brought me out of my thoughts. "I am glad that you have acknowledged a need to improve your leadership abilities. However, we were a long way from the finish line."

I was feeling confused; my headache returned at that moment, especially when I remembered that I could be jobless in six months.

We took a break and I took that opportunity to gather myself and refresh my makeup. When he returned to our table, he informed me that he got permission from the manager for us to stay until 11:30. *I can't believe we've been talking about me for more than three hours!*

The Magic of Unity

Ron encouraged me to relax and enjoy a fresh cup of coffee, while he regaled me with another parable of leadership. In his warm storytelling voice, he said, "A company facing the possibility of extinction needs a bit of 'magic.' I worked for a company that went from the brink of bankruptcy to being highly prized very quickly because of unity facilitation."

Mac's Place (MP) launched itself into a highly competitive field but one for which it had high expertise and experience. When I first encountered MP it was 18 months into its existence and short by $500 million in working capital. The company had a seasoned senior leadership team consisting of Bob, the President and Chief Executive Officer, and Tom, the Chairman of MP's board who represented the investors' interests. It was growing fast, at an average rate of more than 20 percent per year. Bob had an excellent track record in the sales of computer software and accessories. At the time, MP consisted of 50 energetic, committed employees who really believed in the company and its mission. However, not everything was coming up roses for them.

In a similar organization, Bob had been instrumental in building a highly successful and profitable business from scratch and, wanting another challenge, left to start his own company. His global focus was on maintaining relationships with the companies that MP promoted, vendors who were critical to MP's success. Tom spent his time on banking and creditor relationships critical to MP's ability to keep the doors open, but was seriously considering filing for bankruptcy protection because of the severe lack of cash. Both men wanted to stay in business, but a few of the larger creditors were starting to get restless.

When I was asked to sign on as the third member of the leadership team, Tom was interviewing bankruptcy attorneys, but neglected to inform me about how close the company was to shutting down. I willingly took on the challenge to keep them in business.

From my first day on the job, I saw many weaknesses; the biggest was that the company was undercapitalized, meaning that it had outgrown its original cash investment made by the venture capitalists. The employees recognized that the company lacked a common direction, which was concern number two. They were doing their jobs in a vacuum, and the internal system of communications had broken down. Third, there was a growing problem with obsolete inventory, which wasted badly needed dollars. MP lacked someone who could objectively view the company with a global oversight of the entire process in order to deal with the wasted uses of working capital. A fourth problem was that no one would make important decisions. Bob was a bottleneck to both work getting done and decisions being made, yet lacked the time to organize our people assets into a cross-functional oversight group. The departments had developed a silo mentality and were often working at cross-purposes.

When MP was launched, it made sense that its founder, Bob, should be involved in all the daily decisions and know everything that was going on. As the company grew, people were hired to fill the roles of manager and supervisor, but Bob forgot to let go of his responsibilities and delegate to capable employees. Everything still flowed through Bob, who was putting in 15-hour days, 7 days a week, and was always behind. He had reached his Peter Principle point but did not recognize it.

MP's overriding problem was its lack of strategic operational leadership.

My second day on the job, I apprised Bob of the specific opportunities for improvement and suggested that we implement a formal team process as a way to solve the most urgent problems. With some reservation, he agreed to my plan. We immediately formed a team consisting of the managers and supervisors from all sections of the company, and our charter was to absorb the responsibilities of the day-to-day management from Bob. Within a few weeks, the communications breakdown was fixed and decisions were being made timely and effectively. Bob quickly found that by being outside of the decision loop, he had more time to concentrate on key issues and spend with his family. He loved that!

The second team I put together was a cash management group, and the third took over full responsibility for the inventory, which was currently being co-managed by three employees who never talked to each other.

In less than six months, we formed six different employee teams. Employee morale visibly improved, managers assumed leadership roles, and the major problem areas were in the process of being resolved. The real payoff, however, came in two ways. First, employees who were not part of these teams continually asked me when they would be asked to serve on one. They wanted to be part of the creative synergy going on all around them. This enthusiasm was sparked by those who were already part of a team. The second payoff came a month later when MP was acquired by the Northwest's premier software retailer who saw MP as a 'jewel to add to its crown' and made a buyout offer, which the stockholders readily accepted.

MP went from facing bankruptcy to being highly desired in less than seven months. The reason we survived and were subsequently purchased was because these engaged, involved, and focused employees kept the company alive during that difficult time. It took a leader to unify them and give them a purpose.

When he paused for a drink and to indulge in the coconut cookies the manager brought us, I decided to turn the table on my coach, so I asked the question before he could: "What did this experience teach you about leadership, Ron?"

Leadership Lesson

After resting his chin on his hand, he said, "I witnessed firsthand that when a group of employees are united in a common effort, it is amazing what can be done. From the inside it feels like magic, but it's really hard work."

Without a pause he included me in the moral. "And how this relates to your situation is this. Your first leadership challenge is to get everyone engaged in solution creation and owning up to their role in making things happen. There does not need to be a crisis in order to galvanize people for this unity. Your goals—daily, weekly, monthly, even annual ones—will get accomplished when employees are united. It is up to the group's leader to foster and facilitate that unity and to keep it. Joslyn, you need to become that catalyst."

He paused to let me reflect while he finished off his coffee and another cookie. Unfortunately, there was no wait staff around to refresh our drinks. I was tempted to yell at someone to help us, but then remembered my commitment. *No more drama!*

Overcoming a Crisis with Unity

He then said, "You faced a similar situation when you were hired by Neoteric as its Vice President of Sales. I understand that you knew this company was on the ropes. Do you recall the first few things you did to contribute to the amazing turnaround?"

After pulling my thoughts together I said, "That seems like a lifetime ago. Let me think. The first thing I needed to do was to convince my team that there was a real problem. Stephen had been unable to get this message across to the sales employees who always see things through rose-colored glasses."

I gasped involuntarily. "I just realized that I am looking at my leadership abilities through those same glasses. It just hit me!" I tried to hide my surprise by standing up and walking again.

Ron smiled and I think he noticed what was happening within me. He prompted, "You said you needed to get their attention..."

"Right. Right. We had lost four major OEM accounts, and no one in sales seemed worried; many thought we could easily replace customers that had taken years to acquire. My second action was to get everyone looking for missed opportunities. We identified hundreds of leads we had overlooked or ignored because up to that point we were doing so well."

He inserted, "I notice that for the first time you used the word 'we,' even for actions that took place before you were an employee. To me this is a good sign."

I didn't understand his comment, so I continued with my memory of what took place. "The third step, and the hardest, was to convince certain members of the team to work hard without the incentive carrot dangling in front of them. I had to let some sales people go because they demanded to be paid for prospecting in addition to their regular commission. We couldn't afford that. The next thing I did was to go out on visits to the larger prospects with a sales employee who I believed would do the best job of creating a relationship. That was Dawn and she excelled at it. I was there only to open the conversation; then I let her take over. All along I was ego-stroking, dealing with resistance, and rallying employee morale. We had lots of meetings, which they hated but were necessary to ensure we were all committed to this effort. Once we started gaining new accounts and sales, the momentum became self-perpetuating. After 18 months our sales were higher than before the 'crash' and we had 32 percent more customers. Fewer major ones, but the smaller accounts were hungry for our products and tended to be more loyal and profitable. I decided to promote Dawn, a great employee, to a vital position."

I sat back glowing in self-satisfaction.

He allowed my smugness before he said, "Now I can see why Stephen wants you to succeed; you supported him in his time of crisis. He told me how the two of you fixed the production problems that led to the loss of those large accounts. Sounds like you and he teamed up very well."

"Yeah. Good times. Well…not really. My marriage suffered from the long hours and constant travel. Stephen and I both got very ill afterward, probably from the stress. Yet I was so proud of what my team accomplished in such a short time."

I noticed that I started out smiling at this recollection, and then my mood changed. "That is why I'm so frustrated with Jackson! He was instrumental in the turnaround and his support was unwavering. Now, it's like that never happened!"

Realizing that I was very upset, I sat back and breathed deeply, trying to let the feeling go.

He let me stew in silence. *He seems to know what I need.*

The Beginning of Needed Repairs

"Joslyn, as you know I plan on having one-on-one meetings with many of your key employees as part of this coaching program. We will also conduct a company-wide survey of employees' feelings and concerns. I can guarantee I will be able to supply you with insights that could help you repair every key relationship."

"Right. Right." I was unconvinced.

He ignored my skepticism and continued the conversation. "Let's talk about your key employee, Jackson. Do you think there is a future that includes the two of you working in sync again?"

I think his question was designed to get me past the anger.

"I would like to, but I think it's up to him." I pursed my lips together until my cheeks hurt.

Smiling, he said, "Repairing the damage will be up to both of you. If you both are willing, you can get back to that closeness you once had. Someone has to start rebuilding the bridge of trust."

He paused to let me dwell on this thought.

Looking at his watch, he announced, "Our time is almost up. Let's figure out what you will work on for next week's session. You will really like the location and it will be fun. The work we are doing is heavy, deep, and real, so I want you to enjoy the process, too."

I was curious. "Where will we meet?"

"That is a secret I am keeping."

I glared because he refused to disclose anything, and he laughed at me! But I felt better. I was simultaneously scared and in awe of what coaching was doing to me. Today I was elated, angry, and wistful several different times, but overall I knew I had accomplished something, although I couldn't define it.

Despite the silent messages the wait staff was sending us that we should leave, we worked together for another 10 minutes to finalize my next action steps.

My Assignment

Ron instructed, "Before we meet again I would like you to write out your answers to eight questions." He handed me a sheet that contained them.

PROVOKING QUESTIONS

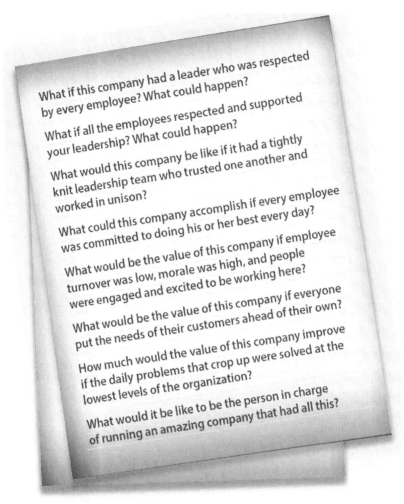

What if this company had a leader who was respected by every employee? What could happen?

What if all the employees respected and supported your leadership? What could happen?

What would this company be like if it had a tightly knit leadership team who trusted one another and worked in unison?

What could this company accomplish if every employee was committed to doing his or her best every day?

What would be the value of this company if employee turnover was low, morale was high, and people were engaged and excited to be working here?

What would be the value of this company if everyone put the needs of their customers ahead of their own?

How much would the value of this company improve if the daily problems that crop up were solved at the lowest levels of the organization?

What would it be like to be the person in charge of running an amazing company that had all this?

"This will be part one of your application assignments. Part two we covered at the start of our session and that is to pay attention to when you feel the urge to point the finger of blame. Even if you don't verbalize it, stay aware of the desire. Describe for me what happened and who was involved."

I nodded while writing this down.

He asked, "Will you commit to me that you will follow through on this every day for two weeks?"

I wanted to say "no" because I had so many other things to get done in the next few weeks, but I said that I would. He said nothing further. *He is trusting that I will do it.*

As he stood up, Ron announced, "It's time to leave."

The Club was filling up fast with members meeting over lunch. The rain had stopped and I noticed as I drove away that stylish golf carts filled the greens like cattle in a spring meadow. Men and women in bright clothes seemed to be enjoying themselves. Maybe I am too. Maybe?

*****

Ron's Assessment of Joslyn's Progress

The little bridge of trust I've been building is slowly emerging.

I thought this as I buckled myself into the car. Before I started the engine, though, I used the quiet to dictate a note for Joslyn's file. This is what I said to my recorder:

> *Joslyn experienced some breakthroughs today and shifts in her thinking about herself. She is beginning to own her culpability as a poor leader and recognizes the cost of her need to blame others. She realizes, I hope, that her team doesn't trust her because she makes them the scapegoat for her reluctance to lead.*
>
> *Today's session was fruitful. I will follow-up with Joslyn in two days to make sure she stays committed. She is in a vulnerable and raw stage, and her growth is quite fragile.*

Driving back to my office, I cleared my thoughts so that my intuition could do its work and assist me in finding ways to get her past the ignorance to the havoc she was still creating.

*****

Bottom Line of Leadership

In every organization, people look to the CEO and other members of the management team for guidance. This leadership body must model the cooperation and trust they want from those they lead. This requires that leaders be highly skilled in facilitating unity, which means the ability to unite people for a common purpose. However, the behavior that quickly undermines cooperation and mutual trust is the Blame Game.

A high road leader doesn't engage in blaming anyone, but instead gets people focused on the cause of the problem and then guides them toward a solution. This method is not easy because humans crave drama and prefer to pass blame. Blaming is the path of least resistance and defers the person's acceptance of any culpability for the problem.

When a leader uses blame to hide his or her shortcomings, it fosters an atmosphere of negativity, a cost you cannot afford. Negativity in the workplace decreases employee enthusiasm and creativity, and adversely affects performance and productivity. Worst of all, United States companies lose $3 billion a year due to the impact of negativity on performance. Negativity is contagious because employees with a bad attitude can spread the negative attitude to others. While you may not be the one with negativity, the bad attitude from others may affect your work. Unchecked negativity can harm an employee's mental state and physical health.[14]

In the workplace, only 29 percent of employees are fully engaged while disengaged employees have reached 26 percent. This means that nearly three-quarters of employees are not fully productive. The number one factor the study cited influencing engagement and disengagement was "relationship

---

[14] John Zenger & Joseph Folkman, *The Extraordinary Leader: Turning Good Managers into Great Leaders*, McGraw-Hill, 2009

with immediate supervisor." The Bureau of National Affairs estimates U.S. businesses lose $11 billion annually due to employee turnover.[15]

When a leader strives to be a unifier, bringing different people together to work cooperatively toward a common purpose, miracles can be accomplished. Employees enjoy their work and appreciate one another. When conflicts arise, the team knows how to deal with them constructively.

---

[15] A poll of 1,000 U.S. adults in March 2007 by the Employment Law Alliance *The High Cost of the Bad Boss*, American Management Association website http://www.amanet.org/training/articles/The-High-Cost-of-the-Bad-Boss.aspx

Chapter 4
Courage

*"I admire Joslyn as a person but
disliked her as my boss."*

Time Remaining: 22 Weeks

I decided to mix things up for Joslyn's session because we would be exploring an area—self-awareness—where she was very uncomfortable, and I decided our sessions would be at locations where she could relax and pace. For today, I knew the ideal place to discuss courage. Joslyn obtained her MBA from Stanford but attended the University of Washington for three years, so it was where we would meet. As she preferred to walk and talk, the Seattle campus provides plenty of places to roam. Today, Seattle would hit a whopping 89 degrees.

The two important issues I had to present included information she would not like, yet needed to hear. One was about a chance meeting with Lauren, her former assistant, and the other was the list of the board's concerns about her performance.

The Board's Dissatisfaction List

The previous week, I met with members of Neoteric's board, and from that session, left with a list of specific areas they thought Joslyn needed to work on. It is jarring and humiliating for any employee to discover that their boss is unhappy with their performance, and yet the person usually finds out just before he or she is tossed out the door. I know it's unfair and it happens often with reluctant leaders. I experienced this early in my career.

That meeting with Neoteric's board demonstrated that incomplete and disconnected communications were a problem within the board, and between them and Joslyn. I believed this culture defect was a contributing factor to why Joslyn lacked awareness of their anxieties, for which she was only now being held accountable.

After leaving that meeting I made a note to discuss my disquiet about this culture weakness at an appropriate time with Stephen.

As I sat waiting for Joslyn, enjoying a crisp apple, I looked over my notes. To ensure she remain as their CEO, Joslyn had to provide the board with proof that she could:

- Communicate broadly and widely
- Willingly discuss her personnel plans with them before carrying them out
- Be a unifying force in the company
- Develop internal leaders so she has time to be more strategic
- Inspire higher levels of performance at all levels of the organization
- Build more empowerment and accountability all across the organization
- Build an empowered leadership team who is then able to empower others
- Foster trust throughout the organization
- Foster win-win attitudes among employees
- Build a culture of loyalty and dedication
- Lead by vision, not by fear

I could tell from this list that some of them had developed their desires from reading the current 'hot' leadership books.

"If Joslyn had been given this list when she was hired, things would certainly be different," I thought out loud,

"Maybe they did and she ignored them. I'll need to find out." Nearby, two students who heard me babbling smirked at one another about this 'old dude who talks to himself.' I noticed they walked away as fast as they could. I chuckled somewhat quietly.

Joslyn found me in U of W's Red Square next to the statue to George Washington. I was easy to spot because while there were dozens of students hanging out, I was the only person who wasn't dressed like one. Joslyn's bright outfit announced her arrival from 200 yards away. Today, she was completely in red, in a pantsuit and wearing shoes that resembled Dorothy's ruby slippers. Her small red attaché seemed to glow. Joslyn's long blonde hair was held in place off her neck by a clip with red carnations. To make the theme complete, she carried a red coffee cup! *Maybe the red is a sign that she has not lost hope.* She lifted her cup in greeting and then sat gingerly on an ancient bench. I guess she didn't want to stain her suit.

Joslyn stared at the ground in silence.

Afraid to Face a Problem

"Good morning, Joslyn! It's a pleasure to see you. How are you today?"

"I am tired. I'm mad! I worked until 1:00 a.m. last night and have been putting in long hours all week. I am so upset that I want to fire Jackson right now!" A person walking by looked up in surprise at this outburst; Joslyn noticed and blushed.

"What's going on? What did he do…or didn't do?"

"Jackson has been out of the office on sales calls and mentoring some of his low-performing sales people. He doesn't delegate well, so all the calls and questions he would normally field are being routed to me. The only time I can get my work done is after hours. Worse, he doesn't return my calls or respond to my emails. It's like he either wants to ignore this part of his job, or he's sending me a message."

I asked, "What about Isaiah? I thought he was Jackson's lieutenant. Why isn't he taking on those duties?"

"He should be, but with the vacancy in the COO position, he's been spending a lot of time with Latisha, helping her manage production. Orders are up by 11 percent, and we've been hiring factory workers like crazy."

"Production was Dino's responsibility, the VP who resigned a few months ago, correct?"

With a look of chagrin communicating she didn't want to be reminded about him, she replied, "Yes. We need someone in Dino's seat since production has increased by 7 percent, but..."

She got lost in her thoughts and I hoped she was dwelling on why both Dino and Kelly (the COO) quit—out of protest for her leadership style.

I prompted, "But?"

"But since YOU took away my authority to hire and fire, I'm doing the best I can with the resources I have!"

She continues to ignore her contributions to the problem, while scapegoating others.

I reminded her, "Stephen did not say you could NOT hire someone; he just wants you to consult with him and Angela before you make any personnel changes because..."

She cut in, "Because none of you trust my judgment!"

"That is not a true statement. Allow me to explain why he took that drastic step." I breathed deeply to remind her to do the same. "If Dino wanted his job back, would you rehire him?"

"Yes," she said with reluctance. "But..."

"No buts. Would the company benefit today from Dino's talents?"

"Yes."

"And if Kelly wanted to return as COO, would the company benefit from her talents?"

"Yes."

"Stephen wants assurance that the company does not lose any more good people, and until you prove you are the leader he needs, he reserves the right to question what he perceives as your impaired judgment, especially since Neoteric lost two assets in Kelly and Dino. He agrees with you that the company might be better off if they were still on the payroll. Do you understand his reasoning?"

She hesitated. Hopefully the message sank in that she was making others serve as scapegoats for her poor leadership. "Okay, I get it. I am the one who screwed up by driving them away."

Ah, maybe she is taking accountability. This thought raced through my brain just before I heard, "Even though I didn't do it intentionally!"

We still have work to do, I lamented silently.

"Let's find another place to sit where it's more private." There were now about 100 students milling around. I pointed to a distant spot. As we walked there, I breathed in the fragrance of lilac wafting from a nearby garden. We began the core of this session on a cleaner bench under an ancient alder tree.

Before we sat down she took a long drink from her red cup and then pointed to it. "Lemonade, not vodka!" *She is very sensitive about a lot of things.*

An Inspiring Vision

In the background I could hear students laughing and talking. I asked her to read me the answers to the assignment she committed to two weeks ago.

Pulling a notepad from her red case, she said, "I had mixed feelings about doing this and I'm not sure why. At first, I felt blue but as I wrote I got excited. Any guesses why?"

I responded, "We can explore the reasons for your mixed feelings, but first tell me what you wrote."

"I'll start with the last first." She smiled at her confusing words.

What would it be like to be the person in charge of running an amazing company that had all this?

"I wrote:

It would be easy, less stressful, and I would have more time to be strategic.

"This is where I noticed my excitement. If work could be like this, I would be in seventh heaven every day."

"That was the intent of the question, to get you excited. Good work. Now tell me about the answers to the rest of the questions."

As she read each answer I noted her reactions. She shrugged her shoulders and her face showed no emotion—not even anger. This told me the questions touched her heart and she was not pleased about it. *She might be approaching the sadness stage and why she feels 'blue.'*

Joslyn finished, and I suggested, "Would you like to recap those thoughts into a single sentence?"

Value of Cooperation

After a moment, she said tersely, "I think MY COMPANY would be worth three or four times what it is now IF we trusted each other, we supported each other, we had a singular customer focus, and we worked in concert. A little voice said to me, 'We would be amazing if my people acted like this. Nothing would be impossible.'"

I noticed her phrasing of 'my people' instead of 'we.' This signaled that she had yet to believe that she could create this scenario.

I shifted my position on the unforgiving bench before I said, "Would it help you if we address your sadness and its potential cause?"

She perked up at the question. "Yes."

"What contributed to the good feelings when you started writing?"

"Uhmm...The thought that my job could be less stressful, that I'd have time. That felt exciting."

"Is your job like that now?"

"No!"

"Imagine that a magic genie gives you a wish and you ask for a tropical island to live on. You rush out there with a vision of a tropical paradise and you arrive to find a windswept, arid, uninhabitable rock."

"Okay."

"How would you feel?"

"Disappointed. Angry. Like I was conned."

"Would you feel a sense of loss because there was a gap between what you imagined and the reality?"

"Of course, along with the other feeling I mentioned."

"As CEO, is your job to make good things happen?"

"Yes."

"Do you think you are able to do that now?"

"No!"

"Does that feel the same as finding that your tropical paradise didn't exist?"

She paused to consider this then responded, "Yes. Yes. It does feel the same."

I waited for her to process this.

"Are you saying that Stephen is a genie who promised me paradise?"

"No but what if your title of CEO is the genie?"

"Uhmm. I get it. You said a CEO makes good things happen, right? And I'm not doing that. So if the title is the genie and it conned me...Oh, I get it."

From the look on her face, her mind must be racing. I waited.

Joslyn was looking up at the sky. "Could it be that part of me recognizes what could be possible and that's why I felt exhilarated with this vision? But I'm frustrated that I don't have it?"

"What a great insight! May I add to it?"

She nodded, even though she was still looking up and thinking.

"You most likely think that creating that vision of the future is impossible. That is why you lost the exhilaration. This gap between a dream and reality created the sadness. As I've mentioned, you are experiencing a sense of loss of a previously held image as a successful CEO. It is natural for you to feel that way. It's a sign that you are moving forward."

"But what can I do?" At that moment she sounded like a child instead of an adult.

I knew I needed to be forceful to get her prepared for the news I had to deliver.

I said as gently and firmly as I could, "You asked what you can do, and the answer is to accept the reality you are facing. The tropical island is not what you imagined. You are not the leader you thought you were." Here goes. "The sooner you accept that you both created the situation AND have the power to shift it, the sooner you will feel better."

Her intense glare at me informed that my message had its effect.

She replied forcefully, "You still have to prove to me that it's my fault." She was retreating as I feared and had forgotten the lesson about blame vs. culpability. I made a written reminder to return to her lapse later.

After spending a few minutes getting updated on Joslyn's current projects, I presented her with the list of the board's concerns. As she read it, she trembled as if experiencing a chill. *She is really scared,* I noted. *I must redirect her attention.*

I stood up; she did too. We began walking the campus.

She said, "I haven't been back here since transferring to Stanford. I forgot how peaceful and green it is." She pointed to a building. "My favorite class was there. It was on marketing, and the instructor is the person I credit for my decision to go into sales. She had amazing stories, and listening to them I visualized doing what she talked about."

"So she's to blame?"

Doing a double take, she looked at me and saw my smile. It took her a second to realize I was teasing. She tried to return the smile but it was forced.

After a few minutes of silent walking she asked me what my biggest concern was that I took away from my meeting with the board. I explained, "Some of these desired traits or conditions they presented came from complaints the board received from members of your team, who obtained promises of anonymity. I am certain that the board and employees have been exchanging emails complaining that you are not listening to them. To add fuel to the fire, Angela told me she is extremely disappointed in you because you treat her disrespectfully." *I knew ignoring Angela's phones calls would come back to bite Joslyn.*

She walked over to a nearby bench and sat down. She said nothing but her body language spoke volumes. She stared at the grass and fidgeted like a child called before the principal. I let her cope for a moment then I started walking again. She followed.

"Right now you probably are thinking that you want to take that document, throw it back at them, maybe informing them, 'You can shove your list where the sun doesn't shine!'" That got her laughing, as intended.

I continued, "Now that you have imagined what you must NOT DO, tell me what you...I mean, what a leader would do with this list of concerns."

Hesitantly she said, "I guess I have two choices. Quit or live up to those expectations."

"Before you decide which, let's cover what you will need to make that important decision, and that is courage."

I handed her a bright white Ping-Pong ball with the number **3** written on it.

Inner Leader Trait – Courage

"The next inner leader trait or Ping-Pong ball is courage. I know that you have courage because you wouldn't be so successful in sales without it." She nodded in agreement. "Why do I believe that you have courage?"

Looking up at the sky, she said, "In sales, you face rejection, have doors slammed in your face, and are told 'no' a lot. Frequently, you have to crash through obstacles such as red tape that get put in your way."

"Yes. All that and even more. In leadership, you must tap into that courage because it will carry forward the momentum of your leadership energy and the desire to bring people together. Tell me, what does courage mean to you?"

Pausing she said, "Umm. Courage is being unafraid. If a person has courage she can face things that would normally scare her. Heroic people like a pilot, firefighter, or ER physician are courageous."

I nodded, knowing she needed validation when doing introspection.

"Why does a person such as a senior leader, you or someone else, need courage? Why is it something that you need to be skilled at? Why must a leader be comfortable displaying it?"

She picked up her pace, so I followed. "In sales, rejection is an everyday occurrence, so I need courage to get past that and go for the sale. As a sales executive, I had to say 'no' to deals and to customer requests. As the CEO I now have to say 'no, you can't do that' a lot. That is where I think I need courage. Is that what you were looking for?"

She then turned her body toward me, causing herself to walk backward, which looked funny.

Trying not to laugh, I responded, "That makes sense as it relates to sales but in leadership, it goes far beyond that. As a leader you are put to the test repeatedly. You are the one making things happen, and if your plans go awry, all eyes are directed at you! Leading others requires immense courage, yet leadership of others starts with leading yourself. Self-leadership is defined as the internal ability to lead oneself to make the best choices and decisions on a moment-by-moment basis throughout the day. That act requires courage."

She stood next to me, asking, "Describe for me what you mean by leadership courage? I'm a little confused."

Courage Defined

"People universally define a person who is doing something great, yet risky, out of love or necessity as being courageous. We think of the soldier entering into a gunfight with the enemy while risking personal harm to save a buddy. We think of the person who grabs a boy off the street to prevent him from being hit by a bus. We think of someone who coaxes a gun-toting bank robber to surrender. This is what we imagine as courageous. The term *courage* specifically calls to mind having fortitude in the presence of physical danger, as in a battle and other dangerous situations. However, that meaning is far too limiting because many dangers you face daily are not physical. It takes courage to be the only one standing up against a boss who wants to take a less than honorable path, for example."

I continued. "Individual courage, as I define it, is interrupting your own status quo. You need it when performing important leadership responsibilities such as openly talking about sacred cows, acknowledging a problem no one wants to address, and even accepting a or painful reality like you just did. It took courage to listen to your board's concerns and Stephen's advice to get coached."

She nodded.

"Now more than ever a leader needs to be courageous," I said. "This is a theme I hear repeatedly when I interview accomplished leaders. It takes great courage to be a leader, which is why today it is a foremost leadership trait. You are the primary influencer, a direction- and tone-setter, and your company's conscience. These roles require you to have unshakable confidence in yourself. This type of confidence requires courage to make tough decisions. Each day you must make difficult choices involving standards, risks, morals, ethics, and accountability. Leaders, especially in times of crisis or difficulty, must lead with consistency and extraordinary courage."

"I thought I had unshakable confidence until...all this happened!" She spread her arms out wide in a dramatic fashion.

"Let me table that thought for a second." I continued with the lesson, "Today, just as 50 years ago, the leader must be able to:

- Exude positive energy
- Create momentum and execute
- Play the heavy, sheriff, or bad guy
- Build strong, supportive, empowered teams
- Apply discipline
- Counsel
- Confront people's behaviors
- Set standards
- Raise the bar on everyone's performance
- Terminate people
- Innovate and adapt
- Trust people explicitly
- Say 'no' often

"You must be the solid rock of confidence that both your firm and your team rely on to thrive."

"Right. Right," she responded without conviction.

I needed to hit a pain point for her to really see what I meant. "I've noticed that you don't face tense issues like Jackson's not responding to your requests. I have seen you walk away from employees when you don't agree with their suggestion. You rarely meet face-to-face with Angela. This implies to me that you lack the courage to face tough challenges, especially when it comes to dealing with your people-related issues."

That hit a nerve because she sucked in her breath through her teeth.

"You thought you had unshakable confidence, but this confidence was based on the belief that you are doing the right things. When you discovered you are doing the 'wrong' things, the ground beneath you crumbled. You have a personal status quo that you must shake off and outgrow, and that is the perception that since you are right everyone else must be wrong."

She winced.

"To succeed at Neoteric, or anywhere else you work, you must act more like a true leader and less like a tyrant." By studying her face I knew my words had the desired impact.

Reasons to Be Courageous

After suggesting and finding a place to sit so she could take notes, I said, "The primary argument as to why a true leader, which you are becoming, must be courageous boils down to seven primary reasons."

1. The Right Choice Is Unpopular

"True leadership is not a popularity contest. At times you will take an unpopular stance. You will be criticized either openly or quietly for decisions you make and things that you do. Facing unfair criticism without being swayed or affected by it takes courage. Refraining from getting retribution against your critics is a courageous act. You do not allow personal insults or slights to be a distraction.

2. The Buck Stops with You

"As their leader you have ultimate accountability for the actions of each of the people who work for you. When an employee makes the wrong choice or does the wrong thing, it ultimately reflects back on you, the person who leads that employee. Not flinching when people point the finger of blame at you requires courage. Coaching and counseling someone who proves unreliable takes courage.

3. Lack of Support

"Despite your position of authority, employees will intentionally withhold support from you or attempt to undermine your efforts. This happens most often in dysfunctional groups and companies. An inspirational leader refuses to commit her team to a cause or project that has no obvious support, and strives to gain support if the cause is a worthy one. The refusal to commit before gathering support requires tremendous courage. Gaining support from your team without demanding it or using fear takes courage.

4. Delayed Gains
"You must be willing to sacrifice immediate gain to turn your vision into positive results. Unfortunately, today's leaders are focused on short-term bandages and quick gains, to the disregard and neglect of the long-term impact of their choices. As a leader you need courage to avoid succumbing to this popular no-win trend.

5. Leaps of Faith
"You must be willing to use methods that are untested, be courageous and willing to blaze a new trail. A leader role is a risk-taker, even if you don't define yourself as one, because what works today may not work tomorrow. You focus on the greater good as a way of not allowing fear to stop you from taking risks. You take on each challenge with confidence that comes from courage.

6. Reliance on Other's Expertise and Experience
"You cannot be an expert in everything. You need to openly acknowledge skills and knowledge you lack and to understand your limitations. You fill gaps in your abilities by asking others to become involved.

7. Realism Is Ground Zero
"You must truly want and accept the unvarnished truth from the people in the trenches. You must do everything in your power to get employees to be honest with you. It takes courage to ask and to hear their responses, which may not be what you want to hear. Leadership is grounded in reality."

Joslyn rapidly wrote in her notepad.

After a pause I quipped, "At times, reality bites! Just like the news you heard today."

She groaned but kept writing. When she paused, I continued. "There is another fear-inducing aspect of leading, and that comes from a battle many leaders have within themselves regarding uncertainty and control, which is one of many leadership paradoxes.

Leadership Paradox

> Leaders must take risks as they face the unknown. However, leaders exist to reduce uncertainty.

"Dealing with this paradox of leadership demonstrates the importance of courage that is required of a great leader. This is where experience leads to good judgment, which creates a willingness to step into the unknown. Not all leaders understand this paradox."

It was nearly noon so we decided to dine in the student union building. Joslyn found us a table in the shade where we could talk privately. All around us was a whirl of activity generated by the students and faculty whizzing by on their bikes and skateboards. Nearly every student was hunched over with an overly large backpack growing out of their back. I wondered, *Will any of them ever walk with a straight spine?*

After dispensing the food and drinks, she sat across from me, ready to listen.

I said, "The starting point for you to be more courageous is to frequently ask yourself this question: *What message will people take from my response to this situation?* When you are their leader, people are always watching you. In the face of adversity, such as Isaiah sending nasty emails to you or Angela chastising you in front of the board, if you chose to run away, blame someone, or make excuses, those watching will lose faith in your ability to lead them. On the other hand, in the face of adversity, if you chose to take wise risks, challenge the status quo, and act with confidence, you will reinforce the faith people have in your ability to lead them. Your own view of leadership courage begins with how you perceive yourself. This is because of the next truism about leading, the 8th **Natural Law of Leadership**.

> **You cannot lead others
> until you can lead yourself.**

"What does this truism mean to you?"

She stopped eating her salad. Pointing a fork at me, she replied, "Well, it maybe says that how I deal with fear and uncertainty in the small things affects how well I deal with the big ones. If I lack the courage to, say, hold my daughter accountable, it will be hard to hold Isaiah accountable."

I could see a lightness fill her eyes. She just had a breakthrough moment, but I would wait to find what it was. I nodded and said, "That's a great insight."

Payoffs of Courage

After finishing our meals, I continued with today's lesson. "A true leader gets things accomplished on time and on budget. You can deal with obstacles and challenges because you can see beyond the horizon and dream of the future. You can face up to any challenge, even when it's a problem not of your own making. You move forward with little regard to the personal cost."

She finished off her drink to free her hands to take notes.

"A true leader imagines a better future and makes it a reality, and in doing so you look at your own work with thoughts of what could be possible. With the confidence that comes from courage, you can understand the risks and be willing to take them. You can act thoughtfully, carefully, and prudently, even when you need to leap into the abyss of the unknown. You can make calculated decisions by weighing the odds and valuing the prize. You can assess options, weigh priorities, and consult your advisers because you strive to make an objective decision. With courage, you are both a dreamer and risk-taker. Why can you do all this? Because the true leader is inspired more by the anticipation of success than by the fear of failure.

"Finally, a leader needs courage to be ethical. You always choose the ethical and accountable High Road, and your onramp is courage."

We finished our meal and I carried the various items to the recycle and compost bins. In environment-conscious Seattle, nothing is thrown away.

High Road Leader's Definition of Courage

She was still tense as we walked around the campus again. Because it was quite warm, we stayed close to the tall trees, where it was cooler.

I continued the lesson. "To better understand the level of your own courage, you start by examining what drives a person to act in ways that take her beyond her perceived limits, which is another way to define courage. For the person holding a position of leadership, courage in action is:

- challenging the unsatisfactory status quo
- tapping into the power of one person and one team
- slaying sacred cows
- speaking out and speaking up

- standing up to bullies
- being honest and telling your truth to others
- owning up to and admitting your mistakes
- looking less than perfect and still retaining your confidence
- questioning prevailing assumptions or conventional wisdom
- being intentional while overcoming your fears

"All these can be summed up as rising above one's self or refusing to take the easy way out."

I checked to see if she understood all of this, and she did.

Costs of Courage

"I have mentioned before that a majority of people in a leadership position are reluctant to lead, and the primary reason for that is the cost of being courageous. Reluctant leaders tend to claim *I am not a leader* even when they are. They somehow intuitively sense the high price attached to owning the label."

She nodded that she understood.

"Courage requires risk-taking. Each time you take a risk and go into the unknown, you are being courageous. Only the passage of time determines whether an act is courageous or rash. Leading requires you to face your emotions because courage either exists or doesn't and is based upon how you feel in the moment. In most courageous acts you lead with your gut."

She interrupted, "I understand that a leader takes risks and I've always been willing to do that. What else is the cost for me to be courageous?"

"Yours is an insightful question. The other cost involves your personal values. You must have a clearly defined sense of what is both valuable and worth fighting for. Courage is an emotional commitment to an ideal. However, your gut-level feelings must be based upon a defined value. The adult who saves the child reacts without thinking because one of her previously defined values is that life is sacred and every child is worth saving. The soldier who saves his buddy faces immense risk because he believes that no one should be left behind and that the cause he is fighting for is a worthy one."

"I see but I don't always feel that brave when it comes to dealing with people. I'll admit that things I do might create chaos, yet I shy away from other people's chaos and drama."

Smiling big, I responded, "Congratulations! That is important to know about yourself. Realizing that is the halfway point toward tapping into the courage required to stop running from those messy people situations."

A nice smile showed on her face.

Actions that Help You Become More Courageous
"Are you ready to continue?" I asked.

She said she was.

"This is the perfect moment for us to address your fear of other people's dramas. When you make a fear conscious, you lessen its power. May I take you through a quick exercise that will make your fears conscious, so that you can feel powerful over them?"

"I guess so."

I led her to a private shady spot to sit where she could focus and relax.

When she was ready, I instructed, "Please close your eyes and answer each question without thinking.

"Are you willing this minute to talk with Jackson and Isaiah and Curtiss about their insulting behaviors?"

"No."

"Are you willing to talk honestly and openly with Angela?"

"No."

"Are you willing this minute to discuss with any board member their concerns?"

"No."

"We are done. I can tell you're tense, so please relax and breathe."

"What was that about?" she asked.

"I made you face your fears—conversations that you don't want to have and will avoid having. Now that you know what they look like, fear's power over you will be lessened. Not immediately but the confidence to take these actions will grow."

"Okay." Her voice sounded doubtful.

"I took you through that as a precursor to the growth steps you will assign yourself."

She looked at me sternly.

"I want to accomplish something that enhances your courage before we agree on your growth steps."

It was now extremely hot and perspiration showed on both our faces. We headed toward a building in order to find a cool spot to land. Along the way, we passed a group of 15 students, and the reason I noticed them is that while they were sitting very close to one another, shoulder-to-shoulder or holding hands, none were talking to the other. Each had their attention tuned to at least two different pieces of technology. I commented, "I am concerned because that is how the next generation will show up at the workplace: spending an inordinate amount of time communicating via technology yet not having the ability to communicate one-on-one or have normal conversations. I apologize for getting off track."

She said, "My daughter is like that. Sometimes the only way to get her to respond is with a text message, even when we're in the same room!"

By that time we had found a quiet area to sit and work. Just then, a custodian with a squeaky cart went by so I waited until she could hear me.

Sitting across from her, I said, "Where was I? Oh, yeah. Anyone can increase their ability to face tough issues, have difficult, dreaded conversations, and feel confident when things don't look hopeful. All it takes is a commitment, a plan, and practice. Let's brainstorm ways that you can practice courage in terms of your specific daily habits."

While I wrote and prompted, Joslyn paced the hallway and spoke her thoughts out loud. When finished, these were her suggestions for herself:

- Tell the truth to others and especially tell it to myself
- Conduct a daily review of my personal courage
- Face my fears and do it anyway
- Be accountable for all the things I am and have, because in some way I fostered them
- Stand up for what I believe and stay consistent in those beliefs
- Be more open-minded because many of my beliefs are someone else's opinion that I adopted as my own without question

- Know my leadership intention and more specifically those things I value as a leader
- See myself as a confident person who displays courage whenever and wherever it's needed

I handed the sheet to her. "Through these eight actions you can grow bolder; practicing them becomes your path to greater courageousness."

As a reward for this hard work, I related a story about courageousness, while she sat down, sipping from her red cup. The sweet smell of lemonade surrounded us.

Lauren's Words

"Lauren, your former assistant, was at the board meeting and asked to speak with me."

"Why?" I could tell that the news alarmed her.

"She wanted to talk about you." At this Joslyn swallowed hard but remained silent. "Doing that took a lot of courage on her part. Lauren is now the daughter-in-law of Travis, the board's legal counsel. She married his son two weeks after she left Neoteric."

"Is she going to sue me…us for wrongful termination?!" I understood her fear.

"Hold on and relax. There is no bad news in what she told me. She still cares about you and wanted to know how you are doing. Travis must have informed her I was working with you. She felt an obligation to provide me with some insights about you."

Relief came into her blue eyes, along with curiosity.

I asked, "Do you recall the reason Lauren gave for quitting?"

"Not really. She was just unhappy all the time."

"That is part of why she sought me out: to clarify what happened. My guess is Travis said something which perhaps compelled her to come to your defense. She had nothing but praise for you as a person. However, she had to resign because when it came being your employee, she said you acted like The Hulk."

Joslyn allowed a small laugh to escape.

I continued, "She admired you as a woman but she felt extremely disrespected in return. She felt scared each time you raged at her. She tried her best to please you and do what you asked, but you were never satisfied. She added, *I like her as a person, but not as my boss.* She had planned on inviting you to her wedding but thought you had burned that bridge. She had tears in her eyes when she spoke about the wedding."

Joslyn was deeply touched but didn't know how to respond.

I inquired, "How would you describe the relationship that existed when she worked for you?"

Her face flushed as she thought. "I liked her. She was outgoing and did whatever I asked of her without complaints. I...We didn't have a close relationship, though it seemed like she wanted one. I didn't know she was scared of me...of The Hulk!"

"What do her comments tell you about yourself?"

"That I have a problem."

I laughed. "That's obvious to both of us, but please be more specific."

"I guess...since we are talking about courage, I made it so that she couldn't find the courage to talk to me about how badly I was treating her."

"It's natural for an employee to feel uncomfortable speaking to her boss about disrespectful treatment. Imagine how much harder it is when the person you need to confront about disrespect is the CEO!"

"I can see that now but I was simply her boss." This came out as a whine.

I needed a deeper reflection from her. "Think about her feedback as it relates to your courage. What are your thoughts?"

Contemplating my question brought a frown to her lightly tanned face. Slowly she said, "I didn't have the courage to ask Lauren what was wrong." More rapidly she continued, "I was not willing to examine what was hurting our relationship. Until the day she said, 'I quit,' I assumed things were fine between us, though I was peeved by her occasional incompetence."

"Was it incompetence or maybe something else?"

"What do you mean?

"Could what you perceived as a flawed employee be your unrealistic demands? Could it be your never-ending dissatisfaction?"

She held her spine erect and looked up. "It hurts to admit, but it was most likely my demands and…" She paused to think. "It was also my not knowing how to reach out to her." This confession was hard for her, so we walked the space. She needed a pause to recover her poise.

I asked, "What would be a courageous action to take now that you know how Lauren feels about you? Think about this while I share an experience."

Courage in Action

A firm where I worked put in place a cash-based incentive program which was designed to reward employees when the firm reached a certain level of profit for the year. The calculation of each employee's share, which was complex, was weighted toward the employees with more tenure at the organization.

That year we exceeded the profit target so Alan, our CEO, and I set aside time to determine the amount each employee had earned. Alan gave me a prepared spreadsheet to use and, following his format, I calculated the amounts that each person earned. Before my team issued checks, I ran my calculations by Alan, who agreed with them.

I thought we were done!

About 90 minutes after the checks were issued to very happy employees, Alan raced into my office and shouted, 'You need to get those checks back from everyone!' I was in shock. 'What do you mean? Why do I need to get the checks back?'

'I made a mistake in my formula and everyone's amount is incorrect,' he replied. I thought he was exaggerating the emergency.

Alan showed me his spreadsheet assumptions and where the calculations when awry. I could see that there were ten payout errors out of 50 employees we paid. While the total payout was correct, six received more than they were entitled to and four were underpaid. The most any employee was overpaid was $25. Most of the corrections ranged from $3 to $7. Each correction was meaningless when compared to the total each employee received.

I argued, 'We don't need to do anything about this. This is not a problem.' Again, Alan insisted that I get the checks back from everyone, or at least the ten people impacted.

I could have acquiesced but believed I needed to take a stand. I refused to ask employees for their checks and explained why. 'By now everyone has deposited or cashed their check, and to insist that they write us a check for a few dollars would be both ludicrous and insulting. One thing I know about people is that once you make a financial commitment to them, never go back on your word. The errors will not hurt the company in any way, but making it known to the employees that we made a miscalculation would cause more harm than good. We cannot mess with what now has become an entitlement!'

Alan again demanded that I take their checks back or ask the ones who were overpaid to write us a check. Again, in a very polite and respectful way, I said that I would not and was firmly set against doing so. We argued for almost an hour. I continued to explain why I believed it would be both improper and send the wrong message for us to make corrections just because of a few dollars. Finally, Alan backed down and let the matter go. I don't think that he was ever convinced of my reasoning. He was an engineer, and everything had to be accurate down to the last penny.

"It took a lot of courage for me to take a stance on something that could get me fired, courage that I did not know I had. I took the stand because of my strong belief in the importance of people's contributions to the company and their feelings."

Leadership Lesson

I asked what she got from this story.

She replied, "I see your story from the CEO point of view. If I were your boss, I would have canned your butt! Or at least that would have been my customary way to deal with you. Looking at it from an employee view, meaning you are Lauren in this story, I understand why Lauren stood her ground. This is coming out awkward. What I mean to say is, except for a few people, no one has ever stood up to me." She thought for a moment. "Even if they had I wasn't ready to hear it."

She was having another breakthrough so I signaled for her to continue.

"Maybe they did try and I took it as rebellion or meanness or even defiance." She massaged her eyes. "I have a lot to think and rethink. Oh, and write. I have been writing in my journal but not regularly."

I smiled and nodded to send the message that I understood and was glad. "Your leadership journal is where you can find your inner truths by being honest with yourself."

Joslyn's Assignments

"You do a good job of showing me the truth…even when I don't what to hear it. I know you must be honest with me, and it stills hurts when you tell me the truth I've tried to hide from. How about if I make it my assignment to come up some ideas to improve relationships? I will run them by you so you can give me feedback so I won't make relationships worse."

She needs to show courage. "As I see it, you have some important relationships to mend, which will test your newfound courage. I encourage you to give yourself assignments that are more than ideas. Tell me actions you will take."

She cringed but made suggestions anyway. "I will decide how to make amends with Lauren. I'll first run my plan by you and then carry it out right away."

"Great."

"I will decide the best approach with Jackson now that I realize that he is probably reacting in kind to my treatment of him. He is probably like Lauren, doing his best to please me but receiving my displeasure instead. He wants to talk with Joslyn but I give him my Hulk instead."

I laughed.

After chuckling at herself, she continued. "My third way for challenging myself is to develop a plan for improving communications with Angela. I'll email my thoughts to you and, after you bless them, I will carry them out. I dread this one.

I have to ask this. "Will you commit to me that you will do these?"

She started to shrug but caught herself. "I commit." She sounded firm.

Facing Up to the Board's Expectations
"Those are all courageous actions to take. I would suggest one more. Based on what we covered today, you still need to deal with the board's expectations. It's a long list but you need to start immediately to take this seriously. How will you turn that rocky island into a tropical paradise?"

She was at a loss and began biting her lip.

"How about you start with one thing on their list?" I showed it to her. "Select one that you think is most important."

After studying it, she surprised me with her answer.

"There are two I can start today. Lead by vision and communicate that vision broadly."

"Excellent! What can you accomplish over the next two weeks?"

"Well, first I can redo the two assignments you gave me regarding vision, and second, talk to employees and my team about what Neoteric could look like years from now."

"That is a great start," I said. "May I offer one final insight?"

"Yes."

"Your overall growth step this week is to repair relationships so that trust can bloom again. Four plans and four relationships. I believe you will find parallels among all four plans. Look for the common threads. Write about them in your leadership journal."

"Will do, coach!" she said in a playful way.

It was now hot in this hallway and I knew neither of us wanted to return to work sweaty and sticky, but that's life. Most of her hair had fallen out of the clip and was clinging to her neck. I felt how wet my shirt had become. We moved into an empty classroom where the air conditioner worked to finish out this session.

Paul's Tale

"One more story before we end today's session. It is about how much harm a leader lacking courage can do to an employee who cares."

Paul emailed me this story after meeting him at a leadership conference I spoke at. He asked for my thoughts, which I openly shared. I will tell this in his words:

I was an accountant in a big organization and my responsibility included entering accounts payable and expenses into the general ledger. I also handled a small petty cash fund for our business unit. I noticed that a sales employee was doing something funny with the receipts for the cash reimbursement requests he turned in. It looked to me like he was doctoring them, and this happened several more times. I was fresh out of college but I knew this was inappropriate behavior.

One day, after this employee turned in another apparently altered receipt for several hundred dollars, I contacted the vendor and asked them to fax me a copy of the original receipt. I now had proof of the alteration designed to ensure this employee was reimbursed for more than he paid out. It was a small amount but I knew his action went against company policy.

I took my concern and evidence to the manager of our business unit, who promised that it would be handled. Later, I heard that the employee was terminated.

But that is not the end of the story! The company's CFO—my boss's boss—called me on the carpet for worrying about immaterial amounts. He said, 'You must not have enough work to do if you're wasting time questioning someone else's expenses.' Soon after that, the people I worked with referred to me as 'the company snitch' behind my back. Each time I applied for advancement in the company, I was turned down.

I don't regret what I did. I could never trust my bosses again because they made me out as the bad guy for doing what I felt was part of everyone's job. As soon as a good job came up outside the company, I took it.

I wrote back to Paul: It is clear to me that the people you worked for were not leaders. They knew they had a problem but rather than have the courage to deal with an unethical salesman, they relied on the tried-and-true blame game. Basically they shot the messenger who told them the truth. What you did, Paul, was take the high road, and I acknowledge your courage.

Leadership Lesson

She said when I was finished, "Tell me the lesson, Joslyn."

I knew she was mocking me but she was entitled, based on what I took her through today.

She continued, "Lauren and probably Jackson feel like Paul. Even though Lauren's gone, I can do something about my communication breakdown with Jackson."

I nodded that I agreed.

She contemplated this story a little more and I saw that light come on in her eyes again. *Good sign.* I could tell she wanted to ask me more questions, but we had other places to be.

After agreeing on the location of her next session, I accompanied her to her car. Walking together we shared snarky comments about the clothing and grooming trends of the students. Yes, it was impolite, but we chatted about how each generation chooses their badge of honor through their clothing choices. She laughed when I described my generation's long hair, tie-dye, and bell bottoms. We both mocked her generation's love of mullets and big hair, acid-wash jeans, and parachute pants.

As she eased herself into her late model BMW, I quipped, "I am willing to bet $1,000 that we will see all those outdated styles become the rage again."

Joslyn smirked and raised her eyebrows.

As we said our goodbyes, I was thankful she was in a better frame of mind, which I attributed to Lauren's feedback. After making two mental notes—to send Lauren a thank-you gift to reward her courage, and to contact Paul to see how he was doing—I joined the huge traffic crawl heading east.

*****

Joslyn's Assessment of Her Progress

"I am surprised how good I feel, all things considered." *I normally don't talk to myself out loud but I'm doing it.*

"Yes, I have only five months to turn things around. Yes, the board expects more of me than I've given. Yes, I'm scared but I'll show them what I am made of. Ron helped me to see what I thought is courage is something else, maybe anger. I am mad.... who am I mad at? Why am I so angry?"

Traffic was moving slowly so I turned on the radio so I could relax with music. I took three deep breaths like he taught me. It helped.

A tear came to my eye because I was thinking of Lauren and how much I affected her. That is when I had the realization that I was mad at myself. *I've done this to myself, haven't I?*

For the first time in a long time, I felt there was a light at the end of the tunnel, but I would need to find my courage to get to it and I knew a train was bearing down on me.

*****

Bottom Line of Leadership

The greater the challenge, the sweeter is the accomplishment. Despite any fear, the High Road leaders rise to the occasion because they know that the long-term rewards far outweigh the costs of facing the challenge. This is based upon their vision for a better tomorrow.

Courage is a non-negotiable trait of a CEO and anyone in a leadership position, because no one else can fight your battles. As a leader of people, you will engage in battles for support, cooperation, accountability, and taking the honorable path. Courage arises from recognizing within yourself any small challenges so that when you need to rise above yourself, you have the confidence necessary to do so.

Poor leaders have a substantial influence on an organization's success. They consistently achieve less-effective results, create greater turnover, discourage employees, and frustrate customers. Good leaders will achieve good results. Great leaders produce great results.

In one well-studied, multi-leader organization, poor leaders actually lost money for the company while good leaders in the same organization made a reasonable profit, substantially more than the poor leaders. The extraordinary or outstanding leaders nearly doubled the profit generated by the good leaders[16].

Courage is required to turn a group of mediocre leaders into a team of committed and caring movers and shakers. People who are reluctant to be influencers need courage to rise above their inclination to let others take the lead.

---

[16] *The State of the American Workplace: Employee Engagement Insights for U.S. Business Leaders*, findings from Gallup's ongoing study of the American workplace from 2010 through 2012

Chapter 5
Self-Awareness

"I am afraid I will fall down again. I've lost my stride and not sure if I'll ever get it back."

Time Remaining: 18 Weeks

A Crisis in Faith – from Joslyn's Viewpoint

Trying to find some comfort I thought, *I am feeling the pressure and I don't have any place to hide.*

This was my rationale for arriving at Mr. Rael's office an hour before my appointment. After having several meetings there, I regarded his office as an oasis in the midst of chaos.

I could tell that his assistant, *what was her name?* was unsure about letting me sit in there until he arrived, but he'll understand. Crap! Another text message from Isaiah. Why can't he handle things without me?

I told myself, *Calm down.* I tried relaxing on his comfy leather couch as I went through the 64 emails I received since this morning. I was so engrossed in this that I didn't hear Ron enter the room until he dropped his keys on the floor.

"You startled me!" I shouted at him.

"Good morning, Joslyn. How are you today?"

I raised my head, shook my shoulders, and looked at him. He stood patiently looking at me as if studying me. I hoped he wouldn't notice that my eyes were rimmed in red and bloodshot.

As Ron repositioned a chair to sit next to the couch, I had to confess. "I haven't slept much in the past few weeks. I keep going over in my mind the board's concerns. I keep working on the plan you approved but I'm not sure it's working because I fear the board's ignoring me! Now Stephen just texted that he wants to meet right away, but...I don't want to face him alone. Can you be there? Could you be an intermediary? I am so exhausted that I think I will lose my temper and get into a shouting match."

In my agitation, I knocked over the mug his assistant gave me, spilling coffee on his grey carpet. "I'm sorry. I'm so clumsy." *What's wrong with me?*

He took charge of this problem calmly and soon the mess was gone and I had a fresh cup in front of me. *I wish my team supported me the way his does.*

Cause of My Angst

Ron said in a warm and calming manner, "Please relax, Joslyn. We will have a productive session once you are centered and back in your body."

He took me through a series of breathing exercises followed by repetitive affirmations. Normally I hate this woo-woo stuff, but within minutes I felt calmer and grounded. It felt good.

In his calm way he asked, "May I share my thoughts with you?"

"Yes."

"I believe I have insight into what might be going on with you. Do you recall the change curve I showed you at our last session?"

I nodded that I did.

"You are moving into the bargaining stage of this transformation but have not yet fully transitioned out of the angry phase. Add in a small dose of depression and that's a formula for sleepless nights. In any significant loss, a person will do anything (like you are doing) to be spared the pain of transition. You want to bargain as a temporary truce. You are likely to engage in 'what ifs...' as a tactic to avoid the pain you're feeling. It is natural for you, in this third stage of loss, to want the clock to be reset to avoid feelings of guilt. In this state, you would do almost anything to avoid the pain of swallowing your pride while remaining anchored in the past and attempting to negotiate your way out of the hurt. You could even be experiencing a large dose of depression, another stage of grieving. We often think of the five stages of grief transitions as lasting weeks or months, yet each phase of loss is a direct response to your feelings that can last for minutes or hours as you move across the spectrum of change.

"How does this speak to you?" he asked.

I replied, "I can go along with most of it, except for the depression. I feel like I've been in a car crash and everything hurts. It's a pain I can't relieve."

"What do you think that I can do to help you get past this painful feeling and move through this stage?"

"You once told me about visualization. Can we do that?"

He asked me to lie on the couch, close my eyes and take ten deep breaths. He instructed me to clear my mind of all thoughts and focus on my breath and stay present. Then I was to imagine a serene setting and see myself there.

As I breathed through my nose I could detect the wonderful scent of plumeria, which I hadn't noticed before. I imagined myself on a beach in Hawaii, lying in the warm sun. I heard the crashing surf. I don't know how long I remained this way but when I 'came to,' I felt better, calmer.

He said gently, "Today, any time you feel anxious, close your eyes, take three deep breaths, and recapture that scene. Will you do that?"

Instead of responding, I closed my eyes again and took one more deep breath.

When I opened my eyes, Ron looked at me with a grin and said, "You want me in your meeting with Stephen. Why do you think I need to be there? You are fully capable of meeting him on your own. I sense that your normal self-confidence has vanished again. What has changed?"

I blinked slowly, recapturing the feeling of relaxing in the warm sun. "Well, until you presented me the board's list of demands...I mean, concerns...I thought I was on solid ground, at least with some members of the board. Now I know I am not. I think that if I go meet with him, I'll have to beg...I mean, negotiate...for my job. Is that true?"

"Did Stephen tell you why he wants to meet with you?"

"No."

"Then how do you know why he wants to meet with you? You are making a huge assumption about his agenda."

"Umm..." *He's right. I am.*

Problem with Assuming

Not waiting for a verbal response, Ron slipped into his peaceful coaching voice. "I recall a professor I had in a college math class who assigned us a complex problem to solve. The next day, when I presented my answer, he asked, 'How, Mr. Rael, did you arrive at this solution?' I attempted to explain myself, yet he expressed confusion at my reasoning. Again, he asked me how I came to my conclusion and, defending myself, I said, 'I assumed...' and went on to explain my thought process.

"Then in front of the entire class, he walked over to the board and wrote ASS U ME. 'Mr. Rael,' he said in a tone that one uses with an unruly or petulant child, 'Let's dissect this word.' Pointing to each part he said mockingly, 'When you assume something without evidence or asking for help, you make an *ass out of you and me!'*

"I was so embarrassed I wanted to disappear. Of course, the class laughed at my expense."

After relating this tale, he added, "While I am not calling you the alternative name for a mule, the sentiment still applies. By assuming something without proof or asking for more information, you are making a fool of yourself regarding whatever Stephen wants."

I nodded but remained silent.

"Let's take a minute and talk about your current mood. Up until a few weeks ago, you were a very confident and mostly capable executive. Today, you seem to have misplaced that poise. What is really going on, Joslyn?"

Faltering terribly, I said, "It's hard to explain." Unconsciously, I had curled into a ball and only noticed when I saw my reflection in his office window. I straightened my spine and sat up. "As you know, I am a runner. Being a CEO is like running an ultra-marathon every day. Before your coaching started, I was confidently running the race with my normal stride. Now that I know the board is unhappy with my performance, at least some aspects of it, it feels like I tripped and twisted my knee. Now that I am running again, I feel like my once-comfortable stride has gone because I am protecting my leg so that I don't stumble again. Actually, I am afraid that *I will fall down again, and I'm not sure if I'll ever get my stride back!*"

"What is this fear about? What does your analogy represent? Please try to be specific."

I stood up and began to pace nervously; I didn't notice until later that I was barefoot, having slipped off my shoes while lying on the couch. "Well. I'm afraid of losing my job. Being fired is brutal and embarrassing. I guess I'm embarrassed of what my employees think of me as their boss. I am afraid that I cannot change and be the leader you want ME to be."

"I appreciate the honesty. Do you want to change, Joslyn? Do you feel the need to lead differently, to shift the ways you behave?"

"To tell you the truth, I am not sure. Maybe I do and then again I don't. Could I just have someone to take care of these softer issues, like employee morale, while I focus on sales and customers?"

"Yes, you truly want to negotiate your way out of this mess, not wanting to face up to your self-created problems."

I didn't have a response. While his accusation—feedback, he calls it—stung, I knew in my heart he was right. Without thinking, I sat back down and stared at my phone and began to text Isaiah. When I realized that I was intentionally ignoring him, I placed the phone in my briefcase and apologized.

Ron nodded his acceptance and said, "Joslyn, I have another story that may explain what is going on with you. May I proceed?"

I nodded my approval, though why he needed it, I didn't know.

The Vacation

A colleague, Terry, told me about a trip she took as a teenager with her parents to visit the Grand Canyon. They lived in Vermont and, at the time, a road trip from there to Arizona took three days of intense driving. Terry said that her dad had a specific itinerary in his head and followed it for the entire three days. He knew, according to his charts and maps, where he needed to be at any certain time. All during the drive he consulted his watch and drove the exact speed limit and even used a stopwatch to reduce the time it took to fuel up. Terry and her mom grew bored with the long hours on the road so they began to linger at the restroom and meal stops he built into his timetable. Whenever he thought they were taking too long, her dad threatened to leave them behind.

On the morning of the fourth day, they finally reached the Grand Canyon. Terry's dad located one of his designated scenic points and parked their car. Tired and bored, Terry and her mother got out to stretch and enjoy the view. They noticed that her dad stayed in the car looking at his watch.

After about 15 minutes, he walked over to where his wife and daughter sat and announced, 'Okay. Get in the car; it's time to start the trip home.' Terry told me, 'I was shocked, appalled, and embarrassed. This was the first of the world's natural wonders I had ever visited. I wanted to stay there and enjoy it because we had paid a high price to get there.' Luckily her mom put her foot down, and in the end they spent three days sightseeing and hiking before heading back. 'While Mom and I were enjoying ourselves, Dad was sitting in our car with smoke coming out his nose and steam spewing from his ears.'

Terry believed enjoyment and relaxation were the purpose of this vacation, while her father's purpose was to follow and beat a predetermined schedule, thus missing the whole point of visiting a place of wonder. He focused solely on the endpoint and schedule, while Terry and her mom focused on the experience or journey.

"You want me to tell you what I took away from your story," I said before realizing it. His coaching was affecting me in so many ways and I felt a little like Pavlov's dog but in a good way.

He waited for me to answer my own question.

Leadership Lesson

I said, "There is a line in a Paul Simon song: 'Slip Slidin' Away.' That's what came to mind. Seems that the closer your friend, what was her name? Terry? I mean, the closer her dad got to his destination, the less he cared about it. I think that is what Paul's lyric means."

He replied, "That is a very insightful analysis and right on the mark. I will add how my story relates to your current situation. Are you ready to learn what you can do to regain your comfortable stride?"

I nodded that I was.

Ron went into his teaching mode. "My point, as it relates to leadership, is that while one aspect of being a leader is to get your organization to a certain place, such as achieving sales targets or profitability levels, it is not the main point of running a business. Sales growth is a point on your journey but not the destination. A CEO and her team lead a business to create an 'experience' for the shareholders, its partners (i.e., customers and vendors), and the employees, in the context of what the business is about."

I nodded, though I was confused.

"The behaviors you display to your employees and board are like Terry's father. You are so focused on the top and bottom line that you are missing the point of the whole journey. The board wants you to focus on the journey, rather than specific points or milestones."

I started to reach for my crutch again—the phone—then decided against it. "I think I understand, especially if I identify with Terry. My Daddy is a bit like that, a man who was very strict and demanding, who seemed to miss the meaning of life, the emotion and the passion. I guess I turned out more like him than I am willing to admit."

"Your attempt at a smile tells me that you have returned to your body, which is important because the work we will do today will get intense quickly."

I felt my smile grow. A small laugh popped out of me.

Inner Leader Trait – Self-Awareness

Ron walked over to his desk, grabbed another white Ping-Pong ball and placed in into my clammy hand as he sat beside me again. I stared at it, noticing it had the number **4** written on it in black ink.

Waiting until he had my full attention, he said, "The next inner leader trait or Ping-Pong ball is self-awareness. To me, this is among the most important leadership traits because without it, any leader can fail quickly."

I felt myself flinching at his comment.

"Without self-awareness, you don't know if the other inner traits are being activated. You also don't know what sort of impact your actions are generating—positive, neutral, or harmful."

I felt myself biting my lower lip so I eased up and breathed deeply.

He paused before continuing. "As a coach I serve as your personal mirror. I hold up this mirror and reflect back what I see without judgment. I show you the truth that you reveal to me. If you do not like what you see in this mirror, you have three choices. One, you could break the mirror, a nonproductive act because you are still the same. Two, you could search for a better mirror. That one might tell you the truth and it might not. Three, you could do something about the person whose reflection you see."

I nodded, but said nothing. *I trust that this will make sense soon.*

"A few sessions ago I suggested that you make a list of how you would describe yourself as a CEO, identifying areas where you excel and areas where you think you need to improve.

May I assume you did it?"

I couldn't resist. "What did you just tell me about assumptions?"

It was the first time I saw him embarrassed. "I apologize. Guess I was slip slidin' away!"

As my laughter joined with his, it felt good. He succeeded in putting me at ease.

I opened my notebook and scanned the list. It had been a while since I completed it, and the first thing I noticed is that I had listed more positives than negatives.

How will my list compare with what the board told him? I felt fearful, but couldn't dwell on it because he said, "Please read what you wrote."

I read from my first list.

I am good or great at:
- *working with customers*
- *negotiating long-term contracts with customers and vendors*
- *getting things done on my terms*
- *following up on my goals*
- *conducting meetings*
- *communicating what my needs are*
- *getting others' input*
- *holding down expenses*
- *making my company profitable*
- *keeping operating costs low*
- *increasing revenues through sales promotions, pricing options, and discounting*
- *managing the company as a whole*
- *being accountable.*

Feeling some trepidation, I read the second list.

Things that I think I can improve upon are:

- *keeping my employees' concerns in mind*
- *getting people to cooperate with me and with one another*
- *understanding why people do what they do*
- *selecting the right employees*
- *balancing my needs with the needs of the board.*

His silence added to my unease. Then he looked over my shoulder and pointed to a specific strength—*communicating what my needs are*—and asked, "What is your proof? How do you know that this is something you are good at?"

I was puzzled by his inquiry. "I just *sense* that I am good at it."

He pointed to several more and asked the same question. I quickly realized I was unable to describe some specifics, meaning I had no proof that most of my plusses were true. He then directed my attention to an area where I thought I was deficient—*selecting the right employees*—asking, "How do you know that this is something you need to improve?"

That got to me. "How am I supposed to know? No one tells me anything!" I glared at him and wanted to leave.

Ron let my storm pass and walked over to his desk. I wasn't sure if this was meant to calm me or him. He grabbed a document and a book.

Leadership Self-Awareness

Placing the document in front of me, he adopted his peaceful persona, which I envied at that moment. *I wish I could be like that whenever my employees are angry with me.*

He said calmly, "A leader must always be aware of her impact on the people around her. Those impacted by your actions extend beyond your employees; you have an effect on Neoteric's customers and vendors, your shareholders, the general public, and even strangers. Do you want to know what many in these groups think of you right now?"

His change in topics was so smooth that I relaxed some.

After a deep breath I responded, "I really don't want to hear what they think about me, especially our shareholders. I have produced profits for them, so they should be more than satisfied. We continue to gain good profitable customers, so obviously I'm okay there and we still work with the same select vendors. What do I care about what the public thinks about me? And I certainly don't think it's important to pay attention to what employees think about me."

"May I point out something?" Without waiting for a reply, he said, "That last statement contradicted an earlier one where you claimed *I am embarrassed by what my employees think of me.* I take this as another symptom of your lack of self-awareness. I perceive confusion."

I felt rattled and looked at the floor.

Gently he continued. "I respectfully disagree with what you said about not caring what others think but rather than debate why you need to care, I think it's time for a story."

He pushed my coffee toward me, I guess as a signal for me to relax. *Hmm. He uses his stories as a calming device.*

"Do you recall the fable about the Emperor's new clothes?" He pointed to a children's book that he laid on the couch.

"It's been so long since I heard it that I don't recall what it was about."

The Emperor's New Clothes[17]

Once upon a time there lived a vain Emperor whose only worry in life was to dress in elegant clothes. He changed clothes almost every hour and loved to show them off to his people.

Word of the Emperor's refined habits spread over his kingdom and beyond. Two scoundrels who had heard of the Emperor's vanity decided to take advantage of it. They introduced themselves at the gates of the palace with a scheme in mind.

'We are two very good tailors and after many years of research we have invented an extraordinary method to weave a cloth so light and fine that it looks invisible. As a matter of fact, it is invisible to anyone who is too stupid and incompetent to appreciate its quality.'

The chief of the guards heard the scoundrels' strange story and sent for the court chamberlain. The chamberlain notified the prime minister, who ran to the Emperor and disclosed the incredible news. The Emperor's curiosity got the better of him, and he decided to see the two scoundrels.

'Besides being invisible, your Highness, this cloth will be woven in colors and patterns created especially for you.' The Emperor gave the two men a bag of gold coins in exchange for their promise to begin working on the fabric immediately.

'Just tell us what you need to get started and we'll give it to you.' The two scoundrels asked for a loom, silk, and gold thread, then pretended to begin working. The Emperor thought he had spent his money quite well: in addition to getting a new extraordinary suit, he would discover which of his subjects were ignorant and incompetent. A few days later, he called the old and wise prime minister, who was considered by everyone as a man with common sense.

'Go and see how the work is proceeding,' the Emperor told him, 'and come back to let me know.'

---

[17] Story by Hans Christian Andersen, The Hans Christian Andersen Center
http://www.andersen.sdu.dk/vaerk/hersholt/TheEmperorsNewClothes_e.html

The prime minister was welcomed by the two scoundrels. 'We're almost finished, but we need a lot more gold thread. Here, Excellency! Admire the colors, feel the softness!' The old man bent over the loom and tried to see the fabric that was not there. He felt cold sweat on his forehead.

I can't see anything, he thought. If I see nothing, that means I'm stupid! Or, worse, incompetent! If the prime minister admitted that he didn't see anything, he would be discharged from his office.

'What a marvelous fabric,' he said then. 'I'll certainly tell the Emperor.' The two scoundrels rubbed their hands gleefully. More thread was requested to finish the work.

Finally, the Emperor received the announcement that the two tailors had come to take all the measurements needed to sew his new suit.

'Come in,' the Emperor ordered. Even as they bowed, the two scoundrels pretended to be holding a large roll of fabric.

'Here it is, your Highness, the result of our labor,' the scoundrels said. 'We have worked night and day but, at last, the most beautiful fabric in the world is ready for you. Look at the colors and feel how fine it is.' Of course, the Emperor did not see any colors and could not feel any cloth between his fingers. He panicked and felt like fainting but luckily the throne was right behind him and he sat down. When he realized that no one could know that he did not see the fabric, he felt better. Nobody could find out he was stupid and incompetent and the Emperor didn't know that everybody else around him thought and did the very same thing.

The farce continued as the two scoundrels had foreseen it. Once they had taken the measurements, the two began cutting the air with scissors while sewing with their needles an invisible cloth.

'Your Highness, you'll have to take off your clothes to try on your new ones.' The two scoundrels draped the new clothes on him and then held up a mirror. The Emperor was embarrassed but since none of his bystanders were, he felt relieved.

'Yes, this is a beautiful suit and it looks very good on me,' the Emperor said, trying to look comfortable. 'You've done a fine job.'

'Your Majesty,' the prime minister said, 'we have a request for you. The people have found out about this extraordinary fabric and they are anxious to see you in your new suit.' The Emperor was doubtful about showing himself naked to the people, but then he abandoned his fears. After all, no one would know about it except the ignorant and the incompetent.

'All right,' he said, 'I will grant the people this privilege.' He summoned his carriage and the ceremonial parade was formed. A group of dignitaries walked at the very front of the procession and anxiously scrutinized the faces of the people in the street. All the people had gathered in the main square, pushing and shoving to get a better look. Applause welcomed the regal procession. Everyone wanted to know how stupid or incompetent his or her neighbor was but, as the Emperor passed, a strange murmur rose from the crowd.

Everyone said, loud enough for the others to hear: 'Look at the Emperor's new clothes. They're beautiful!' 'What a marvelous train!' 'And the colors! The colors of that beautiful fabric! I have never seen anything like it in my life!' They all tried to conceal their disappointment at not being able to see the clothes, and since nobody was willing to admit his own stupidity and incompetence, they all behaved as the two scoundrels had predicted.

A child, however, who had no important job and could only see things as his eyes showed them to him, went up to the carriage. 'The Emperor is naked,' he said.

'Fool!' his father reprimanded, running after him. 'Don't talk nonsense!' He grabbed his child and took him away. However, the boy's remark, which had been heard by the bystanders, was repeated over and over again until everyone cried: 'The boy is right! The Emperor is naked! It's true!

The Emperor realized that the people were right but he could not admit to that. He thought it better to continue the procession under the illusion that anyone who *couldn't see his clothes was either stupid or incompetent. He stood stiffly on his carriage, while behind him a page held his imaginary mantle.*

At his pause I asked, "You are going to ask me the moral as it relates to me, right?" I had paid attention because I knew he would ask what my take-away was.

He nodded for me to proceed.

Leadership Lesson

"I think you're implying that I am the Emperor. Everyone sees that I don't know how to lead and either I'm blind to this or don't want to acknowledge it."

He responded, "That is a fair assessment. How do you feel about that?

"I don't like it at all! I feel angry, ashamed, and, and..." I felt a light flash in my brain and had to stop. His silence allowed me to process my thought.

When I felt composed, I said, "The Emperor was in denial, correct? He was so concerned about his image that he could not bring himself to admit that he was wrong. I now see the connection to the purpose of today's session."

I felt giddy for a second or two because it felt like a weight had been lifted off of my shoulders.

"See. You can learn because you are a very smart and talented woman."

I wanted to say thanks but couldn't get the word out. *Hmm.*

Ron added, "Allow me to share another lesson from this tale. It is easy for any human to be blind or insensitive with their own traits and abilities. You and I could perceive a personal trait as a detriment—say, communicating only when necessary—while others might see it as a plus. Similarly, you and I may believe we are good at something—say, being sensitive to an employee's concerns—yet others think we *suck* at it. Sorry. I don't like that word. Most of your employees think that you *Hoover* at being sensitive."

I laughed with him at this play on words.

He said, "The moral of this fable is that when a person lacks honest feedback and self-awareness, he or she will become blind to things they need to improve and the impact they have on others. This blindness or myopia is severely worse for a leader to have because the leader is only trusted when he or she has congruency among her words and actions and her behaviors and intentions."

I drained my coffee cup, so we visited the coffee station to refill and then returned to his cozy and quiet office. As I eased into the comfy couch, I asked him, "What do you mean by incongruity?"

Leaders Can Easily Fool Themselves

"A few weeks ago, Jackson accused you of lying at the staff meeting. Remember how embarrassed you felt?"

I nodded.

"I met with him to better understand this tense situation. He explained that he asked for your approval for him to update the sales commission and incentive structure, and you replied, 'I do not care if you do or not, it's your area of expertise.' Do you recall telling him that?'

I nodded in the affirmative even though I was apprehensive about what else Jackson told him.

"In the very next staff meeting, when the topic of policy updates came up, you told the group that YOU had initiated the review of the incentive program and assigned Jackson to do the work. This is why, in front of everyone, he called you a liar."

I hung my head, recalling my actions.

"I am willing to wager that you have a track record of altering the facts or taking credit for other people's accomplishments." He held up his hand to forestall my protest. "You don't need to defend yourself. I have verified these poor leadership behaviors with every person on your executive team."

Waiting until I could return his gaze, he added, "Could you explain why these incidents took place? I am not asking you to justify, but rather tell me why you feel the need to engage in this behavior."

"I don't know what to say!" I glared at him in silence. My stomachache returned.

He was relentless and said, "You, like every leader and CEO, have behaviors and habits that need improving. To do this you must become self-aware about your specific limitations and blind spots. According to the employees I met with and the results of the employee survey, you appear to lack all self-awareness of how you are impacting employees. Your acting like the Emperor is Stephen's greatest concern and why he has you on a short leash and gave you only six months to make your behaviors more congruent. Ask yourself, *Why am I acting like the Emperor?*"

I felt anger and embarrassment simultaneously. *Why do I keep feeling like this? I hate it!*

I rose from the couch and stood by the window. Ron could probably tell that I was shaken by this feedback.

I turned back toward him, sighed, and asked, "What else do my employees say about me?!" This came with more venom than I intended. *I guess I do care what they think about me!*

My Employees' Feedback

Ron waited patiently as I collected myself and returned to the couch; he sat to my right and opened up a notebook. Together we went over the results of his interviews of selected company employees and from the company-wide survey. Ron's report said:

The members of your executive team describe your leadership style as:

- *dictatorial (aka Attila the Hun)*
- *lacking compassion*
- *control-driven*
- *autocratic or not team-oriented*

The confidential employee survey shows that employees in general describe your leadership or management as:

- *nonexistent*
- *inflexible*
- *dictatorial/autocratic*

In our survey we asked employees a question about how they would describe you as a person, and they responded that Joslyn is best described as:

- *cold and uncaring*
- *distant and aloof*
- *menacing*
- *demanding*
- *unsympathetic*
- *negative*

I was stunned by this feedback and collapsed into a ball. *I've tried so hard to improve!* I closed my eyes and shook my head. I was close to tears but willed myself not to cry.

Trying to calm the obvious storm within me, he said, "You are facing this news more stoically than I expected. I admire your courage to listen to your critics."

Probably sensing that I needed to get away for a while, Ron suggested a lunch break. We talked about a lot of things unrelated to my leadership and Neoteric. I asked him questions about how other CEOs act, especially female ones. I inquired about the people he had coached and what changes they were able to make in themselves.

It never occurred to me before today to ask these questions. *I guess I haven't been taking this coaching too seriously.* Due to his feedback, I committed to myself to pay attention because my career depended on it!

When we returned to his office, we were both in a more pleasant mood. Chocolate cake does that for me.

Ron led off with, "We still have more work to get done. To ease us back into the right frame of mind, allow me to relate a story about my initial lack of self-awareness as an emerging leader.

Mark's Performance Evaluation

I was promoted to supervisor for the first time at the age of 27 and knew nothing about how to be one. The promotion went to my head and I began to act very self-important. For example, I took on only projects I liked and delegated those I didn't. I was bossy to employees who were formerly my peers. The two men I worked for were not sure how to deal with my change in attitude but didn't believe that firing me was necessary. They were also extremely uncomfortable challenging employees on their unprofessional behaviors. However, they devised a plan that would help me to become self-aware of my self-important attitude.

I supervised Mark, a member of my team, whom I described as slightly arrogant and strong-willed. At Mark's one-year review, I was assigned to do his performance evaluation and to convince him that his self-importance was a problem. As I prepared to do this difficult task, I saw the light! Mark was behaving exactly how I was behaving and by having to come up with a solution for his problems he was causing, I was being forced to face myself and the problems I caused.

"To this day I am thankful that my bosses took this approach because I learned more about how to be a leader from this experience than from getting fired or being demoted."

As per his plan, I was more relaxed and hopefully ready for exposing myself to more feedback.

Importance of Self-Awareness to a Leader

Noticing I was ready, Ron began to coach again. "A leader must remain self-aware. This means she pays attention to her impact on others. She also understands that healthy, open relationships must go two ways. Unfortunately, Joslyn, according to employees, you have one-way relationships. You care about how people impact you, but you fail to care about how you impact them. My granddaughter, at the age of three, acted this way because she could not see the world outside of herself. You as an adult know that the world does not revolve around you, yet this is how you come across to your employees and members of your management team."

I nodded in understanding, but wasn't prepared for what came next.

His voice took a more serious tone. "Let's examine your behavior when you first arrived here today. Darcy, my assistant, said that you basically hijacked my office without asking for permission. Take a moment to put yourself in her shoes. How might Darcy interpret your actions?"

"Uhmm. I would think the person was rude and did not care about anyone's boundaries. Is that how I come across?"

"Darcy could answer that better than I could but did you think how taking over my office might be inappropriate? Did you consider how you invalidated Darcy's authority? Did you consider that whatever opinion she may have had about you before today has now been lowered?"

I shook my head, suddenly realizing that these thoughts had never entered my mind. *I am the Emperor!*

He let his questions sink in before continuing. "It's a simple case of cause and effect. When you treat people like they don't matter—the cause—then they will in turn treat you like you don't matter, which is the resulting effect. All I need to do is look at the survey as proof. Phrases like *distant, uncaring,* and *unfeeling* are feedback that the relationship you have with employees is one-sided. Yet I know from our work together that this is not the real you. So there is something that triggers this behavior when you are in the presence of your employees or people that you believe are of lesser importance to you. We will delve into the causes soon, but not today."

I didn't know what to say; all my energy was preventing the tears from flowing. Ron mentioned in a prior session this interesting fact: In leadership, crying openly is perceived as a weakness, which leads to a lack of trust in that leader. This affects both men and women, but because women innately relieve stress with tears, we are perceived as wimpy because of it. Ron allows me to express all my emotions, but because I was already branded as a weak leader, I felt the need to remain as stoic as I could.

To hide my feelings and get grounded again, I wrote my thoughts into my notebook while he asked Darcy to bring us iced tea and lemonade. As she placed the drinks before us, I smiled and said, "I am sorry for what I did this morning." Already smiling, she replied, "Apology accepted." She touched my hand gently and left.

Her touch and kindness sparked a thought that I had to share. "Uhmm. I flashed back to your story about assumptions, and as a result I now know why I feel like an ass. I've been assuming that I am acting as a leader should. Your...I mean, my employees' feedback tells me my assumptions have been wrong for a long time." It felt good to admit that.

"You have experienced another shift. Congratulations!" I noticed a similarity between Darcy's smile and his. *Is she his daughter?*

Process to Grow Self-Aware

After taking a few sips I asked, "How do I become self-aware?"

He was ready. "You have three opportunities to grow in self-awareness regarding your impact on those you lead."

1. Pay Attention

"First, when you are interacting with people, pay close attention to facial expressions and body language along with verbal clues such as the tone of voice and what they are not saying. These all provide data points about your impact on them. Here's an example. At our initial meeting, you basically ordered your new assistant, Brian, to get you a fresh cup of coffee. He rolled his eyes and had a pinched facial expression, which communicated to me that he thought you were a pain in the rear end. Did you notice him doing this?"

I defended myself. "No. I didn't. Was it obvious?"

"He did nothing to hide his responses and yet I could tell his actions never entered your awareness radar. Since the day of my first visit to your office, I have witnessed incidents where your employees respond with obvious feedback; some ignore you; some purposely avoid you. I've also noted that at times when they are with you, the person usually wears a frown and generally acts like your presence will burn them alive."

That hurts!

2. Use a Mirror

"The second thing you must do is to proactively seek out unfiltered feedback. It is frightening for any CEO to ask for feedback. He or she will often erroneously believe they don't need feedback or they are above reproach. Everyone needs this information to grow, improve, and course-correct. I think of feedback as a mirror that you and I use to study ourselves to determine if we are doing things appropriately or not."

"Assume that you are about to lead an important meeting of shareholders. You do not know that you have a large tear in the back of your skirt."

"You enter the room to make a presentation, unaware of your wardrobe malfunction. I guarantee that many people will notice the incongruity or flaw (even though you don't) in your professional appearance. All during the session people will focus on the flaw and miss what you are saying. What is worst of all in my scenario is that people are silently wondering why you don't care about your appearance! Even though you really DO care about your appearance, without the feedback a mirror could provide, you have unintentionally embarrassed yourself and lost credibility."

"Now imagine yourself in this scene and play close attention to this question."

He paused to let me reflect before asking, "Would you want someone to inform you about your torn skirt?"

"I would definitely want to know right away."

"I would, too, except I usually don't wear one in public."

I laughed at his silliness.

"Therefore, before you go into this important meeting, you would check your appearance in the mirror for vital feedback to determine if anything is amiss, thus giving you the opportunity to self-correct. Does that sound accurate?"

I replied that it did.

"In leadership, this mirror-like feedback comes from people you work with, listen to, and trust. For them to give it to you freely, they must trust you, believe that you want to know, and that you won't chastise them for being honest. As you improve, you prove to them that you value their feedback. Even though you are the top person in the organization, you have traits, character quirks, and behaviors that need addressing because they are diminishing your leadership. Unless you value and seek out feedback, you will remain blind to how you are impacting others."

3. Do Proactive Follow-ups

"The third way to become self-aware is to do consistent follow-ups on all your important communications. Assume that you meet with Kendra and ask her to prepare a report that requires extensive research and analysis. After describing for her what you need, she leaves to go do the work. You assume that she now knows exactly what you want and how you want it, but..."

"But she most likely does not. Is that what you were going to say?" I somehow knew what his point was, because this had happened with several members of my staff.

He replied, "Yes. Odds are high that she won't fully understand her assignment; therefore, it would be appropriate for you to describe the task, then, instead of sending her off immediately, ask her to provide feedback to you regarding your instructions and find out if she has any questions. Give her a time by which you want the report, and ask if she can meet that deadline. About halfway to the deadline, conduct a follow-up to understand how Kendra is doing and assess if she fully understands what you asked for. Timely follow-ups provide you feedback on the clarity of your instructions, if you provided enough background, and if mutual understanding took place. You also engage in conversations so you stay aware of the impact of your communications. Following up provides the time to make corrections in your communications and in her understanding, thus ensuring you both win."

I nodded but I guess he wanted to verify that I truly understood this because he asked, "Explain to me the three ways you can gain the feedback so you grow to be more self-aware about your impact on others."

I did my best to summarize his information, and he clarified a few things I left out. He told me that he was modeling a technique that I could adopt and practice which would help me become more self-aware of my impact on others.

To my utter dismay he announced, "To help you do this and to know specific areas to work on, next week I will observe you in action to see how people react to you and how you react to them. I will be your shadow for a whole day."

I audibly gulped. "If that will help me to be more self-aware, then I guess you have to." I know that I said this in a petulant way but couldn't help myself.

Our time together was nearly over and I still sensed something was missing but was not sure what it was. Before I could say anything, he said, "At lunch we talked about leaders you admire. May I share a story about one of them?"

I nodded because I really enjoyed his stories and their meanings.

Alan Mulally's Problem[18]

'I came to Ford to help turn around a global and American icon.' This is how Alan Mulally described his intention when he was hired away from Boeing and given the top spot at Ford.

---

[18] Strategy + Business magazine summer 2013, *The Wise Leader* by Prasad Kaipa & Navi Radjou and other sources

When Mr. Mulally took over Ford's leadership reins in 2006, his arrival rattled Ford's management team. He found a very insular culture filled with bureaucratic processes, kingdoms, silos, and infighting. The culture was generally hostile to any new ideas, with a history of 'organ rejection' or spurning outsiders. Prior to his arrival, part of the problem was that Ford managers were told what to do, not to think on their own. Alan wanted them to be empowered while sharing ideas and resources. Early on, Bill Ford told Alan Mulally that Ford 'is a place where they wait for the leader to tell them what to do.'

Described as 'relentless,' Alan has a laser-sharp focus on a simple vision that he drills into the organization. Every member of Alan's team was issued a laminated card with his tenets to remind them of his plan that he named "One Ford." Alan's leadership intentions for this unifying strategy are: 1) working together, 2) accepting reality, and 3) developing new models that buyers really want.

But Mr. Mulally was not always a good leader. Early in his career at Boeing, he received some intense coaching, at the strong urging of his boss, Boeing's CEO. Alan had earned 'high marks from his employees for coordinating Boeing's supply chain and hitting production goals' but he was criticized for 'leaving much of his team out of the loop.' He failed to earn the trust and loyalty of his team due to some poor leadership qualities. Alan credits this coaching as helping him to become a much better leader. Alan learned that 'leadership is not about me. I wasn't going to succeed if my team did not succeed.' According to Alan, 'Ford's the toughest environment I've ever seen but we will make it through if we stick to the "One Ford" plan.'

Alan succeeded as an outsider in Detroit because 'there was no grandiosity when he came in, there was a sense of urgency and enthusiasm.' He faced up to the risk of managing people's 'expectations as people create a messianic image of him.' Mr. Mulally does not want people to think he is infallible and says that he now values feedback because it helps him know where to correct.

I felt compelled to speak first. "I didn't know that about Alan. The first part of his story sounded just like mine. So even leaders who are larger-than-life can lack self-awareness, too?"

Ron responded, "Yes, they can and often do. A person generally needs a large dose of self-esteem to get to the top of the heap, and this condition can lead to leadership hubris and myopia. My goal is to ensure that you can become more self-confident without engaging in these two sins of leadership."

My smile and good mood had returned. *That's why I felt incomplete.*

He had a wide grin which told me he was up to something.

"Before we determine your growth assignments, I think it's best to end this session on a higher note than it started, with a funny story. Ready?" Ron then told this story.

Mal Hygiene's Problem

Someone who trained me early in my career, while working for a finance company, was an Assistant Manager whom I shall call 'Mal Hygiene.' Mal was good with customers and had a smooth, easy-going way of getting his customers to pay even when they didn't want to. I did my best to emulate this skill, but it was hard because he was not self-aware.

Mal Hygiene was eager to run his own office so that he could be promoted to Manager. He lobbied hard and was finally given one. I was quite inexperienced about leadership, but even then could tell that Mal was not a leader and would probably never be one. His technical and selling skills were polished, but he lacked certain professional attributes.

Every day, Mal showed up at work looking like he had slept in his clothes. His shirts were always wrinkled, his slacks were frayed, and his out-of-style tie and sport coat were stained with bits of food. Mal had a scraggly mustache that he rarely trimmed. I joked that Mal 'only bathed on days with the number 13.' He reeked of cigarette smoke which, when combined with his bad breath, killed any fly that came near. *Behind his back, employees and customers would poke fun about Mal's poor hygiene, inattention to grooming, and inability to dress professionally. As if that was not bad enough, I believe it was another of Mal's habits that really turned off employees and customers. At least fifteen times a day, Mal Hygiene would pick his butt. He was totally unaware that he habitually reached back and tugged his pants and underwear away from his skin. What was sad was that no one—not his boss, wife, or brother—were willing to tell him this was inappropriate.*

I tried hard not to laugh but couldn't help myself; a generous giggle shook my body. He joined in my mirth. *Now I know why he was grinning.*

"I'm sorry," he said. "I know Mal's habits sounds disgusting; just thinking about him turns my stomach. I tell this story because it demonstrates how the lack of feedback can undermine anyone's effectiveness."

I felt carefree for the first time in a long while. I breathed in the good feelings.

My Assignment

Ron turned serious. "Your next application step contains two action items. First, I suggest that you pay close attention to each interaction you have with key employees. Pay heed to their facial expression, their body language, and other clues about how your conversation is going. Are you willing to do that?"

I nodded in agreement, even though I knew this would be hard for me.

"I suggest that your second action be to stay present throughout your day. I see you as a human tornado blowing into the situation with a tremendous amount of energy. I suggest that you slow down and will yourself to be calm and centered. For the next week, pay close attention to your actions as you enter each meeting. Think about the impact that you are having on the people in the room, especially the impact that you want to have."

Catching my eyes, he asked, "Will you do that for me or should I say, will you do this for yourself?"

After taking a deep breath I said, "I will do my best to try."

He laughed and responded, "I could quote Yoda's saying about either doing or trying, but I won't. I am suggesting that you take these actions seriously and do more than just try. One thing I know about you, Joslyn, is that you follow through on a task once you've set your mind to it. So please set your mind to doing this."

Despite my hesitance, I said that I committed myself to doing this.

Before I departed, I asked if it would be okay to speak with Darcy and apologize again. He left that up to me. It felt good doing this. Darcy complimented me on several things, behaviors that I engaged in but didn't realize. As I drove to my office, I contemplated other behaviors that I was not aware of, and this reminded me of the commitment I had made to take Ron's assistance to heart. After taking three deep breaths, I felt somewhat optimistic that I could change. *Where did that come from?*

*****

Ron's Assessment of Joslyn's Progress

Because of her persona as a human tornado I felt exhausted, so I shut the door to my office and sat quietly for a while. Talking to myself out loud, I said, "Joslyn is progressing but it's hard to tell if she really wants to change. She tells me she does, but often reverts to her bad habits. I know she tries and her small victories so far are fragile. I knew the session where she would listen to her employees' unfiltered feedback would be the pivotal point of no return."

I entered today's notes in her file and made a list of other issues we needed to explore. I was cautiously optimistic. *I want her to succeed, but the final outcome is up to Joslyn and her willingness to stop being reluctant.*

*****

The Bottom Line of Leadership

Without self-awareness, the leader can easily believe they are being effective. Many leaders fool-heartedly fall into the trap of self-delusion. These normally smart people adopt a childish belief that seeking out other people's opinions on how they are doing is demeaning. In reality, seeking honest feedback is an indication of both courage and humility and self-esteem.

Universally senior leaders exist in a self-imposed bubble which prevents them from really seeing the impact they have on their company, team, and employees. That is sad because as Ken Blanchard wrote in his ever-popular *One Minute Manager*, "Feedback is the breakfast of champions."

One area that is of greatest concern to a company's striving to be an employer where people want to work is how extensive bullying is in the workplace. Even if it is not the leader who acts like a bully, without the trust created by open and honest feedback, non-leader bullies rarely get caught. The size of this problem is appalling.

Approximately 44 percent of American workers have worked for a supervisor or employer whom they consider abusive. This abusive behavior includes:

- Sarcastic jokes (60%)
- Public criticism of job performance (59%)
- Interrupting in a rude manner (58%)
- Yelling or raising one's voice (55%)
- Ignoring or treating employees as invisible (54%)

According to a recent analysis, 35 percent of American workers have experienced bullying firsthand. Approximately 62 percent of bullies are men, while 58 of targets are women. Women bullies will target other women 80 percent of the time. Approximately 68 percent of bullying is same-gender harassment[19].

What is most alarming is that bullying is four times more prevalent than illegal harassment, as defined by existing labor regulations, so by not addressing it you expose your organization to numerous lawsuits and legal claims.

By remaining self-aware and seeking out feedback from the people they work with and impact, a leader can uncover when and where employees are feeling bullied. Removing an atmosphere of fear from your workplace will lead to lower turnover and higher-quality job applicants.

How would you feel if you had the reputation as the company bully? Without adequate feedback you would never know until it was too late.

---

[19] *The State of the American Workplace: Employee Engagement Insights for U.S. Business Leaders*, findings from Gallup's ongoing study of the American workplace from 2010 through 2012

Chapter 6
Good Stewardship

"While that woman has a thick skull and thin skin, she has the heart of a warrior."

Time Remaining: 13 weeks

The tension in the plush conference room was as thick as a slab of country bacon. I could tell the ten employees waiting there were doing their best to hide their nervousness, but the body never lies. Jackson sighed frequently as he slouched while tilting his chair back and staring at the ceiling. Latisha beat a steady rhythm with her foot against the leg of the oversized mahogany table. Occasionally she relaxed, but then clicked her long nails on the table. Despite downing a Red Bull, Aaron fell asleep and snored softly. Kendra drank enormous amounts of coffee, gulping and refilling her personal coffee cup three times in the 20 minutes we'd been here. I laughed silently because Kendra's mug read "Caffeine: breakfast of non-sleepers." Curtiss shuffled papers, frequently changing the top paper, while checking the clock on the wall every 30 seconds. Pindar, looking the most relaxed, tapped on the top of his notebook with a pen.

Listening to this combination of his tapping, Latisha's clicking, Aaron's snoring, and Jackson's sighs I realized that I was the only one who seemed to notice that they had inadvertently created an interesting rhythm. The building's air conditioner was attempting to cool off the stuffy room but failing miserably.

We were waiting for Joslyn to show up to her weekly staff meeting. *I can see why she lacks their respect. She is wasting valuable time, and they resent it.*

As part of her coaching program, this day I would serve as Joslyn's shadow, observing her in a day packed with meetings. *Was her tardiness an omen of what the day would be like?* The first meeting was a weekly executive 'war council' session, as Joslyn referred to it; the name was fitting because everyone in the room looked like they would lay siege the moment she arrived.

The Human Tornado

Suddenly, the meeting room door opened and in rushed Joslyn, dressed in a royal blue pantsuit. She threw a halfhearted apology to the room, headed for her seat at the southern end of the table, and took a stack of papers from her dark blue briefcase. As she plunked them on the table, she announced sharply, "Let's get this show on the road!" Her hair was carelessly braided as if done in haste.

If feelings were visible, I imagined a death ray beaming out of everyone's eyes and landed on her. Noting their stares and scowls, she flinched a little, then stood tall like a warrior ready to do battle.

Then, Joslyn did a double take when she noticed me, as if she had forgotten that I would be in attendance. Immediately she dropped her warrior stance and shrank within herself. "I apologize to each of you. My car had problems and I had to wait on AAA to get it going. While my husband might be a genius in some things, he is useless with anything mechanical. I know you all have busy schedules, so let us get through the agenda quickly, and we can get on with our day." She took her seat and looked down.

I wondered if she was acting passive only for my benefit. Her behavior seemed to appease Jackson and several others, although I noticed none made direct eye contact with her for the rest of the meeting. As the group moved through each agenda item, their actions seemed choreographed. Joslyn would describe the agenda item and call upon the executive to report. Then as the employees presented, she would interrupt him or her with petty questions. *She is treating them like they are stupid*, I put in my notes. With each interruption, the employee's frustration was evident, while Joslyn seemed oblivious to the reaction. That observation also went into my notes.

They covered a lot of ground quickly, but I noticed that not much got resolved. It was as if she expected them to make a decision, and in turn the group was waiting for her to decide. It was painful to watch, and this tension-filled meeting was a waste of 90 minutes. I sensed that many wanted to leave the room but fear prevented them. The moment the meeting was adjourned, everyone except Joslyn exited as if their clothes were on fire. Joslyn walked past me toward the door and remarked sarcastically, "That certainly went well!"

The next meeting on Joslyn's schedule was one she dreaded. She and Jackson were to have a one-on-one meeting disguised as a marketing status session, but it was really Jackson's annual performance evaluation. When Joslyn informed me about the real intention, I asked, "Why use subterfuge? Why did you feel the need to lie to Jackson about the purpose of this meeting?"

Joslyn had an unopened energy drink in her hand and she held it so tightly I thought the cap might pop off. Turning away from me, she responded, "I am scared. Jackson can be intimidating, and I know he will be upset about my feedback. If he knew this was meant to be a performance evaluation he might fly off the handle. He has a temper."

"Do you think he might be rational and calm if he knew the topic beforehand? Ambushing him will be more upsetting. Could this be another reason why Jackson called you a liar?"

She ignored my question.

To underscore the seriousness of her deception, I informed her of the **9th Natural Law of Leadership.**

> **Positive intentions create positive results.**
> **Negative intentions beget negative results.**

I said, "Because you are expecting the worst, you will create a situation where nothing positive would result." Overly focused and anxious, she ignored my advice.

Joslyn's Lie

Joslyn chose to meet with Jackson in her office; she apparently wanted to be on safe ground. I sat in a club chair away from the table where they would sit. Jackson entered her office three minutes early. The cologne he wore had a pleasant musky scent, but his easily identifiable nervousness caused the scent to intensify and it filled her spacious office. Joslyn was to explain why I would be included in this meeting as a test to see how she defined my role.

"Jackson, you've met Mr. Rael, who is giving me pointers on how to be a better leader. I have given him permission to observe me today. Do you mind if he sits in on this meeting?"

He rolled his eyes when she said *better leader* but I don't think she noticed. He looked at her and said, "I have no problem with it, as long as he is not here to give me advice." I could tell he wanted to say more, maybe something critical, but held himself back.

Since the meeting was of a confidential nature, I won't disclose the specific aspects, but I can summarize what resulted. Joslyn asked Jackson to describe his plans for managing the sales group during this growth spurt. They argued over the overall strategy and disagreed on several issues. Despite her semi-aggressive tone, I could see that her body was vibrating with anxiety and she was sweating, constantly wiping her hands on her wool slacks. I couldn't tell if Jackson noticed this due to his anger.

As anticipated, when she got to the performance evaluation aspect of the meeting, he was shocked. He stated unequivocally, "My performance over the last year has been outstanding," and yet she gave him only an above-average rating. He grew even more defensive and confrontational. After 15 minutes of arguing, he claimed that he had an important appointment with a customer and stormed out of the session, demanding that she rethink her evaluation "or else." *He has an ace up his sleeve. Jackson isn't worried that he could be fired.*

I quipped, "That certainly went well." I intentionally mirrored her sarcastic remark from earlier, but she didn't notice.

Joslyn must have sensed that Jackson was hiding something when she confided, "I am not sure what I would do if he quits because he is indispensable to me and to the company."

I thought about Natural Law 9 and how I might use it today.

My Meeting with Jackson

Later that day, in between Joslyn's meetings, I was approached by Jackson, who silently nodded his head in the direction of his office. He wanted me to meet with him, but didn't want to publicly announce it. As I settled into a very comfortable chair, he closed the door.

In his deep sonorous voice he said, "I need to get something off my chest. I know you're here to try to help Joslyn because well, Stephen and I had many conversations about her before you started, and we still do."

So that's why he takes her rage without much pushback, I thought.

"And I don't know how much you know about our history, but at one time we were pretty tight, Joslyn and I. She taught me, she molded me, and she made me realize I was good at sales. For what it's worth, she is still at the top of her game when it comes to selling stuff and working with customers. However, she is a terrible leader!" He took an audible breath and leaned back into his chair. "If it wasn't for her I wouldn't be making a comfortable living. I was heading nowhere fast, but she saw something in me and brought it out. On one hand I am just so upset with her and the way she treats me, but on the other hand, I think I owe her. I sure hope she gets her act together because she's making my life miserable. Thanks for listening."

I thanked him and as I got up to leave, he added, "Two more things. She told me you told her to patch things up with me, but it's been like one step forward and two steps back, hence my frustration you saw earlier. On the plus side, while *that woman* has a thick skull and thin skin, she has the heart of a warrior. I've seen her face some of our toughest customers who thought they could intimidate her, and she didn't back down. She never flinched. She turned some of our most demanding customers into our most profitable ones. I just thought you should know."

Leaving his office I thought, *At least he hasn't written her off but is he being groomed as her replacement?*

Fly on the Wall

For the rest of that day I observed Joslyn in five more meetings. I was amused that she carried the energy drink with her all day and never opened it. This is what I noticed about her interactions with her employees:

- She treated most meetings as a confrontation
- She could not always be straightforward, often circling around the message she wanted to convey
- She rarely attempted to understand the other person's point of view

- She did a majority of the talking and did not listen very well
- She rarely said anything appreciative to the person about their ideas, successes, or contributions

After what felt like a very long and physically taxing day, we had 90 minutes left for today's coaching session. After a short break I was to debrief Joslyn on what I observed. While she was making phone calls in her office, I reviewed five pages of notes in the conference room, the same one where the day started. The room was cooler but the scent of stale coffee remained. *How do I whittle this list down to the essence, and then highlight the areas she needs to work on?*

As I sat there staring at the wall, looking at nothing, I received an inspiration through an image of Joslyn as a child cowering as a large mob of tall, angry people surrounded her. Then the words *good shepherd* popped into my brain. Quickly, I jotted down a few talking points and waited for Joslyn to show up. *If she is late, she is afraid of what I have to say. The later she is, the more worried she is.*

Twenty-two minutes after the scheduled start time, Joslyn joined me, carrying that same energy drink and a royal blue notepad. She stated tersely, "Give me your summary of what you noticed," as she sat down, obviously nervous and exasperated. Her suit was wrinkled and hair in total disarray, making her resemble a soldier after battle.

Leadership Outcome – Good Stewardship

"Today we will switch metaphors. Think back to the pinball machine your father had. By the way, that baseball pinball machine was also my favorite game."

Joslyn said, "One day when I have the time, I will buy one. I'd like to teach Jayna how to play."

"What was your favorite part of playing pinball?" I inquired.

"When the shiny silver ball would ricochet around the game board, getting bounced by the bumpers, those mushroom-shaped things. Or when it hit certain activating areas and would get pushed backward or forward. I was less concerned about racking up points than I was about seeing how long I could keep the ball caroming around the game board. That was my goal."

To get her on track, I handed her a bright silver ball, one directly out of a pinball machine. It had "stewardship" handwritten on it. She clasped it after I handed it to her.

I started today's leadership lesson. "So keeping that rebounding pinball image in mind, we will now place the focus of your leadership development on the outcomes that the outer leader produces. As your pinball bounces around, it activates energy from each of the bumpers, and that energy in turn keeps the pinball in motion. These energy blasts produce specific results which are highly visible and which you and your followers can see. These results can be beneficial, like improving employee retention, or detrimental, such as driving away good employees." Her lips tightened but she remained silent.

I wonder if she is thinking about Dino's or Kelly's resignation letters. Stephen had shared Dino's scathing critique of Joslyn.

I continued. "These outer leader traits can also activate the people you lead, so they can use their talents to produce fruitful results. Today, we will cover good stewardship, which is an outcome and also a trait that continuously renews your leadership energy. Stewardship can activate positive energies within the people you lead."

Meaning of Stewardship

She asked me, "What do you mean by stewardship? I've heard of stewardship in regards to the environment, but what does it mean in relation to leadership?"

"Imagine a shepherd keeping watch over her flock of sheep in a meadow. She stays alert making sure that nothing bad happens to the animals under her care. She has stewardship over the sheep and their environment. As a leader, you are a steward or shepherd of the employees and other assets that belong to this great organization. As the CEO, you are looked to as a person ultimately responsible for protecting all of these assets. In addition, your leadership role is to turn those assets into something beneficial, such as producing sales, adding to profits, expanding a brand, and securing for the company a positive reputation."

"I get it. As both a salesperson and a sales manager, I had custody over products, and my job was to position them into the minds of our customers so that they bought from us, not just once but again and again."

"Based on your expertise in sales," I continued, "you understood that narrow level of stewardship. Today, you have the ultimate stewardship, which is both deep and broad. A leader is a steward of assets. The assets you have been given to nurture, protect, and grow include the people you interacted with today and everyone else in this organization. However, you have yet to realize that you treat these assets with disdain. Today, I witnessed many times where you did this."

She started to protest but stopped herself and instead rolled the ball in her hand. *She's not taking notes.*

The Rental Test

"Joslyn, I'd like you to imagine that you inherit a rental property, a house built for a family. This house is located in a growing and prosperous part of the city, the same neighborhood in which you currently reside. In this neighborhood, where the rental house is located, all the surrounding homes have manicured lawns and beautiful landscaping. The neighboring properties are well maintained and the surrounding area has plenty of public parks and play areas for children of all ages.

"Young families are attracted to this neighborhood for its high-quality schools, plentiful recreation facilities, and safe environment. The house you inherit has been a rental property for many years and currently has a large number of problems:

- The tenants turn over every few months
- The house and yard have not been maintained for years
- The large unfenced yard is filled with junk, weeds, and dead plants
- Some of the windows are cracked
- The roof is covered in moss
- The paint is faded and cracked

"Your new asset is habitable, but just barely! Due to the home's condition, the current tenants, which you also inherit, pay only $350 a month. Similar homes in the neighborhood command rental rates between $1,000 and $1,500 a month."

I checked to make sure she was keeping up. She was, so I inquired, "Now that this house is yours free and clear—no debt or liens—what would you do?"

Without hesitation she said, "I would fix the place up so that it can live up to its full potential, such as turning it into a desirable, upscale rental house, redesigning it as a place for my family to live, turning it into a home for a family member, or, better yet, sell it for a quick profit." She laid her ball down and began to toy with the still-unopened energy drink.

Leadership Lesson

"Your response defines the most fundamental purpose of leadership, which is the **10th Natural Law of Leadership**."

A good leader creates more good leaders.

This idea caused her to put the bottle down, grab the notebook, and start writing.

I continued, "When you live up to your full potential as a leader, you enable yourself to facilitate your followers into fulfilling their potential.

"Today, through your various meetings with employees, you had numerous chances to act as a good steward. Your behaviors determine whether they want do something *for you* or *against you*. Your actions and decisions affect their actions and decisions. Your leadership affects how they relate to this organization and whether they contribute or not. Your impact on them can be a positive experience or a distracting one."

She seemed to be partially listening; I needed her complete attention, so I loudly cleared my throat.

"From what I observed today, the impact you have on your team and other employees is not always positive! You resemble the wolf that the shepherd tries to protect her flock from. The good news is I also observed members of your team acting like good stewards of *their* people."

She twisted her body to face me. I could tell this feedback affected her; she showed more energy.

Grabbing my notes, I said, "To describe what I mean, I've broken my observations of today into four different points. Each one is an important area that you need to work on."

Point 1: A Leader Treats Each Employee as an Asset
"As a leader, above all else, your words and actions must foster trust, because without it you cannot obtain cooperation. It seems as if every one of your employees is angry with you, and in this state resists your direction. Due to your unfounded fears, you have not fully empowered them, and as a result they rely on you to spur them into action. You lack courage when things get tough, which may contribute to why some doubt you or don't trust you."

Point 2: A Leader Uses a Tremendous Amount of Positive Supportive Language
"Much of what you say to your employees is negative and derogative, and this approach closes people off from wanting to help and interferes with their listening to what you have to say. You tend to use what I refer to as 'killer phrases' in your regular conversation with your employees."

Point 3: A Leader Seizes Opportunities to Help Employees Feel Worthy
"Several times today your employees created an opening for you to enhance their self-esteem, but you failed to capitalize on that. I heard many great ideas and suggestions from them, and even though you usually made note of it, you failed to see this as an opportunity to praise and thank the person. I perceive you as either unwilling or unable to build people up."

Point 4: A Leader Strives for Win-Win Outcomes with Employees
"You tend to play a win-lose game with each person. You must realize that success is not a zero-sum activity where achievement requires someone else's failure. A true leader knows that she can only be successful if her followers feel successful. Your employees probably feel like they can never be successful around you. Imagine a game you play against someone who makes all the rules, enforces all the rules in their favor, and does everything to ensure that you will lose. How would you feel about playing that game against that individual?"

She responded instantly, "I would refuse to play that game because I would know for a fact that I could not win. Is this how I act with my employees? Is that how they perceive me…that they will always lose?!" Her shoulders drooped.

"Only you can answer that question, but I'll give you some help to find the answer. Close your eyes and mentally go through each of today's meetings and see it as a game with you on one side and employees on the other. Ask yourself, *Did I help them win or did I help myself win?*"

In a shaky voice she responded, "I am terrified to close my eyes because…because based on your feedback, I already know the answer."

"Then we will make that part of this week's assignment, which I encourage you to complete within the next 24 hours. I suggest that you mentally go through each meeting and imagine it a game. I'll expect you to email me your findings by tomorrow afternoon. Are you clear on what I've asked you to do?"

"Right. Right."

I knew I was being tough but I had to be. If Stephen had been her shadow today, she wouldn't have a job at this moment.

"Let's continue." We spent nearly an hour going over the details about what actions she could take as a good steward.

Courage to Face Yourself

"In a previous session," I said, "we talked about the importance of courage to a leader, and I defined it as stepping out of your comfort zone and rising above your normal tendency. Right now, with all the feedback that you've received about your leadership ability, you will need courage to face yourself. Once you face yourself and clearly recognize the ways you've been undermining your effectiveness and harming your people, then you can do something about it. What is your reaction to applying courage to improving your abilities?"

Pausing her writing, she said, "I am conflicted with this because I feel brave when it comes to dealing with certain issues. Yet when it comes to people—the daunting part of leading—I don't feel quite so certain that I know what I'm doing."

"You will get there, but for now we will start simply by having you pay close attention to how you act and how you speak with employees. The first step to stewardship is to be aware of how often you put employees down with the use of killer phrases."

A Leader Avoids Using Killer Phrases

"You need to pay attention to how you speak with your employees. Any leader can quickly banish great ideas and drive away creative thinking, and they do it by repeatedly using killer phrases. Inexperienced and untrained managers and supervisors use killer phrases that harm relationships and destroy innovations.

"Whenever you use negative-sounding phrases when conversing with employees and colleagues, you are shutting down the flow of creative ideas because you're communicating that 'your idea is not worthy of my respect and attention.'"

I handed Joslyn a document with information so that she could follow along. "These are examples of killer phrases. Each time you use phrases such as these you demonstrate you are closed-minded or unwilling to improve what's not working. In the process, you harm relationships because people will stop sharing their ideas and label you as a naysayer."

This is what Joslyn saw on the sheet.

KILLER PHRASES

You may have a good idea, but...
- it needs more study.
- we haven't the time to waste on bad ideas.
- it's not in the budget. Or it's too expensive.
- we've tried that before. It won't work.
- let's form a committee.
- do an in-depth report.
- let's shelve it until a later date.
- if it fails, it will be your fault.

Your ideas won't work because...
- while that may be a good idea elsewhere, our company (culture) (way of doing things) is different.
- we've never done it that way.
- there are better ways to do it than that.
- it's against our policy.
- we are not ready or willing to change.

Your idea is...
- too academic.
- too hard to administer.
- requires too much paperwork.
- too premature.
- not good enough.
- too modern.
- too old-fashioned.

Don't be ridiculous...
- that idea might be all right in theory, but I don't see how we can put it into practice.
- somebody would have suggested it before if it were any good.
- we can't step on anyone's toes.
- it has been this way for twenty years, so nothing good can come from your suggestion.
- who do you think you are to suggest such a thing?

While your suggestion may have a sound foundation...
- let's discuss it at some other time.
- you don't understand how things work around here.
- we're too big (small) for that.
- our senior managers won't understand it.
- the experienced people won't use it.
- we have too many projects now.
- I just know it won't work.
- let's be practical.
- it doesn't fit our unique needs.
- let's get back to reality.
- why start doing things differently now?

I like your idea but...
- what you are really saying is (and you put your own spin on the idea).
- prove to me who else in our industry has tried it.

If you discover that you use phrases like these examples in your daily conversation, you are a buzz kill! People will stop listening, sharing their ideas, telling the truth, they will forget to invite you to their meetings, and possibly stop talking with you altogether.

Solution: Use positive, supportive, and uplifting language instead.

After allowing her time to read the material, I handed her a highlighter and requested that she highlight any phrase she remembers saying to employees. I watched as she marked about half the phrases and saw a realization set in.

She exclaimed, "Oh! I thought I was being supportive when I said things like that. I guess I may do some of this, but I am not sure what harm it causes. I'm challenging them!" Joslyn retorted with a haughty expression.

I said nothing. *At least she's open to the possibility that she does demean people's ideas.*

Leadership Lesson

I summarized why I suggested she use this tool. "Even when you are not aware, employees are paying attention to how you communicate with them through your words and actions. If you want employees to share ideas, be empowered, and tell you their concerns, they need to know that you will honor whatever they say. All too often, a leader will inadvertently and sometimes intentionally make an employee feel less valuable through the use of killer phrases and other sorts of putdowns."

I added, "My suggestion is that you keep this sheet handy in every meeting you attend for the next three weeks, reviewing it before and after. Notice the ones you use most often, and do your best to either stop saying the phrase or, better yet, convert it into a supportive statement."

She protested, "But I'm not sure what you call a supportive statement."

Because I knew she would not like that assignment, I was ready and handed her a list that described what a supportive statement looked like. "May I suggest that you use your leadership journal and write out alternative ways to say what you mean using these guidelines? Then read it aloud several times until you get comfortable saying them. Are your ready to move on?"

She nodded.

Capitalizing on Talent

I said, "Let's return to good stewardship. The most efficient and effective way to use your people's assets and convert their ideas and energy into positive results is through employee engagement."

"Maintaining employee engagement takes effort and commitment from the top first. Fear and uncertainty can erode the organization's health; however, when leaders step in to keep the level of engagement high, the organization will respond quicker to challenges and be less impacted by bad news. Employees who are highly confident about their employer's financial future are nine times more likely to be engaged than those with lower confidence, according to Gallup research."

Joslyn rose from her chair and walked over to a small refrigerator tucked in a corner under a small mountain of papers. She reached in and grabbed two bottles of water and handed one to me. She gulped hers down in seconds. She seemed to avoid the energy drink.

After saying "Thanks," I continued. "Caring is the lifeblood of employee engagement. Caring is defined as the feeling that your boss or someone at work cares about you personally, that someone encourages your development, and that the people you work with care about the work they do. Caring is always an essential aspect of employee engagement and a primary leadership obligation, because whenever employees feel threatened or insecure about their jobs and livelihood, knowing that someone cares is enormously important. Caring implicitly requires individualization."

"However, many leaders today are hesitant to show that they care about their employees. Somehow they mistakenly think that expressions or demonstrations of caring will undermine professionalism, make difficult decisions harder, or have a negative impact on their employees' performance. In fact, caring does just the opposite. Research shows that the more that leaders or managers know about their individual employees, the higher those workers' performance will be. Showing that you care for employees will keep engagement alive."

"Employee engagement is an emotional attachment between the employees and the workplace. Employees are more likely to become engaged when key psychological needs are met, such as feeling cared for, having necessary equipment, and knowing what's expected. Your primary responsibility as steward is to constantly enhance employee engagement throughout the company."

She protested, "But getting people to all go in the same direction is hard! I've tried."

I was curious. "What is hard about getting people to go in a singular direction?"

"Even though I tell everyone what to do about something, most ignore me and go their own path."

"Maybe a different approach would get employees engaged."

She thought with a frown on her face. "What do you mean? Different how?"

I was ready for that question. "I notice that you said *I tell them*. Employees will engage when their leader sells them on the vision and asks for their ideas on the best ways to fulfill the vision. Employees need to buy into the destination and then be allowed to drive the bus. You see yourself as the driver."

"Right. Right."

I could tell she was not ready yet to explore that way of leading, so I made a written note to bring it up at a later date. I simply informed her, "You can do it...get everyone to go in the same direction."

She was still doubtful. "You think I can?"

"You have the potential to do it, but maybe you lack the desire. Every leader's basic challenge in getting employees to engage is getting past defining your employees as a singular tool and instead embracing them as a portfolio of diverse assets."

She nodded, so I continued.

The X Factor of Leadership

"Leading people to accomplish something is often like herding cats, seemingly impossible! However, that is what leaders exist to do—take people from one place to another so that their followers can get to the desired destination 'safely,' enjoy the journey, contribute or add value, and grow or improve in the process."

"I coined the phrase *the X Factor of Leadership* to describe the unpredictable and hard-to-control nature of humans. Despite our best efforts to shape a person's behavior, people always have the capability to do the unexpected. We see frequent examples of this, such as the person of integrity who commits an act of fraud, the dependable employee who suddenly becomes flaky, or the loving parent who unexpectedly abandons a family."

"As a leader you must be aware that despite your best effort to lead people toward a specific destination or place, certain individuals may opt out of the journey. You must not take this personally or see it as a poor reflection on the quality of your leadership. If you are striving to be the best leader you can, just view these moments as an X Factor."

Just then a loud crash came from somewhere outside of her office. Before she could leave her chair, Brian opened her door, poked his head in, and said, "Don't worry. It's nothing!" As he shut the door again, she rolled her eyes and sighed deeply. "See what I have to put up with?"

We still have a ways to go...but she might surprise me.

Renee, the Helicopter Boss

Her next words did. "I am beginning to grasp what you have been telling me from the day we met about how I treat people. I just recalled an incident from many years ago. It struck me that what you are trying to tell me about my attitude is similar to my experience with a boss I had."

Renee was a Senior Vice President of a group of young marketing researchers in a small technology company I worked for in a past life. Due to the specific needs of this company, Renee was hired even though she lived 8 hours away. As part of her employment agreement, she was allowed to work from her home office and flew in twice a month to work onsite. The team to which I belonged was a well-oiled machine and, for the most part, we didn't need any close, hands-on management from our new boss. At first we didn't mind her infrequent visits. Renee was extremely bright, and had a very accomplished career. The primary reason she would not relocate was that she had three young children and a husband who worked long hours.

Whenever Renee arrived at our office, her presence was immediately known. She carried herself with a pretentious air, sort of like a queen. We began to feel as though she didn't value our hard work, dedication, and long hours. On each of her helicopter visits, Renee demanded our complete attention the whole time and that included jamming us into a tiny conference room for many hours of preaching at us, which prevented us from getting our work done. Because of this, she had us work later than normal. Although she had dinner brought in for us, she lacked any consideration that we had families and lives outside of work.

On several occasions during these marathon triple-overtime sessions, Renee would disappear. Later, we found out that she was making personal calls on her cell phone while we were working our tails off. Worst of all, she demanded respect from us, but through her actions proved that she didn't respect us.

She paused because this memory seemed to overwhelm her. To relieve the turmoil she was experiencing, I related two examples of bosses I worked for during my formative years.

Lucy, the Confrontational Yeller

'You do what I tell you without question, boy, or I will fire you!'

If I had a dollar for each time this was screamed at me, I would have been a very wealthy college freshman.

Lucy, the store manager for Cut-Rate Drugs, taught me about leadership, but in a perverse way. Lucy was a very inconsistent person. One minute she was nice to me and the next minute she was screaming in my face. She acted this way with all of her employees, but as the only male working for her I believed she used more venom on me than any other employee. It might have been my overwrought imagination or timidity that led me to think that way.

I never wanted to be around her because I never knew what to expect.

Tom, the No Confrontation Yeller

Tom, my boss, managed through intimidation. His decisions were frequently based on his current emotions. He was secretive and often had hidden agendas. Despite being an accomplished soldier and lifetime Marine, the colonel somehow never learned the lesson that the leader needs to be the truth teller. The moment a leader distorts the truth, it opens the door for others to do the same.

When I went to work for the colonel as his assistant, he explained that it was important that we work together as a team. Our joint responsibility was to support our dedicated and talented sales staff and to manage the $10 million inventory of specialized construction equipment. I was excited at learning about how a business runs from the inside, since at the time I was obtaining my business degree and learning from textbooks. I would be able to compare what I learned with what I experienced.

The colonel was patient with me, tutoring me well, and I quickly mastered my responsibilities. He taught me about the business, invited me to attend some sales meetings, and occasionally allowed me to accompany our sales people on customer site visits. I got to 'crawl around' the inventory and learn what our products were used for. I absorbed a lot of relevant business information from him during our two years together. However, my specific wisdom about leadership came whenever the colonel got mad at someone, which was frequently.

The colonel had a temper and when he thought that someone had failed him, he would get visibly upset, but the colonel hated conflict so he never addressed the problem with the individual directly. Soon I discovered what my true role was, which was to be his personal bearer of bad news and chastisements, doing his yelling by long distance. Here is how it worked.

The first time this occurred, it involved Jack, an employee in our service department who failed to complete some paperwork required for a sales transaction we had just finished. The colonel had already called to remind Jack about his oversight, to which Jack promised to send the documents right away. Two weeks elapsed and still no paperwork. I was not aware of all this when the colonel called me into his office, shut the door, and told me sternly to sit down. I was somewhat nervous because he had not done this before. Previously, when a boss called me in like this, it usually meant I was in trouble.

For the next ten minutes or so, the colonel raged and ranted about Jack's lack of follow-through. In a loud voice he complained about how 'certain' people's incompetence and disrespect made his job difficult and as a result he looked bad in front of his boss, Wilbur.

While trying to mentally protect myself, I was clueless as to why I should be the recipient of his rage about something that was obviously his problem. Soon my question was answered. The colonel composed himself, sat behind his desk, looked me in the eye and said, 'Ron, take care of this for me and go harass Jack for that paperwork. Don't come back until you have it!'

Having learned from prior experiences not to question my boss's directives, I left the office. I did not have to go *far because Jack's office was in another building across the street. The whole time I was scared, even though I had no reason to be because Jack was a friend.*

This situation occurred every other week during my time with the colonel. I soon realized that while he knew the action that needed to be taken, he could not bring himself to face the unpleasantness of person-to-person conflict. I wondered, 'How did he survive 25 years in the Marines, if he was so fearful of confronting another person?'

Later, I found out from someone who knew about his history that while he served in the Marines he had a reputation as a poor leader. Early in his career the colonel was pigeonholed as a paper-pusher and he was promoted up through the ranks for his competence and administrative skills only.

Joslyn pondered these descriptions and then inquired, "Which one of these people am I most like? Do I act like Tom? Do I act like Lucy?"

"Which sounds most like you?"

With a shaky voice, she said slowly, "I hate to admit it but based upon what you told me today, I'd say a little of both."

I laughed. "By this time next week you will know for sure after you listened to your direct reports describe the sort of relationship you now have with them."

She visibly winced.

Joslyn's Assignment

I looked at my watch and noticed our time together was nearly over. Meanwhile, Joslyn eyed the still-unopened energy drink and then tossed it into her trashcan. *Clang.*

I said, "You will determine what your growth step assignments will be. Based on what we covered today, what should you work on?"

She looked up from her notes in surprise.

"I...I am not sure."

I could tell she wasn't prepared for me to step up the level of trust.

I prompted, "We covered treating every employee as an asset to nurture and grow."

"I will begin to see each employee as an individual and stop seeing them as a homogeneous blob."

Yikes, that sounded harsh, but she does think of them as one big blob!

I said aloud, "We covered helping employees feel worthy."

"I commit to finding more complimentary things to say."

"We covered win-win outcomes."

"I could spend time after each meeting reviewing to see if I allowed them to win."

"We covered how you speak to employees." *This is making her nervous.*

She stopped fidgeting with her pen and replied, "I can use your killer phrases to monitor my language."

"Anything else?" I asked.

"I can't think of any more."

I handed her my notes about what she just committed to do.

"You are relentless...and thorough." She said this and placed the sheet into her coaching folder, but she was smiling.

I hoped she would be smiling after this bit of news: "You agreed weeks ago to a major growth step that will take place next week when I sit down with each executive. To prepare for this, I need you to block out two consecutive days when every executive is in the office. I will meet with each of them for 15 to 20 minutes to assess the sort of relationship they have with you now and what they want to improve."

Her eyes grew wide.

"Yes, I know this is scary and yet it is the only way for you to find ways to rebuild trust with each member of your team. This will feel intimidating, so tell me what you're thinking right now."

Panting as if she finished a race, she said, "Just thinking about doing that is overwhelming, so I guess I need to work through my fear with courage. I know it has to be done," Joslyn sighed, rubbing her forehead.

I needed to redirect her thinking before this session ended, so I employed an effective coaching technique.

Joslyn's Moment of Rediscovery

I asked, "Describe for me your overall learning from today."

"I guess I do put people down. That's not it!" She put her face into her hands again and breathed deeply three times. Composed, she continued, "It is hard to put into words but I will do my best. I believe I am starting to get back in touch with the true me. Inside of me is a person who does care about her employees, yet there is some disconnect. What I mean is that my feelings of concern do not seem to go past the feeling stage. I've led salespeople for years and I've never had these types of issues that I'm having now with my team and the company's employees."

I remained silent until Joslyn added, "Do you know why that is? Have you worked with other people who have the same problem?"

"What you describe, this disconnect, is a common problem among all leaders and even CEOs. We are weeks away from uncovering the specific issues, but each time we meet you are getting closer to that inner truth. You will know exactly when you've uncovered it because you will feel extremely vulnerable and yet euphoric all at the same moment. Just have a little more patience because we're almost there."

I paused before asking, "Are you writing regularly in your leadership journal?"

"Yes! No, that's a lie! I write sometimes. That's also not true. I haven't had time." She hid her face in her hands. I let her reflect on what she had just done.

"Oh, I see why you're asking. You are suggesting that I write about Stewardship?"

"Would it help you to become a better steward of these X Factor assets?"

She groaned and said, "Yes, it could."

She needed more so I said, with intentional emphasis, "The reason I brought it up is that IF you write what you are going through, the REAL you will show up on the paper. Many of the answers you seek will emerge. Trust me on that. Remember the first part of Natural Law 9? Positive intentions produce positive results. Being HONEST in your writing will prove this truism. Just as the second part of that law applies in your language because by speaking negatively to and of your employees, they will respond negatively to you."

"I see that now. Thank you. It's dawning on me that you are a good influence on me."

I started to gather my belongings. "While you have actions to take, I suggest that you forget about them and relax. Simply dwell on what we covered today. Start by doing that visualizing exercise again."

"I will," she said eagerly.

As I walked out of her office, she sat on her couch, removed her shoes, put her feet up and stared at the ceiling.

*****

Joslyn's Assessment of Her Progress

Every part of my body aches! Maybe it's the flu.

But that inner voice which I have ignored for too long said, *No. You're not ill, Joslyn. It's the pain of change.*

I needed to think and relax. By rearranging the pillows, I was able to make a comfortable resting place on my settee. I shed my heels because that brought some relief.

I think I know what my employees will say about me. That won't change because they will comment on who I was, not who I am changing to. It hit me that I had admitted to myself, *I am changing.*

The body pain eased and I felt a flutter of hope. As I lay back, trying not to fall asleep, I reviewed the day and the meetings and I saw myself as the wolf hunting down innocent sheep who had faces of employees. The image was alarmingly funny but I needed to see it. When done indulging in that exercise and feeling refreshed, I peeked out of my office and noticed I was alone. I texted Harold that I would be here another hour and then shut off my phone and computer.

I took the notepad that was my leadership journal out of my briefcase. For more than two hours I wrote and wrote and wrote! On my drive home, I surprised myself: I felt elated and grateful.

*****

The Bottom Line of Leadership

Success is not a zero-sum activity where achievement requires someone else's failure. Yet many managers seem to buy into the falsehood that if they are treated well, employees will take advantage and get sloppy, so they treat employees like a number. The research shows just the opposite will take place. Howard Schultz, CEO of Starbucks, said, "Every dollar you invest in your employees falls to the bottom line." He has proven since 1978 that when you treat employees as assets, they prove you right. Practicing good stewardship as a leader not only boosts profits, it pays off with an engaged workforce.

An engaged workforce can also boost stock price. Gallup's researchers found that organizations with more than 9.3 engaged employees for every one actively disengaged employee, experienced 147 percent higher earnings per share (EPS) than their competition. Organizations with an average of 2.6 disengaged employees for every engaged one had 2 percent lower EPS than the competition.[20]

Companies that have the highest level of employee engagement are twice as likely to report their organization is hiring new workers when compared to organizations that have lower levels of employee engagement. The companies where employees are emotionally disconnected from their work and workplace are far more likely to report their organization is experiencing employment cutbacks when compared to companies with high employee engagement.

Employee engagement is vital to your success. Here is what Gallup has discovered in its recent and ongoing research into workplace issues:

---

[20] Research conducted by Development Dimensions International, *Fascinating Numbers: How Much Does Good Leadership Affect the Bottom Line* by Robert Tanner http://managementisajourney.com/fascinating-numbers-how-much-does-good-leadership-affect-the-bottom line

- 70% of today's employees are disengaged
- 20% are actively disengaged (defined as openly miserable)
- Only 36% of managers and executives can be described as engaged

Boosting employee engagement links to financial performance in several ways. When comparing the business units in the top quartile versus the business units in the bottom quartile, these findings came to light. Units with the highest employee engagement have:

- 12% higher customer advocacy
- 18% higher productivity
- 12% higher profitability

Comparing the business units in the bottom quartile against business units in the top quartile showed that the units with the lowest employee engagement experience:

- 51% more inventory shrinkage
- 31% to 51% more turnover
- 62% more accidents

It is up to each leader to practice good stewardship because it pays off.

Chapter 7
Caring and Compassion

"No one is allowed to question what a CEO does or says."

Time Remaining: 9 Weeks

Source of Role Confusion – from Joslyn's Viewpoint

I invited Ron to join me for lunch at a 1950s-style diner north of Seattle. This memorable place was filled with noontime guests, and the clatter of dishes made it hard to engage in conversation. Normally I prefer a library-like place for a meal meeting, yet the noise level at this place was like a rock concert. I felt compelled to be here and didn't understand why. This place smelled of burgers, grease, and coffee. As I stared down at the table and listlessly played with my salad, he asked why I chose this establishment. Before I could answer, I felt a teardrop and saw it fall into my salad, yet I couldn't stop how I was feeling. Normally I am much better at controlling myself. *Maybe coming here was a mistake!*

I give kudos to Ron because he didn't press the question, choosing to study the décor. After a few minutes of awkwardness between us, I recovered my poise. Then I explained.

Family Memories

"This place reminds me of my parents. Every Friday, after he got his paycheck, Daddy would bring the five of us to this restaurant. We sat over there," I pointed out a booth in the corner, "and in turn we would place his quarters in the jukebox. As I recall, music seems the only way he could relate to us on a personal level. With each song, he would ask the person who selected it questions about what it meant, and for about 2½ minutes those were the best conversations that I had with Daddy."

"Your father worked for Boeing as an engineering manager, correct?"

"Yes, he is a very smart man and can design or fix anything, but he cannot tolerate people! Let me restate that. People, with their feelings and foibles, befuddle him. If Jillian, or Josh, or I went to him with a problem, he would tell us to talk with Mom. Then he would go out into the garage and tinker. He waited until the storm or problem passed before he surfaced." Even in this bittersweet memory I attempted to smile but couldn't.

"Tell me more about your father." I saw curiosity in his eyes.

As I spoke, it took tremendous effort to raise my voice above a whisper. "Daddy left Brooklyn to relocate us out here, and I guess his parents didn't like that. He rarely talked with them and as far as I know, never saw them in person again once he left the neighborhood of his birth. He did return for my grandparents funerals. For some reason, Gramps never forgave Daddy for 'abandoning his family.' That's what he told me, anyway, but I suspect he was just as much at fault for the estrangement. I left New York when I was six and never got to know my grandparents. Oh, they wrote letters and sent gifts to Mom, my siblings and me, but not to Daddy. This estrangement worried me and still haunts me a little."

"Why?"

"When I started my career, I was so scared that I was like Daddy, unable to relate to people. Holding resentments. Hiding from drama. That is probably one reason I went into sales. I was also very scared that I might turn out to be more like my mother."

He reacted with a shake of the head, as if my comment surprised him.

With a gentle look, he asked, "Tell me about your mother."

I felt myself relax a bit. "Mom, whom I love dearly, was the opposite of Daddy. Where he shied from situations involving people, she craved them. She needed relationships and worked so hard on them. Almost always, she put everyone else's needs ahead of her own until…until…"

He nodded for me to continue even though I felt my heartbeat in my ears.

"Until she had what Daddy called a nervous breakdown, but I suspect it was an alcohol addiction. She went away for a while…and then *she changed*."

"How did she change?"

"She seemed driven somehow; I can't explain it better than that. Mom enrolled in college, found a passion for law, and upon graduation got hired by a good local law firm. She became tough and assertive, not right away, but it happened gradually. Before this, we kids would always get our way. When she became a paralegal she didn't allow that any more. She set high standards. She set expectations. She demanded something from us each time we asked her for something. Before her 'breakdown' she tolerated my dad's hiding out. Then one day she didn't! He began to hide even more, which made her very angry. Soon, it seemed like she ran the family—a complete change in who wore the pants."

"What about her did you not want to emulate?"

My heart was still racing. "While I admire her setting standards for behaviors and standing up for her needs, I didn't like her intolerance of Daddy's need to run away."

"Maybe you are a little of both. Had you thought about that?" His question caught me off guard.

I took another bite of my salad before replying, "What do you mean?"

"Recall what you have learned about the poor leader-like behaviors which have Stephen concerned. Then, think about your father's and mother's behaviors. I will be quiet and finish eating while you reflect on similarities or parallels."

Normally, I love their Cobb salad, but today I couldn't taste anything, so I pushed it aside. As I thought, I noticed that I was chewing my freshly manicured nails. I put my hands on my lap. Ron studied my face, making me even more anxious. After he finished his chicken Marsala, he suggested I speak my thoughts out loud so he could take notes. He ordered a peach cobbler à la mode for us to share when I stopped to process. *Talking about this feels...feels like I am naked.* I shivered at the image.

When I was out of ideas, he handed his iPad to me. I read what he had entered.

"What connections do you find in what you told me?" he asked patiently.

Releasing my teeth from my lower lip, I said, "I see several connections. *I am demanding and set almost unreachable expectations.* That's Mom. *I run away from drama.* That's Dad. *I hold onto resentments.* That's Dad. *I create needless conflict.* That's both Mom and Dad. *When feeling overwhelmed with people issues, I hide out.* That's Dad. *I lose my temper easily.* That's Mom. *I can be obsessive.* Again, Mom and Dad."

Despite my feelings, I felt myself grin slightly. *I want to deny this but he helped me see the truth!*

He smiled warmly and went into his coaching voice. "You did well, Joslyn. Congratulations. You experienced a major breakthrough just now!"

I hid my vulnerability by nibbling the peach cobbler I ordered.

He said, "However, I want you to remember and hold onto this thought: You also have many good traits which you got from them. Would you agree?"

"I guess I do." *No, I don't!*

"Clearly you do have many wonderful traits that balance the scales. May I state some of them?"

"Go ahead." With pie in my mouth it came out as "Grm hehe."

"I have told you many times that you are smart, a quick learner, and tenacious. Now that I know about your family, I add good problem-solving skills, taking charge, possibility thinking, negotiating, and of course setting high standards for yourself."

"Thank you." *Despite those, I still made a mess of things,* I lamented to myself.

He adjusted his tone slightly. "Are you ready to change directions?"

"Yes." *Let's get the focus off me!*

"Then we will talk about communication and language. I wanted to further test a few hunches about your character makeup."

I was both ready and fearful. I pushed his miniscule share of the dessert to his side of the table. *When I'm nervous I crave sugar.*

Impact of a Leader's Words

The noise level went down once the lunch rush was over, and we could hear one another better. The cobbler disappeared because it's to die for. Now that our table was cleared and drinks refreshed, his teaching persona took over.

He asked, "Tell me what your father told you regarding the important things in life."

"Like the birds and the bees?" I giggled, and he grinned.

"No. I mean, when he talked to you about money and business, what do you remember him telling you?"

I sat back to think. "Money and business. As I recall, Daddy had this love/hate relationship with business. As a union man, he thought all management was clueless and cruel...at least until he became a manager. He then altered his opinion, claiming that all executives were 'evil.' Yet he constantly praised Boeing for its business practices and the way they paid attention to their customers and made high-quality products. That's strange. Now that I articulate this, he seemed to be of two minds, often in conflict."

Ron said, "So he was a blue-collar worker, and you ended up in a white-collar job. I would guess that would lead to some tensions in how you each think a business should be run."

"Yes, it did, especially over the last few years."

Uncle Todd

"At a prior session you told me that your mother's brother was a big influence in your life. Tell me more about him."

He watched as I nervously twisted my curls around my fingers. I noticed and folded my hands on my lap.

"Uncle Todd was a CEO at several different companies. He'd be recruited but get bored after five or six years. Then he would be recruited to another CEO job. He lived in at least nine different states. Mom said he was good at taking a small company public, thus making the founders and himself very wealthy. He was in demand but it was at a high cost. He went through four marriages and never had any children. Even though Daddy was committed to his job, he tried not to let it affect his family. Uncle Todd, it seems, put his career ahead of family and, despite his wealth, is a very unhappy man."

I sighed and continued. "Mom adored her brother so Daddy did his best to tolerate Todd. Daddy always put Mom on a pedestal, even when she was berating him. Sorry, I got off topic. Todd and Daddy used to get into arguments whenever they got together. At family gatherings, they would loudly espouse their points of view about how a business should operate. After a few beers, their words turned angry, and I was always fearful that they might get into a fight. Although they never did, any time they got together I was extremely nervous once they started talking about labor and management." My memory of this created a pain in my chest.

Noticing my stress, Ron paused in his note-taking to form a question. "Are you willing to explore this?"

"Yes."

"I would like you to list at least five things you learned about business from your father. Think about things that he used to say when he talked about business." As before, he typed while I talked.

"Daddy frequently said:

- 'A shareholder makes money by cheating the worker.'
- 'All executives are incompetent and out of touch with reality.'
- 'No one cares about the plight of the average employee.'
- 'Executives, especially CEOs, are extremely overpaid and have huge egos that interfere with their ability to make decisions.'
- 'Management and everyday employees will never see eye-to-eye.'"

He nodded his encouragement. "Good. Let's switch over to your Uncle Todd, the CEO. Tell me at least five things that you learned from him about business."

"That's easy because we had many discussions about business when I was growing up. He emphatically told me in many different ways that:

- 'No one is allowed to question what a CEO does or says.'
- 'The Board of Directors works for the CEO and not the other way around.'
- 'When the CEO says jump, every employee should do it without question.'
- 'Workers usually do not know or care about the big picture, so management needs to guide them.'
- 'Employees are basically sheep and often need fleecing and culling.'
- 'Most employees only care about their paycheck and rarely want to know what the business is about.'"

When I was done he shook his head and rubbed his forehead. "Wow! Those are some strong opinions that I'll wager shaped you in many ways."

Although it surprised me to hear that, I knew his insight was true. "Now that I've said them out loud, I am beginning to see that they may have." I sipped my water to calm myself. *Talking about my history puts me on edge! But I guess we have to do this.*

First Connection

After downing his iced tea, Ron explained. "The reason I asked you to recall these memories is because your perception about running a business is shaped from these two important men in your life. Because they saw it from completely opposite points of view, you were caught in the crossfire. One part of you dislikes or distrusts the rank-and-file employee. This paradigm came from Uncle Todd's words. One part of you distrusts executives, and this paradigm came via your father's words. Yet *you are management!*"

I nodded, though I was skeptical.

"Early in your career you were an entry-level salesperson and then you were quickly promoted into sales management, so you have never been a blue-collar employee like your father. I sense that you are always fighting against yourself. The battles you witnessed at family get-togethers are now fought within you."

"Were you aware of this internal torment?"

"No but now that you state it, it somewhat feels true."

"Maybe because you are not aware of this internal emotional and mental turmoil, you take your anger out on your employees."

He paused to let me dwell on this insight. "Tell me what you are thinking."

My doubts vanished. "That makes sense…except for the part about taking it out on employees." *I don't do that!*

Feeling shame, I needed to change the conversation. "One of my assignments from our last session was to write about the 'real me' and see beyond other people's opinions, ones that I've apparently adopted as my own. I had a hard time thinking of anything to write when it came to my view of running a business. I can now see some opinions that I wrote about are actually my father's or uncle's words. I understand now why you had me do that exercise."

Second Connection

Smiling with encouragement he continued, "Another connection that I see, based on what you told me about your family dynamics, is that you never learned about emotional language."

"What is emotional language?" That phrase piqued my interest.

"Think about how your father reacted whenever he had to face typical human issues such as disagreements, unhappiness, or aggression from his children. What did he do? He ran away from the situation and hid in his workshop. He was unable to cope with it or maybe never acquired a process for handling it properly. That could be why he was incapable of having normal father-to-child discussions except through music. Dwell on that as you look at your own behaviors regarding personal issues that your employees present to you."

That stung! "Are you implying that I run away from disagreements, unhappiness, or aggression from my employees?"

"Do you think that you do?"

"Up until now I didn't think so." I paused to think. "But as I sit here recalling Daddy, our Friday suppers here at this diner along with other memories, I can envision how he would react to the drama in my staff meetings."

He grinned. "What a great insight! Tell me what you see him doing."

"I imagine him reading the newspaper, falling asleep, or even bailing out of the meeting before it's over." *Uh-oh. Here it comes.*

"Have you more than once imagined yourself doing these things in your staff meetings?"

"Quite often." My heart raced, making my head throb. *He knows me too well.*

"Do members of your team behave this way in staff meetings?"

Damn him. "Yes. Yes, they do."

He maybe sensed my unease because he slowed the pace. He thought before asking the inevitable question, "Why do you think they want to avoid meeting with you?"

"I make them uncomfortable."

"Is this outcome intentional? Do you do this on purpose?"

I sighed deeply and rubbed my forehead, hoping to make the ache go away. "I can see how that if I put everyone on edge, I feel like a victor because they can't question me. It's hard to admit, but... but I often feel like I am doing it because I don't know what I am doing. Does that make sense? Is that a source of my anger? Self-doubt?"

"Yes, it could be. Allow me to describe the **11th Natural Law of Leadership**."

> **All leaders have moments of doubt.
> It is what you do with those moments which
> prove if you are a true leader.**

My only response was to agree with him.

He continued to tell me what I know I needed to hear. "This is what I believe you experience in those moments. When an employee asks for help or seeks guidance from you, you get a feeling of vulnerability. Similarly, when you ask an employee or colleague for help or guidance, the same feeling arises. These normally occurring situations cause you to become mad at yourself for feeling exposed until it boils over as anger directed at the person you are with."

He's right. "Asking for help is something I am extremely uncomfortable with!"

"I have seen evidence of that. It explains your initial reluctance to having a coach."

I nodded.

"You just told me: 'Asking for help is something I am extremely uncomfortable with,' right?"

Not sure where he was going, I nodded.

"Allow me to show you a simple and powerful technique to shift that dynamic each time you feel vulnerable. It requires you to reframe how you feel. Would you like to learn this technique?"

"Yes."

"It requires you to rephrase your statement. Repeat after me, 'I am uncomfortable asking for help AND I am able to do it.'"

Reluctantly I repeated his words with my arms folded tightly across my chest. We did this several times until I realized what he had just done with me. I relaxed and sat back, trying not to smile.

Third Connection

Ron continued the lesson. "One behavior I've noticed in my observations is that you tend to shy away from dealing with issues that contain emotional content. In your case, instead of running away as your father would have done, you adopt the persona of Uncle Todd and become abrupt, dictatorial, or you squash the emotions out before they can be explored. Remember Todd told you often, 'No one is allowed to question the actions of the CEO.' That is a very emotion-laden, dictatorial statement. In your interactions with employees you attempt to take control of almost all conversations. I notice that you rarely speak to them at a peer-to-peer level, but instead adopt a servant-to-master speaking style."

"Ouch. That smarts. You saw or heard me do this?"

"Yes. You consistently do that. You even attempt to do it with me, even though I don't let you get away with it." He stopped, studied me, and said, "Tell me your thoughts."

I couldn't look at him. "Yes. I can see that I do that. Examples of it are echoing in my ears. I am so sorry."

I looked up and caught his smile. "I am not the one who needs your apology. You have used this angry, confrontational style with many people. Would you like to learn a more leader-like way to handle yourself in these situations?"

I covered my face in my hands and rubbed my eyes. Taking two to three deep breaths, I looked at him and answered, "Yes."

"That's good to hear. My suggestion is that you relearn how to speak with people and relate to them on a peer level as you reframe how you define your comfort level."

Laughing out loud I said, "Message received, Ron. You would have made a great psychologist."

"I believe that you missed my message." He looked sternly at me. "I will restate what I said. You have an opportunity in front of you to relearn how to communicate. To lead well you must communicate as a CEO does."

This time I didn't miss his message but I could think of only one response. "I don't have time to learn how to communicate differently! I am already too busy!"

I could tell he anticipated some sort of excuse from me because he stared at me in silence. In anger, I shut down.

Gomer's Woe

"Speaking of B.S., that reminds me of a story." He paused to see if I grasped his opinion of my lame excuse.

I rolled my eyes because I did get it.

> A farmer named Gomer was digging a long and deep trench by hand. A hiker stopped to ask for directions. They exchanged pleasantries and their names. The hiker was puzzled as to why the farmer was using a pick

and shovel when a few yards away sat a new John Deere trench digger.

'Gomer, I hate to pry, but why aren't you using that piece of equipment so you can save your back?'

'Well, my son-in-law lent me his trencher and told me how to use it. I tried recalling what he said, but I'm a hands-on type of guy. Since I can't figure out how the darn thing works and I gotta get this done quickly, I go with what I know works.'

After getting directions from Gomer, the hiker left, shaking his head in puzzlement. 'I would bet that if he spent an hour or two learning how to use that thing, he would save that amount of time and more. Plus, he wouldn't have to work so hard.'

Weeks later, Gomer lay in bed resting his aching back, which neither heat nor pain relievers would improve. Through closed eyes he saw himself digging trenches while the trench digger sat idle in the sun. He slapped his head in frustration when he realized how his stubbornness was the cause of his pain.

Leadership Lesson

He wanted me engaged and asked, "Tell me the connection you see between what we just talked about and my Gomer story."

I emerged from my cave. *Yes, I am like Daddy.* "I am Gomer and in my bullheadedness, I refuse to accept suggestions that could make me better. Is that what you wanted to hear?!" I attempted to throttle my anger back but failed. *The sugar is fueling this.*

"I agree. You are just like Gomer in many ways. You complain that you don't have time and you have too much work. Yet if you took the time to use the tools available you would not need to work so hard. You would find that more work gets done with less fuss and stress. You claim to need employees' help but you fail to ask for it and if anyone does try to support you, you belittle them!"

I felt my cheeks flush. *He's so calm even when I am trying to irk him.* I relaxed in my chair.

Leadership Outcome – Caring and Compassion

Reaching into his black briefcase, Ron pulled out a silver ball and a sheet of paper with an image on it, both of which he placed in front of me. The reflective ball felt cool in my hands and measured about two inches.

"Thank you. What is this for?" I asked.

"Today, we will cover the sixth Leadership trait, one that produces forward momentum in the previous five leadership traits. This trait is multifaceted and will vastly improve the impact you can have on those you work with."

I saw the words *Caring* and *Compassion* handwritten in ink on the silver ball.

Using his teaching voice, he spoke. "Many senior leaders are just like you and Gomer. You fail to realize that by investing a few hours regularly to become a better leader, you would:

- Get more done
- Have more ease
- Be less stressed
- Enjoy your job more
- Have more free time
- Be more strategic
- Be better problem-solvers

And, of utmost importance to a CEO, you would become a paragon of leadership who would produce more leaders."

"Today we will delve into another outcome and energy-renewing trait, which is having and demonstrating caring and compassion. They fit together and are connected as one. I see them as a Siamese twin trait. This particular trait is interconnected with stewardship because if you really care about your employees, you will become a good steward of them, and by demonstrating consistently that you are a good steward, people will recognize that you care about them."

We chatted for a while regarding my feelings around compassion and caring. Although I was still uncomfortable doing this, Ron assured me, "Executive coaching generally focuses on business issues, but a really good coach knows that the client will be unable to separate the different aspects of her life because *everything is interconnected*. A personal issue spills over into her business competency. A spiritual challenge negatively impacts personal and business competencies. Emotional issues always undermine confidence and competency in all other aspects."

Eight Competencies of a Balanced Life
Ron then placed a drawing into my hands and I studied the image. "Your life, like everyone else's, is broken into eight different competencies or facets."

8 COMPETENCIES OF A BALANCED LIFE

These are:

1. Spiritual
2. Health
3. Recreational
4. Finances
5. Family
6. Relationships
7. Career
8. Learning or Education

"Like an old-fashioned wagon wheel with eight spokes, each facet is connected to the other seven and defines who you are and how you feel about yourself. A good coach will work with the individual and delve into all eight dimensions to determine how an issue in one competency impacts the others seven."

I was hesitant to respond because I didn't know where this was going.

"You told me that you are experiencing problems in your personal life that are adding severe stress and causing your irritability and sleepless nights. Can we explore one facet of your life—relationships with Jayna and Harold?"

"If we have to." *I sound just like Jayna.*

Jayna is my 16-year-old daughter whom I describe as *purposely failing her classes despite a high intellect.* I admitted to Ron once that my husband, Harold, insisted that I was *uptight and had the warmth of an ice cube. Will I regret these disclosures?*

Calmly he explained, "Even though it may seem that these issues should not affect your competency as a leader, they do. Let's return to the analogy you used about running a long-distance race. What can happen if your shoes don't fit? How is your running affected if your shirt chafes?"

"I wouldn't be able to do my best. Irritants like these would distract my focus and...and...Oh, I get it! If other parts of my life aren't working well, then I can't put my full concentration on my job."

"Exactly."

"Are you saying if other parts of my life—family, health, other relationships—are troubled, the drama could spill over into my effectiveness at work?"

"That is correct. It is difficult to feel like you're a competent runner if your shoes don't fit right. A fight with Harold is likely to foster anger at a colleague."

It felt like a weight was suddenly lifted off my shoulders; the relief was short-lived, however. I noticed that the diner's staff was giving us the eye. "Time to leave," I said.

We grabbed our possessions and walked to my car, where he continued the lesson.

"While these facets of your life could lessen your impact, you cannot use them as an excuse for being a poor leader or for berating an employee."

To my shame, I realized that I was about to throw Harold and even Jayna under the bus for my troubles with Stephen. *He anticipated I'd do that.*

Looking at me over the top of my newly polished BMW, he said, "Your employees also have personal needs, and when they feel cared about, those other seven will usually not interfere with their ability to give you their full commitment. If the employees believe that you, their boss, do not care about them, these competencies will become more important than doing their best for you. A lot of their work time will be spent pursuing interests that will make them feel competent. These behaviors will interfere with their ability to care for Neoteric's customers, harm the quality of their work products, and reduce their productivity."

I listened attentively as we got in the car and buckled up.

During the 40-minute drive back to my office, Ron explained the caring leader to me.

Caring and Compassion to a Leader

He said, "Consider this question: *Why does a leader need compassion?*"

I chose to concentrate on the heavy traffic.

He continued, "Whenever I ask a reluctant leader that question and he or she cannot think of an answer easily, it implies that they don't practice compassion. Yet compassion is an essential character trait for every leader. The reason is not that you lack or do not feel compassion; rather, for the typical leader the challenge is in the word itself. A favorite Zen saying describes it well: 'Make no judgments where you have no compassion.' I have met far too many reluctant leaders who think compassion means either pity or condoning someone's actions. Pity is basically feeling sorry for someone."

Unwilling to take my eyes off the road, I simply nodded.

"I can explain compassion with an analogy. You and Cameron work for the same company. Assume she is someone you admire and are close to. Last year, she hired a payroll specialist who was later caught embezzling $50,000. Cameron failed to closely supervise this person's work, and your employer puts the entire blame on her. In addition to terminating Cameron, your employer contemplates suing both the bonding company and her to recover the loss. Even if they don't sue her, the bonding agency could potentially hold

Cameron liable for their share of the loss. Already having lost her credibility and having to go into debt to pay for an attorney, her woes grow. If Cameron is deemed negligent, she could lose her professional license, which would totally alter her life for the worse. You deeply care about Cameron."

"Tell me what you would say to your friend Cameron."

"I'd probably say to her, 'You made your bed, now you have to lie in it.' That sounds harsh but it's how I'd feel."

"Many reluctant leaders would respond that way. The person who misunderstands or lacks compassion thinks *I don't feel sorry for Cameron because she is the one who made a poor choice and she now has to suffer the consequences of that choice.* Because pity is a feeling of sadness, it is possible for you to feel sorrow about Cameron's situation. This sadness is why people dislike dealing with personal issues because of the emotions involved, especially for those who define themselves as logical and not swayed by emotion."

He paused to let me catch up and then went further. "A person who does not understand compassion could misinterpret it to mean condoning or overlooking Cameron's actions. This person thinks *Yes, Cameron most likely was made the scapegoat, but it was her fault. By feeling sorry for her, I would have to overlook her lack of professionalism and errors in judgment.* That is how some people perceive compassion. However, feeling compassion for Cameron does not give her a free pass, even if she is culpable."

His voice grew softer and he seemed to measure his words. "Compassion is both connection and understanding with empathy. A person with compassion would think this way. *Cameron is a precious human being and I hate to see her suffer. Yes, she made an unwise decision, yet I can understand why she may have made the choices she did. She now has to face the consequences for what happened. I will do what I can to help Cameron through this.*"

He paused before continuing, "Notice the frame of reference the person with compassion uses. In compassion, the understanding colleague does the following: she recognizes Cameron's humanity, feels for her condition, has empathy by walking in Cameron's shoes, recognizes the reality without placing blame, and stays connected by caring about Cameron. This loving attitude toward Cameron demonstrates what compassion is—an acknowledgement of concern and caring for the person at a deep level."

He paused.

Since I remained silent, he asked me again, "Why does a leader need to be compassionate?"

The Compassionate Leader

Traffic was less congested, so I glanced over to understand his expectation then turned my attention back to the road before saying, "Because a leader is expected to make tough decisions and difficult choices and, as you have told me, people have a strong and constant desire to feel confident and capable."

"Correct. Many times you will impact people in hurtful ways such as having to lay off employees in order to save the company or saying 'no' to someone who desperately needs you to say 'yes.' You need to understand the feelings and concerns of the people impacted in order to make a wise decision. You, as the leader, stand on a large stage, and the higher up the organization chart you are, the larger your audience of followers becomes, as does your impact. Today, with the speed of business and change, the person in charge must be able to make quick decisions that can have a lasting or significant impact and which result in unpredictable outcomes."

This makes sense. "So what you are saying is having compassion helps the leader to make these tough decisions without guilt or regret." I felt good and satisfied.

Ron replied, "Yes" and asked more questions to verify if I understood why compassion was a necessary trait for a leader.

As I was pulling into my designated parking space, his next words created a chill inside of me.

"You will need to tap into your compassion over the next two days as you listen to employees speak the 'truth' about their relationship with you. My guess is that you will hear things that are tough and contradict how you might see yourself."

I gulped as I exited my car.

"Are you up to the task?" He held my gaze until it felt comfortable.

It took all my self-control to refrain from getting back in my car and driving away. *I guess it's time for me to face the truth.*

Listening to My Employees

For the rest of the day and most of the next day, I would be fulfilling an application or learning step that I agreed to carry out.

Ron would spend time talking with each of my direct reports to gain a better understanding of my relationship dynamics with them. He had informed me, "The interviews are a vital part of my coaching process for a CEO. I am concerned that you might refuse to participate. However, I sincerely believe that you are committed to improving yourself as a leader, and I know this information would be of value to you. I cannot force you into this—it has to be your decision. My goal in each interview is to uncover insights that could help improve relationships with each of them."

When we talked about it, it seemed a simple thing, but now that it was in front of me, I was terrified!

And here is why I was so scared: I would be required to sit in a remote part of the room and remain absolutely quiet while taking notes about the conversation. I was to be a fly on the wall! Even though the employee knew I was present, I would sit out of the employee's sightline.

Ron had said, "They will be just as scared as you. I talked with each one and I guaranteed that what they tell us is solely intended to help you grow. I promised there will be no repercussions or negative consequences for anything they say." He made me swear that I would never hold what they said against them.

Without any hesitation, I agreed. This was before he told me he would check in with them to ensure that I kept my promise. I knew that I could never hope to be trustworthy if I used their honesty against them.

During these interviews, Ron suggested that I write down any self-discoveries and aspects of the relationship I was previously unaware of. I had to remain absolutely quiet.

In each meeting, Ron asked the employee the same simple, open-ended questions. First: *What do you like about Joslyn and your relationship with her?* (These are listed as pluses.) Second: *What situations about Joslyn and your relationship with her are not working?* (These are listed as minuses.)

Before we started this, I believed that I would rather be burned alive than do this. However, Ron's confidence and encouragement would be my life preserver. I promised to stay strong and (hopefully) stoic. Writing notes in the third person helped a lot.

His first meeting was with Kendra, Neoteric's Chief Financial Officer.

Relationship Pluses
- I admire Joslyn as a person.
- I want her to teach me about marketing and the selling process since she's so good at it.
- I like that she emphasizes and preaches cost management.

Relationship Minuses
- She ignores my advice.
- She allows sales and marketing to spend whatever they want.
- She occasionally belittles my financial acumen.
- She overrides my decisions on issues that affect sales and customers.

The next interview was with Pindar, our VP of Marketing Communications. It was hard for him to be open about me until Ron explained, "Joslyn needs you to be honest so that the two of you can effectively work together from this day forward."

Relationship Pluses
- She really knows our sales systems and our customers.
- She has great relationships with key customers and accounts.

Relationship Minuses
- She belittles my work because she rewrites nearly every marketing copy I give her.
- She fails to keep me informed of changes in policy and direction.
- She confuses the sales team with mixed messages.

Next he met with Curtiss, Director of Human Resources, who reports to Kendra. Curtiss claimed that he couldn't think of any pluses due to his frustration over the way I treated employees. That hurt.

Relationship Minuses
- – Joslyn contributes to high turnover.
- – She creates a culture of fear.
- – She alienates people on the management team, especially me.
- – She ignores my advice on handling sensitive personnel issues.
- – She fails to follow existing Human Resources procedures.

His next session was with Marlene, our Director of Information Technology, who also reports to Kendra.

Relationship Pluses
- – She keeps people in line.
- – She controls costs.
- – She gives me plenty of money to have a world-class information system.
- – She listens to my advice, especially when it impacts sales and customers.

Relationship Minuses
- – She does not seem to want to know me as a person.

Ron seemed to avoid me after the last session of that first day, which I assumed was planned. I felt so vulnerable and raw. I went home that night with a severe headache. I tossed and turned for a while as my employees' comments trampled my brain. I wanted to scratch out his eyes, but then I remembered that he had given me a tool to use. *He must have anticipated I'd feel this way.* I followed his instructions about how to deeply relax to the letter and it worked. I fell into deep slumber. I woke up refreshed yet scared.

Early the next morning, Ron's first session was with Latisha, who, as Vice President of Distribution, also served (temporarily) as our Chief Operating Officer, Neoteric's second highest officer. She serves as replacement for Kelly, who resigned because of me.

Relationship Pluses
- She stays out of my hair most of the time.
- She understands cost structures.
- She helps my team in negotiating long-term vendor contracts in our favor.

Relationship Minuses
- She tries to micromanage Production too often.
- She looks at Production and Operations as adjuncts to Marketing rather than an independent functional groups.
- She disrespects me.
- She hasn't helped me developed as a female leader in a male-dominated industry.
- She acts like a man (instead of being herself).

Latisha added this comment: "Initially I thought Joslyn would make a good mentor, but I have changed my mind. Nearly all the women in management are disappointed in her. We hoped she would be someone we could emulate, but that train left the station in her first month as our CEO." I wrote in my notes: *I never knew that women were looking for me to mentor them.* I couldn't hold back tears that filled my eyes when I heard that.

Ron's next interview was with Aaron, who also wore two hats. In addition to being our Director of Material Acquisition, he was filling in the role as VP of Production, a key position left vacant when Dino resigned.

Relationship Pluses
- She knows our market, our customers, and our products.
- She is always pushing for higher margins.
- She is invaluable in setting production goals.

Relationship Minuses
- She ignores my advice, especially since I've taken over Dino's responsibilities.
- She makes assumptions without consulting me to the accuracy of them. She is often wrong.
- She treats Production as the Sales group's toy, thus not respecting what we are capable of.
- She ignores me and my supervisors whenever she visits the production facilities.

His next meeting was with Paula, who, as the company's Treasurer, reports to Kendra, the CFO.

Relationship Pluses
- She gives me total freedom to manage the company's cash.
- She respects my knowledge and expertise.
- She sets achievable goals on asset management issues.

Relationship Minuses
- She is a poor role model for a female leader.
- She sometimes ignores my advice.
- She puts me in a difficult spot when I have to choose between what's best for the company versus what's best for the customer.
- She allows sales to get away with murder; as a result, we have higher bad-debt losses than the industry average.
- 90 percent of the time she makes decisions in favor of our customers, thus decreasing our profits.

Ron next met with Dawn, an excellent Marketing Director who works for Jackson. I refer to her as a dynamo for her ability to make good things happen.

Relationship Pluses
- She and I frequently visit key accounts.
- The wonderful way she handles customers.
- She has extensive product knowledge.
- She has solid relationships with most customers.

Relationship Minuses
- She is hard to get to know on a personal level.
- In my opinion, she doesn't fully trust me.

Next on Ron's hot seat was Isaiah, who, as our Sales Manager, works directly for Jackson. Despite his best efforts, Ron wasn't able to get any information out of Isaiah because he was extremely upset with me and refused to say anything as long as I was in the room. Ron's calm persistence paid off when Isaiah made this comment: "That (expletive) woman does not give Jackson the respect that he deserves. In fact, I hope she quits and Jackson becomes our CEO." I held my head with sweaty hands. *What have I done*? I could not for the life of me give myself a satisfactory answer.

Ron saved the last interview for Jackson, our VP of Sales & Marketing. He explained why. "Because of the already deteriorated relationship between the two of you, I wanted to spend more time determining if anything could be done to improve the situation. I've met with Jackson several times prior to today. He was very concerned about your impact on the morale of his sales team. He told me that he was feeling betrayed. You spotted his raw talent years ago and groomed him for sales management. When you relocated to the Northwest to join Neoteric, he followed and has been very loyal to you. However, once you moved into the CEO seat, he said, 'It was like her personality shifted 180 degrees. Instead of being my friend, she treats me like her enemy.'"

I genuinely wanted to hear what Jackson thought about our relationship because I really missed the closeness we once enjoyed.

Relationship Pluses
- She knows sales and walks the talk.
- She has good, deep relationships with our customers.
- She puts the sales team's needs ahead of everyone else's.
- She knows the market and where it is headed.

Relationship Minuses
- She pisses me off every day.
- She scares people on my team so I have to work very hard to keep them happy.
- She frequently treats me like dirt or like a gopher instead of a sales executive.
- She steps on my toes by going outside of my authority at times.

Jackson lamented, "I am still very loyal to this company. I'm just not loyal to her."

These interviews wore me out but were worth the time invested because I gained extremely painful and valuable information. I was glad to hear the reality that up until now I had intentionally avoided.

At the end of my notes I wrote: "I commit to improving the relationship with each member of my team."

I wanted to go home and medicate myself to sleep. I hurt all over. However, Ron insisted that we meet the afternoon of the second day to discuss what I had learned.

Importance of Relationships to a Leader

As he entered my office he commented pleasantly, "Was it as painful as it looked?"

"You warned me there would be times when your feedback would feel like I'd been stripped raw, and today is one of those times. I feel...like I just drank from a fire hose and the water was nasty-tasting."

"And that feeling is a good thing!"

I studied his face and realized he was being honest, not facetious. I stood up and paced, too restless to sit.

He spoke calmly, "Congratulations on the work you just completed! Many senior leaders give up on themselves long before we get to this point in your journey. It took courage to both open your eyes to their truth and to peel back the layers to uncover your true self."

"Thanks. I can see why some give up." I grabbed bottles of water for both of us from my mini-refrigerator and paced nervously while gulping mine down.

Ron said, "Why we've devoted so much time on relationships in the last few sessions can be explained by these truisms, the **12th and 13th Natural Laws of Leadership**."

> **It is your people who tell you if you can lead.**
> **You can give yourself the title of leader, but only your**
> **followers will tell you if you are worthy of that honor.**

> **A leader can only be successful when her**
> **relationships are successful. In leadership**
> **it is the relationship with your followers**
> **that matters the most. They grant you the**
> **power to lead them, and place their**
> **livelihood and talents into your hands.**

Even though I was unsettled and hurting, I needed to be truthful. "Well, what they told me through you is that I have yet to earn the title of leader."

He let that comment hang in the air. Then, he asked, "What did you learn about yourself over the past two days?"

I paced as I spoke. "I am a good person with bad habits. I use anger to push people away, put them on the defensive. I have missed many opportunities to use the talents of my team. No wonder people are scared of me because I intentionally scare them. Can I do better?" I hung my head and massaged my aching forehead. I refused to cry.

He approached me and gently placed a hand on each shoulder so that I faced him. "Do you want to do better? That's the real question that you must answer immediately."

"I want to say yes, but I'm not sure if that is my ego talking or the real me."

He let me go and returned to a chair.

A Vote of Confidence

Just as we were about to discuss this further, we were interrupted by my assistant Brian. "Mr. Jackson said he urgently needs to see the two of you. Can he come in?"

I automatically started to react with annoyance but caught myself, let it go, and invited him in. I thought, *Maybe he is going to tender his resignation.* I was not prepared for what happened next.

Jackson entered timidly and apologized profusely. We all sat at my table, with him across from me. "I apologize for interrupting you, but I am leaving early tomorrow for a long trip and believe that what I have to say is so important it couldn't wait." He paused to see if he was forgiven.

"It is okay. What's on your mind?" I did my utmost to be warm and sensitive. I think Ron noticed.

Looking directly at me, he said slowly, "We just finished talking about you." He saw my puzzlement. "I mean, most of the leadership team got together after my meeting with Mr. Rael. We talked about what it meant to have you in the room while we complained about you." Jackson looked at Ron but tilted his chin in my direction, then turned back to me. "Most of us were amazed that you were willing to do something like that, and as we talked, some of us realized that you were serious about changing." He collected his thoughts. "We debated about what it means to this company if you stay or if you leave."

Here comes the bad news.

"Many of us realized that we'd be in a real hurt if you left. What I am saying is that, in a fashion, you just received a vote of confidence from your staff." His laughter rumbled from deep within his body. "It was not unanimous and there are fences you need to mend but as the unofficial spokesman for your team, we are starting to feel hopeful that things between us will improve."

I was stunned and didn't know what to say. My sweaty hands squeezed the table.

He stood up. I could sense his slight embarrassment at being the messenger even though it was good news.

Ron must have sensed my momentary helplessness, so he took the lead. "Jackson, before you go, I have an important question. Can you stay a little longer?"

Facing the Issue

Staring at Jackson, he asked, "Can this relationship be saved? Do you believe that things can work out between you and Joslyn?"

Jackson sat down. He paused for a beat and replied, "About a month ago I would've said 'hell, no' but a little over a week ago I was contacted by a board member." He turned his body toward me. "And no, I can't tell you who it was. I was asked if I was interested in being considered for the CEO position." He paused to let that sink in. "But I declined because I think that I am not ready to assume that much responsibility. I like sales. So my answer today to Mr. Rael's question is *I hope so.*"

Ron studied my eyes to maybe get a read on how I felt. At the moment my feelings were torn between elation and sorrow.

Ron asked me, "Joslyn, do you want a better relationship with Jackson? I ask because the relationship between the two of you is the second most vital one in this organization."

I felt an icy pang of fear but breathed it out. Looking directly at Jackson, I said, "Yes, I hope so. I hope that we can mend fences and maybe go back to the type of relationship we had in the beginning."

Jackson grinned. "That would sure take a load off my shoulders."

For another 20 minutes we each offered Ron ideas about ways to improve our working relationship, and then Jackson left. On his way out, he gave me a hug, something he used to do. It felt good, and I was hopeful.

I knew that Ron would end this intensive session by extracting a commitment or two from me.

My Assignment

Smiling, he said, "Today's action plan for you has multiple levels to it. Are you ready to hear it?"

I nodded.

"The first thing I suggest is for you to deliver a personal apology to your team members. Take to heart what they said about you in those meetings and find something within that to apologize for."

Despite my trepidation, I had to prove to Ron that I could change, so I said I would.

He then surprised me. "It's your turn. Based on your employees' feedback, what other urgent actions do you assign yourself?"

I breathed and took a moment to think. "I believe my second action is to develop an overall plan to improve employees' perception of me. Maybe Jackson and Letitia can give me insights and ideas on how to go about doing this. I will ask for their suggestions."

"Are you truly willing to ask for their help?"

"I think maybe that could work toward repairing the relationship among us. Yes, I am willing."

"Are there any more actions you feel compelled to take?"

"No. I am good." I tried to be funny but failed at it.

"May I suggest one more action item? It is an important one that could help Neoteric thrive in the longer term."

He explained, "You could develop a council of women managers and supervisors to promote leadership. Latisha, Kendra, and Marlene will be important assets in this effort. Encourage them to drive this effort and then solicit their advice on whom to select as participants and mentors."

I liked his suggestion and sat up in my chair. I could only imagine how painful it was for the women leaders on the team to be disappointed that I was such a poor role model. I wrote down his suggestion and made a commitment to him that I would do it. *He no longer asks if I will commit to these actions nor does he follow-up between sessions. He trusts me to do the work. Wow.*

We said our goodbyes as we walked to our own vehicles. It was late and I was tired. I headed home, determined not to think of anything. However, my mind became very clear. *I am their leader, yet I have failed to be one. The anger my employees show is because I failed them. I've been reluctant to take charge, hiding behind the need to sell.*

In my heart, I tried to get in touch with how Curtiss and Jackson and Isaiah might feel when I am in the room with them. It was hard, yet I could sense their disappointment and frustration. I stopped that line of thought because it started to turn into a pity party.

That night I slept the most comfortable sleep in months.

*****

Ron's Assessment of Joslyn's Progress

Even though I was exhausted and wanted to think about anything except work, I willed myself to make entries into Joslyn's file while events were fresh in my mind.

This week was a major growth in her development as a leader. I can see many positive changes and less backsliding. Now that she knows how she is perceived as a leader by those she works closely with, she has choices to make.

Joslyn will have a lot to think about over the next couple of days. I admire her courage and willingness to listen to her employees. I believe she has turned the corner, and her victories are now deeper and stronger.

I anxiously wait to hear how she will go about mending fences with her employees. The next few weeks are crucial if she hopes to win over the entire board.

*****

The Bottom Line of Leadership

Employee morale can be the fuel that drives an organization forward or the fuel that feeds the fires of employee discontent, poor performance, and absenteeism. With low morale comes a high price tag.

The Gallup Organization estimates that there are 22 million actively disengaged employees costing the American economy as much as $450 billion per year in lost productivity, including absenteeism, illness, and other problems that result when employees are unhappy at work.[21]

A 2011 study with responses from 1,897 human resource professionals and 12,423 leaders from more than 74 countries found evidence of the impact of good leadership on an organization's bottom line.

- 50 percent is the difference in the impact of a top-performing leader versus an average-performing leader.
- In the area of key metrics like financial performance, organizations with the highest-quality leaders were 13 times more likely to outperform the industry competitors.
- Organizations with higher-quality leadership experience higher employee retention and engagement, up to three times greater than their competitors.
- One poor leader costs a company more than $126,000 a year due to low productivity, turnover, and dissension[22].

Under strong and effective leadership, employee productivity can increase by 300 percent. In other words, one person is able to do the work of three. Due to the positive influence, employee turnover and unwanted attrition can decrease by 75 percent[23].

A leader who truly cares and demonstrates compassion improves profits because the followers stay, remain committed, and outperform the competition's employees.

---

[21] *The Cost of Poor Leadership* ©2010 The Alpine Link Corporation
http://www.alpinelink.com/Index.aspx
[22] *The Huffington Post* August 6, 2012 along with USA Today June 5, 2012
[23] WebEx event hosted by David Will Program Director, The Ken Blanchard Companies

Chapter 8
Serenity

*"I felt so uncomfortable that I did not know
what to say to Karen."*

Time Remaining: 5 Weeks

Today was dark, cloudy, and wet—a typical Seattle day. The
rain beat a rhythm on my office window, while Joslyn stared
out at the gloominess. I wanted her to sit, but I knew that when
she felt keyed up she needed to be on her feet. A tall glass of
cold lemonade sat untouched, dripping beads of condensation
on my coffee table. I noticed these details as I attempted to
stay calm to counteract her visible agitation.

Fateful Meeting

"Joslyn, you said you ran into Karen at the mall. Remind me
why Karen is so important to you."

As she ran her fingers through her recently cut and styled hair,
she said, "Karen is someone I admire so much. As I was
learning to become a sales manager, she was the person
whom I turned to for help and suggestions. Karen is a member
of the Million Dollar Roundtable and is a master at selling and
marketing. Her impact on me is tremendous because she
shared insights into developing leads, establishing credibility
with prospects, and then closing the deal. Most of all she really
was influential by teaching me how to develop a deep, trusting
relationship with each of my customers."

"She sounds like a wonderful individual, so why do you feel
distraught about running into her?"

"Because I seem to have forgotten the lessons that she taught me about relationships. At the time I was only focused on making sales, and what she advised me worked because I was able to acquire bigger and bigger accounts. In a way, her advice allowed me to get promoted to sales manager. However…"

She paused and walked back to the table to take a sip of lemonade. "With all the work I've done with you regarding my relationships with Stephen, the board, and especially my team, I suddenly realized that I've never applied them to the people I work with. An intense sense of embarrassment hit me all at once. If Karen noticed, she didn't say anything. We chatted about this and that, but I was never able to get beyond a superficial level because I KNEW she would be extremely disappointed in me."

Feelings of Inadequacy

Obviously this is where we need to go to today. Aloud I said, "What is it about your incidental meeting with Karen that brought up those feeling of inadequacy?"

"My brain kept repeating the same thing over again: *I DON'T measure up!*"

"You don't measure up to what?"

"I don't measure up to Karen's expectations of me."

As if carrying a heavy weight, she plopped down hard into a chair and bent forward, staring at the tabletop.

I asked, "And you know she disapproves of you how?"

"Maybe she doesn't. Okay, I am being the ASS in *assume*! But if I had told her the dilemma I find myself in today, then I believe she would be extremely disappointed in me. Somehow I let her down because I'm failing to be that person she showed me I am capable of being."

To calm her down, I gently reminded her about the tale of The Emperor's New Clothes. "It relates to the feelings you have about meeting Karen. Could it be that you think that if she saw how you've been acting, she might say you are undressed in a figurative sense?"

"Maybe."

"Could it be you feel like Gomer did the moment he finally realized that he had the tools to get the job done with less effort but was failing to use them?"

"Hmm."

"Tell me what you think about those feelings."

She sighed deeply and paced again. "Those might describe how I felt. I just think that I let her down in some way." She paused in thought. "I think there is something else…"

I let her dig deep for what she was looking for.

After a minute or two she said, "Karen told me a story that affected me at the time but I'd forgotten it. Seeing her again brought it all rushing back."

"Can you tell me about it?" I inquired.

The Integrity Rock

On a visit to Karen's office many years ago, I noticed a fist-sized smoky gray river rock resting on the top of her otherwise professional and messy desktop. 'Is it a paperweight?' I inquired as I picked it up to revel in its smooth texture.

'No. This is my Integrity Rock!'

'Huh?' That statement certainly got my attention. She laughed as I looked confused sitting in her guest chair.

'I keep it there in plain sight to remind me what to do whenever I get tested. Every so often, an executive, a manager, or even an employee will ask me to do something that goes against the grain. Since I enjoy

helping people and believe treating people with respect is of utmost importance, my first inclination is to naturally say "Yes", I can do that. As soon as I think about their request, at times something deep inside tells me that what he or she has asked me to do goes against my personal code regarding what's appropriate.

'I tell the person, "I need some time to think about your suggestion." I pause for a few minutes and pick up this rock as I ponder my feelings about what I've been asked to do.

'Just holding onto this rock and rubbing it reminds me that I need to be rock solid when it comes to doing things that are both ethical and appropriate. With the weight of this rock in my hand, I remind myself, "Karen, your personal integrity is not up for sale." Soon, I get very clear on at least three things: 1) the aspect of their request that bothers me, 2) the reason why I should not do what's asked of me, and 3) some alternative way to accomplish what they are asking for.'

As she paused, I asked, 'When you get these requests…when you need to rely on your Integrity Rock, are they asking you to do something illegal?'

'No. The request is usually to bend a rule, overlook something, put profit ahead of people, fudge a sales number, or make an exception to a company policy. If their request were clearly illegal, I would say "No" immediately! Those times when I need to rely on my Integrity Rock usually involve a gray area or an action that will give one person or one group an advantage or a free pass. More often, it is a decision or act that will pay off for the company immediately, but could bite us in the butt later, or put customers or employees at a disadvantage.'

'How long have you used this Integrity Rock as your reminder to do what's appropriate?'

'I don't recall when I started using it, but I've used this as long as I have been in a position of leadership.'

Handing it back to her with reverence, I told Karen, 'What a wonderful tool this is, and thanks so much for explaining it for me.'

After listening and taking in her warmhearted tale, I said, "Wow, what a great story. In fact, it will serve as a metaphor for what we need to cover next on your journey toward becoming an inspirational leader."

"Karen was...is inspirational to me."

Leadership Outcome – Serenity

She anticipated what I was up to because she had her hand out as I reached into my briefcase, and she smirked as I handed over another silver pinball.

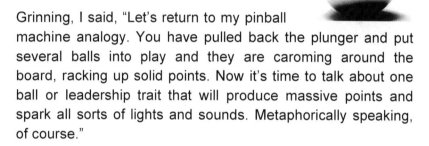

Grinning, I said, "Let's return to my pinball machine analogy. You have pulled back the plunger and put several balls into play and they are caroming around the board, racking up solid points. Now it's time to talk about one ball or leadership trait that will produce massive points and spark all sorts of lights and sounds. Metaphorically speaking, of course."

Each time I mentioned pinball, Joslyn's eyes lit up, and they did again today. She studied the word *Serenity* written on the ball's cool surface.

I asked, "How do you feel now about comparing yourself to Karen?"

"I guess I really didn't need to. Maybe I was feeling sorry for myself and did not want Karen to pity me."

"That is an excellent insight."

"One thing I really admire about Karen is her ability to remain calm even as chaos rains down."

"That is what I call leader serenity."

"Tell me more." She took more sips of lemonade.

I continued, "The ultimate goal of each human is to find serenity by creating the environment that calms us so we can be the best person we can be. As of this moment you do not feel serene at all."

I asked, "How are you feeling? Can you describe it?"

"The best word to describe how I'm feeling is…is agitated."

"How much?"

"Very much so."

Giving her a nod I said, "Agitation comes from many sources, and the major contributor is when you are feeling uncomfortable in your own skin. The inspirational leader generally feels comfortable with herself because not only is she congruent, she understands who she is and why."

Unknowingly she bit her lip as a puzzled look filled her face.

"I know that sounds vague now but in a short time what I'm saying will make sense."

Not knowing what to say, she just nodded.

Leader's Serenity

I went into full teaching mode. "This touchstone leadership trait goes hand-in-hand with courage, forming a powerful bond. The role of a leader is stressful, for reasons both obvious and not. Living up to enormous expectations, constantly holding ourselves to a higher standard, remaining accountable, and being the subject of sniping and often unfair criticism are some of the more visible sources of stress on you. The less visible sources of leader stress include the number of decisions that you must make, as well as the nebulousness of those decisions and their long- and short-term impacts. Another source of stress is the amount of gray area that you must face. Dealing with contradictions and no-win situations can be stressful. Stress also comes from the speed with which things happen. The stress factor that impacts the reluctant leader the most is that nasty six-letter word *change*. Good leaders learn to remain calm and not let their stress get the best of them. Your serenity rubs off on others, even when all hell is breaking loose. Serenity helps you determine the correct path to follow."

She asked, "How does one become serene? Meditation? Yoga? Some other way?"

"Meditation is the most common way to place yourself in a peaceful state, but most people are either too busy to meditate or think it's too New Age. Inspirational leaders who have this sense of serenity about them have found the secret to remaining calm even in the eye of the proverbial hurricane. Your serenity comes from five sources: inner confidence; a positive, uplifting purpose; seeking answers from within; inner peace, and self-definition."

She hastily jotted this down in her lavender notepad.

"We already covered a positive purpose and how it produces your leader energy. Inner peace comes once you let the world and its unpredictable ways unfold, and you cease trying to make the world bend to your will. This is where meditation helps. Through your purpose and by letting go, you get to know the real you. When in this calm state, the answers to all your questions begin to flow from within."

After I paused, I asked, "Have you discovered wisdom and answers when writing in your leadership journal?"

"I believe so, though I'm not always sure."

"It is in there. Are you understanding this?"

She nodded in the affirmative while writing, but I could sense that this information was a bit advanced for her current state of mind (as it is for many emerging and inexperienced leaders).

I went on. "There is one state of mind that contributes to a leader's serenity, and it's the fifth source, namely your self-definition."

"What does that mean?" she stopped taking notes and looked at me with a curious stare.

The I AM Principle

I inquired, "Have you ever heard of the I AM Principle?"

"I am assuming you are not talking about a brand of dog food, right?" She laughed a little, giving me a sign that my information had somewhat eased her tension.

"Why would I be talking about dog food?!" I laughed wholeheartedly to encourage her to relax more. "The I AM Principle is an important key to understanding one's self-definition. I AM is also an equation that looks like this."

I walked over to the whiteboard adorning one of my office walls and wrote:

$$I + A = M$$

She wrote this down in her notes.

"The I stands for Intention, which we talked about several months ago. The A stands for Attention. The M stands for Manifestation, or another way of saying the results that you obtain and produce. Today we will cover the A and M of this important leadership principle.

"This formula is very ancient and sage advice. Every human can get better results by clearly defining their intention and noticing where they place their attention. I know that's a little deep but in a few minutes it will be very clear."

She nodded and kept listening while taking notes.

Our Inner Voice

I said, "Each of us has a soundtrack or an inner voice that describes who we are to ourselves. Each minute of each day you, I, and every other human being define who we are through these two simple words 'I AM.' When you were meeting with Karen, your brain was telling you 'I AM not as good as Karen,' or 'I AM incompetent,' or 'I AM not worthy.' You are not consciously aware that you are doing this. Maybe this is why you feel like you do now, because of what your inner voice tells you."

"This is intriguing," she said. "Tell me more."

"The most powerful tool we all have access to as we strive to change for the better is the phrase 'I am...' The principle of I AM is based upon this timeless truism: *Whatever I think I am, I am.* The power in this tool derives from the combination of your self-talk, your self-image, and a self-fulfilling prophecy."

I had to slow myself down because when I talk about this I get extremely excited and talk rapidly.

After three deep breaths I said slowly, "Whenever any one of us chooses or decides to become something or define ourselves a certain way, we always employ this *'I am...'* statement. *I am a man. I am a woman, I am a wife. I am a husband. I am an uncle. I am a sales manager.* However, we don't say it out loud to the world; rather, we think it repeatedly, like a constantly repeating sound clip or ring tone."

To keep her attention, I used an analogy.

Looking into her eyes I said, "Imagine that you are trying to convince yourself that you look good in a leather jacket and you try it on several times before you decide that it suits you. We try on new labels and through the repetition of our internal self-talk we soon convince ourselves that we are what we label ourselves."

I believed she understood since she was nodding in agreement.

I continued. "Think back to when you first started selling clothing as a teen. You didn't have a concept for that role, but soon someone labeled you a 'salesperson' and you repeated that phrase in your head over and over, and voilà, you become a salesperson and began to think and act like one. The change happened over time, but it started with an I AM declaration."

I paused to drink my iced tea and determine if she was still with me.

Joslyn had an excited look on her face. Almost breathlessly she said, "When I became pregnant with my daughter, Jayna, I couldn't imagine myself as a mom, and I was fearful about how it would affect my career since I was so focused on it. By the time she was born, I had made up my mind that I could be a good mom and still have my career. Is that how this principle works?"

I grinned. "Yes. From the moment you received news of your pregnancy, you thought about and imagined being a mother and the *I AM a mother* self-definition took root, so by the time Jayna was born you defined yourself that way. You changed from *I AM not a mom* to *I AM a mom* through repetitious self-talk."

"And dealing with dirty diapers, and midnight feedings..."

Laughing aloud I added, "Nights without sleep, needless worrying. The practice of being a mom reinforced the thought, just like making sales confirmed your new label *I AM a salesperson*."

"I get it. I suppose you're going to tell me that I failed to use this principle in my role as CEO."

"I could, but for you the I AM Principle applies specifically to not defining yourself as a leader. I sense that back when you were first promoted to a sales manager position is when this new labeling of yourself needed to be applied. Most likely you didn't because the label of *I AM a salesperson* was most comfortable. Wearing and retaining the *I AM in sales* self-definition did not allow the *I AM a leader* label to take root. With each subsequent promotion, you retained *I AM in sales*, and now that label is holding you back while hurting your effectiveness as CEO. You still behave like you are in sales and not in leadership of a whole company."

"That strikes me as so true! Give me a second to let it sink in."

I stepped out of the room to refresh our beverages as she sagged into the chair, deep in thought. When I returned I could sense a tremendous charge of energy in her body. Her eyes were moving back and forth as she looked down.

Is it the breakthrough I've been waiting for? I gave her all the time she needed.

Speaking very rapidly she said, "I see things so clearly now, Ron! Remember that list of things the board said they wanted me to do and be like. I was very angry that they wanted me to be this way and that, but now I realize that I have never taken the time to say *I AM a good communicator* or *I AM in service to the board*. To be honest, all I've been is very self-centered."

Breakthrough, I thought. She lowered her head and rubbed her eyes. From the way she sat and the tone of her voice I could tell that a huge emotional weight had just been released. However, the task of carrying that burden for so long had clearly taken its toll on her body and spirit.

I let her be in that state a little longer. Then I said, "There are two more parts of the I AM Principle you need to understand. The first is the self-fulfilling prophesy nature of I AM, and the second is how to use it to improve, to change for the better."

"Okay. I am ready." Truly, she was eager.

Self-prophesy

I slipped into my teaching mode again. "Almost all our less desirable traits come about because of I AM. After a person puts a label on him or herself, when an opportunity comes along to change that label, we humans very often resist the change by the nature of self-talk using I AM. Let's say a young student is in the first grade and her first exposure to a new topic such as math befuddles her. All it takes is for a teacher to imply or outright say *You just don't have a head for math.* The child internalizes this message and adopts it for herself and keeps repeating over and over: *I'm terrible at math.* Because of the I AM Principle, her incompetence grows but NOT because she can't do math, rather because she BELIEVES she cannot. Even when she surprises herself by understanding a math problem, the repeating sound clip of *I AM terrible at math* reasserts itself, providing false 'proof' to her that she is unable. Without external assistance she will not realize that she truly does understand math, thus missing or ignoring the proof."

I had to check. "Does this make sense, Joslyn?"

"Right. Right."

"In your case, Joslyn, the behaviors that the board and your team want you to engage in are running up against the rock wall of your existing self-labels of I AM, and they—the new behaviors—cannot take root. That is why it's been hard for you to let go of your reluctance to be a true leader."

She nodded that she understood. "You said this principle can be used to change, so tell me how."

She's gobbling this up like a child with ice cream. "I am glad you are ready, because that is where we are going next. I believe we have come to a point in your growth where you need to understand some of these ways you currently define yourself as a person and a leader. I can tell that several limiting labels are interfering with your ability to truly see yourself as the capable leader I know you can be."

"Are you ready to do some more self-exploration?"

"I used to dread this, but now I look forward to it, so hit me."

Discovering Your I AM Statements

"Okay. Let's do an exercise where I ask you to state whatever comes to mind. As before, with these brainstorming techniques we have used in the past, do not edit yourself. Just say whatever comes into your thoughts. I will record them and at the end we will go through them." I grabbed my iPad from my desk and got ready. These are her responses.

(Complete the sentence)

Statement 1: As a leader I AM...

Incapable
Incompetent
Not very well liked
Not very good at it

Statement 2: As a person I AM...

Mean
Hard-nosed
Unforgiving
Not very nice

Statement 3: As a salesperson I AM...

Capable
Competent
Very good at it
A wheeler-dealer
A closer

I said, "Now, we will switch gears. Please complete these sentences."

Statement 4: As a parent I AM...

Confused
Bewildered
Unable to deal with my daughter's problems
Not very sympathetic
Out of touch with what my daughter is doing

I then said, "Let's do it again. Complete this sentence."

Statement 5: As a spouse I AM...

Somewhat neglecting
Sometimes insensitive
Putting my agenda ahead my husband's

I said, "You are doing great! One final time, complete this sentence."

Statement 6: As a CEO I AM...

Confused
Not very good at it
Needing to learn more

I recorded her thoughts as she spoke them.

When we had completed this exercise, we took a short break to return calls or respond to emails, but mostly because I needed Joslyn to be present in her body while reviewing her responses and the meaning of them.

When we regrouped at my work table, I read the responses to her and at the end asked, "What do you notice?"

Her hands fluttered unnoticed as she said, "The first thing that comes to mind is that I am extremely negative toward my abilities. I seem to crucify myself in everything except being in sales. In that role I seem to be in my element and very competent."

"This makes sense because acquiring clients, selling, and negotiating have been your strong suits and where you started from. You are unconsciously competent in this area yet it's in other areas that you are struggling, where you feel consciously incompetent."

She nodded as she sipped more lemonade then asked, "What did you notice?"

She is eager to know. I said, "In your overall responses I notice that you were unaware of this self-talk going on in your head. Parts of it surfaced when you met with Karen. This is a good thing." I said that because she looked sad when I mentioned Karen.

I added, "A part of you currently thinks you do not measure up as a CEO, as a leader, as a parent, and as a spouse. Does this make sense?"

"Yes."

"There is more. What's amazing to me is that most of the areas in my exercise examine where you ARE COMPETENT. Maybe not to the degree that you wish you were and others wish you were, but still you are competent! Therefore, what undermines this competence are the mental sound tracks repeating themselves in your head. Each time you employ the I AM Principle to reinforce what you can't do, you allow yourself to discount your talents and abilities. This is a very common syndrome in high-performing people. Even the most talented and capable CEOs worry that they are inadequate and that someone will find out and expose them. That is why I reminded you of The Emperor's New Clothes. Every leader carries this fear in their head—someone will be the child announcing they are without clothes."

She kept nodding in agreement, then asked, "So how do we, I mean I, become more capable and confident? Why is this coming up now?"

"It is coming to your consciousness at this time because you have grown in self-awareness."

"That was trait number 4, right?"

I responded, "That is correct. You have always had these sound clips repeating in your head. Some were self-created and others were inadvertently placed there. Think about the things your Uncle Todd and father said about business. People who influenced you early in life actually contributed to these sound clips, and very often so did life events."

I paused for a drink and to let her think before continuing the lesson.

"In your case the repeating self-talk like 'As a CEO *I AM confused*' and 'As a CEO *I AM not very good at it*' show up in your everyday actions, thus proving that you are not. This is insidious, and yet this happens to every human being in all eight facets of their life. In your case, the sound clips regarding your ability to sell and deal with clients are very positive. I believe Karen had something to do with your internal message that led to successes in selling. However, in your awkward relationships with Jayna and with most employees, negative messages in your self-talk are more powerful than any efforts to improve those relationships."

"Right. Right. I am sensing that you have been using this concept on me from the beginning."

I grinned. "Yes, I have. The I AM Principle is the heart of the coaching process and is used to understand how you, my client, define yourself. Once I know those labels, I employ techniques to help you let go of those negative self-messages and adopt better ones."

She responded as I'd hoped. "Wow! I never realized the tremendous impact of the self-voice I listen to. So what can I do to get rid of those negative messages?"

Process to Create Better Manifestations

My answer was, "Your goal is not to get rid of them but to replace them with positive ones. Because they are deep in your psyche, they will always be there. However, new positive-oriented ones drown out the old self-limiting ones. Part of your assignment this week will be to create new ones and begin to internalize them. What do you feel about crafting a whole new set of positive and uplifting I AM statements?"

She hesitated. "It feels like it might be uncomfortable, at least at first."

I responded, "Consider this. Your existing self-talk is really made up of adopted I AM affirmations about who you are. They produced labels you used for years, and this is done at a nearly unconscious level. Adopting a new label requires you to make the I AM and affirmation processes conscious in order to replace the harmful ones with positive ones."

"I see." She kept taking notes.

"Are you ready to learn how to create new labels so that you can alter your self-identity?"

"I am eager to learn."

I explained, "As for how to do this, there are three connected solutions to the process."

1. Use Daily Affirmations on Your Intentions

"You start by highlighting your intentions. Do you recall the leadership intention that I asked you to write months ago? That is the starting point; turn it into an affirming self-label."

She opened her notebook to that page and read it aloud.

I am the CEO of a great company. As the primary influence and instigator for change and forward momentum, my intention is to develop a powerful team that creates an even better organization. As a company, we grow in strength by being profitable, capturing growth opportunities, engaging and retaining good employees, and working united under a common long-term vision.

"I see that you have improved it since you shared it with me last time. I like it."

"Thank you."

"Your first step in this process is to develop daily affirmations based on that intention. Start with '*I AM the CEO of a great company.*' Next is '*I AM developing a powerful team.*' You will recite them repeatedly to yourself, which will turn old mistaken beliefs into positive truisms about yourself. For example, instead of hearing your old self-talk say, '*I AM an incompetent leader,*' you will instead repeat at least 40 times a day, '*I AM a competent and capable leader.*'"

"Is that all?" She asked in a way that told me she was somewhat skeptical.

"There are more steps and they won't always be easy because you must FULLY BELIEVE each of these statements and instill in your mind the self-belief that you are both capable and competent in all facets of your life. In order to do this well, you must notice when you are thinking you are incapable and/or incompetent. It is at that moment when these affirmations become vital. There's a saying that you have probably heard: *Fake it until you make it.* That advice is misunderstood because the emphasis tends to be on faking it. In the I AM Principle, faking it really is convincing yourself internally first that you can do it. Believing that turns into actions that prove you are capable of doing it."

2. Place Your Attention on Being Competent

"The second step in the process is to catch yourself doing things right or competently, which is hard at first. Where you put your attention determines what you define as important. The person who feels incompetent will ignore their moments of brilliance and focus entirely on the moments of incompetency. Recall my analogy of the girl in first-grade math. To go from incompetence to competence, you must pay attention to those times when you speak nicely to an employee, when you listen carefully, when you respond to an emotionally charged situation, and when you face a difficult situation compassionately. The more times you catch yourself doing things right, the more your confidence grows along with the belief that *I AM able to do it*."

"I understand. You mentioned there was a third step I could take."

I purposely paused so that she could stay enthused and realize the gravity of what I was asking her to do. Drinking my iced tea allowed me to do this.

I continued. "I did, and that is to handle yourself differently." I stood up and walked over to my computer to print a document. Once it came out, I returned to the table.

3. Think Like a Great Leader
"The third step in the process is to adopt the Attitude of a High-Performance Person. The high-performance individual who believes that he or she will make a positive difference has a unique mindset that others lack. This is especially important to a leader because it directly reflects how he or she uses the I AM Principle."

I then handed her the sheet titled *The Thoughts of a High-Performance Person*, which can be used to develop affirmations. This tool describes the traits of a High Road professional.

I said, "It is imperative that you incorporate these into your daily affirmations and actions, and then practice using them in everything you do."

I gave her time to read it.

THOUGHTS OF A HIGH-PERFORMANCE PERSON

The confident capable person...

Considers themself as a valuable and important person and expects people to like them.

Expects to do worthwhile work and achieve great accomplishments now and in the future.

Controls their reactions toward the world outside of themself and uses the appropriate behaviors to obtain what they want.

Has a fairly good understanding of the kind of person they are.

Has a definite idea of the appropriate course of action.

Is able to exert an influence upon people and events because of their ability and willingness to present and defend these views.

Is regarded as someone worthy of respect and consideration by people who are important to them.

Is able to exert an influence upon people and events because they listen carefully to others' ideas to understand their value.

Is able to exert an influence upon people and events because they expect people to listen to them due to the value of their ideas.

Is able to exert influence upon people and events because they use inclusive language.

Knows that a supported decision made by a committed group is more valuable than one made by an individual.

Enjoys new and challenging tasks and takes all setbacks as feedback on where to improve their efforts.

She let me know that she was ready to continue.

Using the I AM Principle for Congruity

I continued the lesson. "In the self-fulfilling nature of the I AM Principle, your beliefs determine your thoughts, which determine your feelings, which create your actions. It is your actions and behaviors that ultimately determine your results. Therefore, to clearly understand your ineffectiveness as a leader, working backwards, start with what you think about yourself. Currently, your thought of 'I AM incompetent with people' creates a nervous reaction within your body. Therefore, each time you face an employee situation that requires compassion, your nervousness is quite evident. When the employee senses your discomfort they most likely think *she doesn't care about me* or *she hates me*.

"What I am saying is that your undetected thoughts create a lack of confidence that gets communicated outward." I paused to verify that Joslyn understood this complexity. She nodded, so I continued.

"Confidence begets serenity, and serenity leads to your knowing what to do. It is through the way you define yourself that serenity begins to encompass you."

"What do you mean?" Joslyn paused in her note taking.

"Allow me to show it to you visually."

MANIFESTATION OF RESULTS

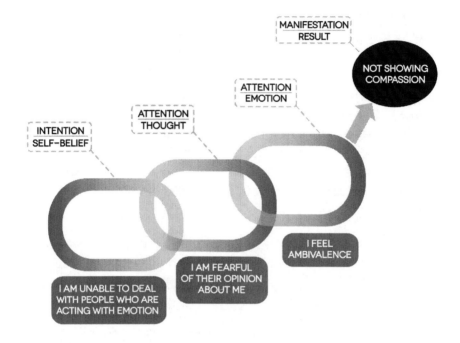

I returned to the whiteboard to sketch a chain with three links. Next, I drew a circle with an arrow running from the third link in the chain and labeled it 'Not showing compassion.' To the side of this circle, I wrote 'Manifestation/Result.'

Next, I added a box above the third chain link. In it I wrote 'Attention /Emotion.'

I asked her, "What are your general feelings about your employees?"

She said somewhat hesitantly, "I feel ambivalence."

I wrote that in a box below the third link.

Pointing to next link to the left, I drew a box under it and asked her, "What do you think about your employees?"

"I am fearful of their opinion about me."

I wrote that under the second chain link, and above the link I wrote 'Attention/Thought.'

Drawing a box under the first link in the chain, I pointed to it as I inquired, "What is your self-belief or inner voice saying about people?"

She was puzzled by this question. I walked toward her notepad and pointed to one of the statements she made about herself earlier. I asked her to read it.

"I AM…unable to deal with people who are acting with emotion."

I wrote that in the box under the first chain link, and above the link I wrote 'Intention/Self-Belief.'

Then I let her study the drawing before walking her through the I AM sequence from the beginning to the end—from link number one to the circle at the end point.

I said, "In your I AM chain, your sound clip or self-belief repeatedly reminds you that you are unable to deal with people who are acting with emotion. It does not matter whether the belief is true or false. The repetition makes it believable to your unconscious mind. This self-belief—the I of the I AM formula—turns into a thought that you do not know how to handle situations like those recent ones involving, say, Angela. With those thoughts, you then self-create feelings of discomfort and fear. Those two emotional states then turn into behaviors in which you communicate to others that you are both ambivalent about them and do not care about their feelings or problems."

I pointed to the word *Attention* above links two and three. "This is the A in the I AM formula. Since your attention is on your fears, all you see are your failures."

I paused, "Does that make sense?"

"It's like the student who focuses entirely on the math problems she can't solve and ignores the ones she understands."

"Right on the mark. Now we come to the M in the I AM formula. The behaviors that your feelings and self-beliefs generate are an apparent lack of compassion. You do and say things that sound to others like you DO NOT CARE, even when you do. You manifest or produce results that are perceived as your proof that you lack compassion."

She studied the diagram for a while, and eventually I could see that it was like a tired bird coming to roost. She understood it. Her body sagged under the weight of this discovery.

I thought we needed to pause to replenish her energy. The rain had stopped, so we took a short walk around the block. Soon we were back at it.

The color has returned to her cheeks and her body is erect. Aloud I said, "Okay, it's truth-or-dare time for you, Joslyn. Are you ready for more personal disclosures?" I said this to produce a laugh and it worked.

I said, "I am going to ask you a very important question, so think carefully before you answer."

I silently counted to 10 before asking, "Do you truly care about the people who work for you?"

I could tell from her reaction that my question was not what she was expecting. I was overly dramatic on purpose.

She sat back in the chair and took a drink of lemonade.

After two calming breaths she said with heat in her voice, "I really do! I care about the people who work for me!"

"Look at this chart." I pcinted to the whiteboard. "Can you understand how this self-belief that you are not a competent leader interferes with your expressing that you care about the people who work for you?"

She did because I could see lightness come into her eyes and her shoulders relax. *Here comes another shift!*

Immediately jumping out of her chair she said rapidly, "Yes, I do see that. I see how by not paying attention to what I am thinking, staying on autopilot has me acting as if I were Daddy or Uncle Todd. Based on some of the things I have been thinking about and recollections that I've recently had about them, I think they both disliked dealing with people, and I adopted this attitude once I became a supervisor, and it continued as manager, and then as CEO. Yet...I somehow never let those beliefs affect my ability to sell!" She stopped abruptly.

I held my breath. *I know she's having another insight that is going to impact her deeply.*

She sat back down and placed her face gently into her hands and in a very quiet voice said, "I now see why my daughter and I have so many arguments."

She grabbed my iPad and found the list of self-beliefs and focused in on things she said about being a parent. "Holy sh--!" she shouted. "I see here that I believe *I AM a bad parent*, and it manifests with not being sympathetic and being unable to deal with her problems and being out of touch with her needs and concerns."

Joslyn took deep gulps of air as if drowning. This turned into a sigh and then she sobbed out, "I do care! It's just that I allow my self-belief that I am...I am an inadequate parent to interfere with seeing Jayna as she really is...connecting with her."

Despite her tremendous self-control, the tears fell. I silently placed a box of tissues near her. *She's finally tapped into some below-the-surface feelings of her current I AMs.*

I let her be in that state for as long as she needed to recover composure.

It was nearly time to end the session, and I could tell that I had taken her as deep as she was comfortable with.

Unexpectedly, she jumped out of her chair as if she had put her finger into an electric socket. She grabbed the cell phone from her pants pocket and looked at it. *What's going on?*

I realized her phone was on silent and she had felt its vibration, which made her jump. I didn't interrupt her since she thought that the message was important. I was concerned.

I relaxed after noticing a huge smile take over her face. Finishing reading whatever was on the screen, she walked over to me and put the phone in front of my face. She was so excited she didn't realize that it was too close for me to read.

She said excitedly, "This text is from Karen." She backed up and read, "I am so proud of you, Joslyn. I knew you were CEO material long before you realized it. I am glad that you have found a good place to challenge your tremendous skills, and I wish you continued success. Your friend and former mentor, Karen. PS: Are you keeping your Integrity Rock handy?"

Joslyn closed her eyes and breathed deeply, holding onto her smile.

I knew that anything I could say would be superfluous, yet I wanted to turn this major victory into a coaching lesson.

I asked as gently as I could, "What are you getting from the message Karen just sent to you, as it relates to the work we did today?"

"I guess..."

I immediately stopped her from saying anything further. "May I suggest that you not guess? Tell me what you are sure of."

She said, "What I am sure of is that there seems to be a gap between how I feel about my skills as a leader and what someone like Karen sees in me."

"Does that apply to Stephen as well?"

After a pause she said, "It must, because he wants me to succeed."

Aha! Inside I was doing a happy dance.

Joslyn's Assignment

"What work do you need to now do, based on what we covered today?"

"First, I need to form new affirmations to replace incorrect self-beliefs.

"Second, I need...I want to start believing that I do care so that I produce new results, more in line with my leadership intention."

"May I offer two suggestions that will help you get a jump-start on these two goals?"

"Sure."

I handed Joslyn a document titled "The Leader's Impact on the Followers," one of our High Road Leadership Tools.

LEADER'S IMPACT ON FOLLOWERS

When it comes to good and effective leadership, you do not need sophisticated, complicated, self-diagnostic tools. You will know your leadership effectiveness by examining this chart.

This comparison chart is prepared from an employee's point of view.

What employees say about the Good Leader:

I am inspired.

I want to join you.

You clarify what is expected of me.

You hold me accountable.

You give me an example to follow.

You allow me to do it my way.

I can translate your ideas into actions and goals.

You specify what my (our) priorities are.

I really like working for you.

What employees say about the Poor Leader:

You lie to me.

You do not back me up.

You do not walk your talk.

You have two standards; one for me and another for you.

You failed me.

You micromanage me.

You never complete what you start.

I never know what our priorities are.

You are a joke.

"It's a two-part tool. Complete the first part where you write about what sort of impact you want to have on people going forward. When it's completed, you will have ideas on how to complete the second part."

"For your second action step—developing new affirmations—I present you with a book I wrote on the subject of capturing possibilities and turning them into reality using the I AM Principle. I suggest you read it to help with your affirmation writing.

"Here is the short version of the technique of developing new affirmations. Develop a list in your journal of between 20 and 40 affirmations that will replace the outdated self-talk. At next week's session we will go through them and narrow the list down to about 10. Meanwhile, until our next session, I ask you to repeat all of them silently to yourself 40 times a day. It won't take you as long as it may seem. Simply use your commute time or your coffee breaks or even the few minutes before shutting out the light at night. Find those opportunities to memorize the replacement I AM statements."

I have to test her resolve. I asked Joslyn, "On a scale of 1 to 10, with 10 meaning *I am ready to do cartwheels*, how excited are you about practicing and adopting new affirmations?"

She bit her lip again as she thought. "I will say I'm at an 8."

"That's a good place to start. The first time a coach suggested I do that, I was at 3." I laughed at myself.

As I accompanied her to the front door, I said, "Remember I once told you that one day you would feel extremely vulnerable and euphoric at the same time? I said it would be at the point where you had a major breakthrough?"

"Yes, I do."

"Tell me how you felt over the last 20 minutes?"

"The same feelings I experienced the first time bungee jumping but more intense. My heart's been beating 1,000 times a minute."

I patted her gently on the shoulder. "Congratulations! Today was the moment you have been impatient for. It will continue to overwhelm you, so I suggest that tonight, if you can, sit by yourself and just let what you experienced today wash over you. The insights you uncorked today will continue for a long time. You need to just be with them. Let a sense of serenity or calmness wash over you. The sort of transformation you are going through is a process and needs time to work its 'magic.' Writing in your leadership journal will help you."

She nodded, uttered a soft "Thank you," and despite the pouring rain walked slowly to her car. I imagined a smile on her face.

*****

Joslyn's Assessment of Her Progress

All the way home I talked loudly to myself. I couldn't keep it in and who cares; my windows are shut.

Today was wonderful! For the first time I see sun shining and the clouds lifting. Ron showed me that I am NOT flawed but that my thinking is. Or should I say my sound clips are flawed. That's funny. The sound track of my life is all wrong! Ha!

I can't wait to get home and do something…anything…to reach out to Jayna and connect with her. Where do I start?

What affirmation can I adopt?

All the way home I sound-tested different affirmations, and I was home before I realized it. By then I had the right one and repeated for the rest of that day and it was on my lips as I fell asleep.

*****

The Bottom Line of Leadership

We hear daily advice from medical experts about the importance of managing life's stresses. If you don't, your health will eventually suffer. In addition, with the ever-rising cost of being healthy, it is better to be proactive in maintaining your good health than treating the effects of unmanaged stress.

Leaders have a tremendous impact on the health and well-being of their employees. Not only does their health, fitness, and wellness affect the company's medical benefits cost, it also impacts employees' attitudes. According to psychologist and leadership consultant Robert Hogan, bad leaders are the cause for enormous health costs and can be a "major source of misery" for many employees. "75 percent of working adults say the worst aspect of their job—the most stressful aspect of their job—is their immediate boss," reports Hogan [24]

The real impact that poor leaders have on their subordinates is huge. Many recent research studies show that bad bosses actually evoke employee suicide, behavioral problems, violence, depression, and post-traumatic stress disorders. A bad boss negatively impacts employees, and those reactive behaviors spill over and affect other employees, thus harming the company's culture.

If you want to be more profitable, turn every manager and supervisor into a good leader, because the specific costs incurred when employees have close daily contact with a poor leader are more sick days, low performance, high turnover, increased incidents of workplace deviance, acts of revenge-seeking, hostility, lack of engagement, and the withholding of creative or innovative impulses and ideas.

Employees tend not to respond to bad bosses with their best self, so the entire organization suffers. Poor management and

---

[24] *The High Cost of the Bad Boss*, The American Management Association
http://www.amanet.org/training/articles/The-High-Cost-of-the-Bad-Boss.aspx

poor leadership lead to a poor organizational culture and disempowered employees, all of which open the door to the forces of entropy. To be successful, you need employees who love coming to work and giving you their best.

Chapter 9
Conviction

"Is it possible that I lack charisma?"

Time Remaining: 3 Weeks

Joslyn's Report

Today I feel great. During my morning run I thought about the changes that have taken place over the last few weeks. First, I now have time in my schedule for activities like running because I spend less time fighting fires. Second, communications among my team have vastly improved, both in the day-to-day activities and in our staff meetings. The company experienced its best month ever in production and sales. Most important of all, I rarely feel like an outsider when meeting with employees.

I did, however, have several nagging concerns that I would need to discuss with my coach today; the most critical one was how to know if the improvements I see are a direct result of me shifting or in spite of me. *I need to know!*

The Joslyn Situation (Code for My Troubles)

I didn't find out until later that at the very hour I was deep into my workout this morning, Mr. Rael was being my guardian angel, meeting with Reese M., who is a much-admired mover and shaker in Seattle's business community.

Reese currently serves as the Chairman of a very large and visible international company and was recently asked to join Neoteric's board, an invitation that he accepted.

Ron explained to me at lunch, "I've known Reese for many years; our paths cross regularly. He devotes many hours mentoring up-and-coming CEOs and senior leaders who seem to gravitate to his natural charisma and confidence."

Stephen had suggested that Ron meet Reese to apprise him of 'The Joslyn Situation.' I think maybe Stephen wanted Reese to get a little more involved in determining alternative strategies if I didn't win the board's vote of confidence.

I felt some despair that I might be unemployed soon, yet I also felt a growing confidence. *What is that all about?*

Ron scheduled his meeting with Reese on the same day as our coaching session because, as Ron informed me later, "I had an idea that I wanted to run by Reese. We spent an hour together discussing Neoteric and your progress. I knew I could be candid with him, despite his recent election to your board, because of our previous encounters and his ongoing work in developing leaders. Of course, I kept certain things confidential. Near the end of this meeting I asked Reese if he would consider mentoring you should Stephen opt to retain you as CEO. He promised me that he would think about it and get back to me. I couldn't tell if he was interested or not, but at least I had planted the seed."

I didn't know all this until later that fateful day.

Meeting at 'The Needle'

When Ron announced the location of our next session, I got excited. We would meet at one of Seattle's crowning jewels—the Space Needle.

Since becoming CEO, I rarely have the time to visit here. Today's azure sky had no clouds, so a 360-degree view displaying the beauty of Puget Sound should be excellent.

I saw this amazing structure through my windshield and thought about the long-term commitments made by visionary civic and business leaders who took a bold risk deciding to develop this untested modern marvel. Opening in 1962, it was built in less than 400 days!

As I rode in the stomach-churning 'rocket ride' elevator that in just 41 seconds shot up 520 feet at 10 miles per hour, I calmed my anxiety by recalling many wonderful business sales meetings I'd attended and hosted here.

Ron was waiting for me on the observation deck.

Today, I wore a green ensemble to show off a little bit. I hoped to walk around the deck either before or after our session so my hair was pinned back to protect it from the breeze. *I actually don't have to rush back to the office to deal with a crisis. Yay!*

Ron greeted me warmly, and then we took the short flight of stairs into the SkyCity restaurant and were immediately ushered to a table. No matter how many times I go up there, I marvel at the awesome view of the city.

After we made small talk, Ron told me, "I can tell that you have a certain aura of confidence and appear to be moving ahead with your CEO plans, no matter what Stephen decides."

"This morning I noticed that feeling of confidence, but I'm not sure why it's there."

"Would you be interested in my take on this?"

"Of course," I said, "because you are usually 98 percent accurate."

"I have to work harder, I guess." He laughed at my jest.

Getting serious, he said, "Based upon my experiences, I believe you feel more confident because you are more comfortable in your role. Tell me what you have noticed regarding your work and your team."

I covered the changes I had discerned that morning and added a few more. "Jackson and I are maybe 60 percent back to the relationship we had years ago. Best of all, meetings with members of my team are focused on what is going right rather than what's wrong. I no longer call them war council meetings."

"That is great to hear. I hope you recall that I said it would be like this once you stepped up and stopped being reluctant."

I nodded then added, "But at the time I didn't believe you."

The conversation lagged while our scrumptious lunches were served.

He picked up the thread a few minutes later when he said, "That is normal. Regarding today's session, I must determine if you are still committed to convincing Stephen that you are CEO material or have chosen another path. He and I have a call scheduled for tomorrow afternoon."

A chill went down my spine so I concentrated on lunch. We dug into our meals in silence. I looked out the window and thought, *It's all up to me.*

Ron broke the silence when he asked, "Have you met Reese, the new member of your board?"

Where did that come from? Aloud I replied that I had.

"Tell me what you think about him."

Between bites of my Crab Louie I answered, "I think he is the most charismatic person I have ever met."

He chuckled, "That is what a lot of people say about Reese. What is it about him that you define as being charismatic?"

"I would say that he is likable, friendly, and has a kindly disposition."

"Anything else?"

I looked out toward the scenery of the Cascade Mountains while he enjoyed more of his chicken dish. I then answered, "Reese seems to have a serenity or calmness about him, the leader trait we covered two weeks ago."

"I agree with you that he is very charismatic."

Ron's next question caught me off guard.

"Do you define yourself as charismatic?"

At that very moment my mood went south. "No. I do not believe I am charismatic…and now as we talk about Reese and I think about myself, is it possible that I lack charisma?"

In his warm voice he reassured me. "You are, in fact, charismatic even though yours is different from Reese's. Every person has a specific type of charisma. May I fill you in on some aspects of leader charisma while you finish your clam chowder and salad?"

"Sure."

Leadership Charisma

After a few more bites, Ron began. "Charisma is a very misunderstood quality. We see it in people like Reese and Stephen because of their outgoing and visible personalities; their likeability factor comes across quite easily. With your slightly introverted nature, your charisma is not quite as readily seen until people get to know you. Think about all the deep relationships you have developed and retained with customers. This is proof that you have a type of charisma and likeability."

He continued after a brief interruption by our waiter, who followed the script by asking, "Is everything satisfactory?"

"A leader's charisma comes from four sources: 1) your own personality type, 2) your feelings about yourself, 3) your convictions, and 4) your global view of the world. Each one impacts your leadership effectiveness AND your likeability factor. As an experienced and accomplished marketer, you understand that your personality type is one that helps you remain successful in selling. At a previous session we talked about your feelings about yourself, which I am glad you are working on and will continue to work on. The focus of today's session is on your convictions."

Leadership Outcome – Conviction

Ron handed me another silver ball he'd pulled out of his coat pocket.

I wonder where he gets these.

Its shiny surface contained the word *Conviction.*

With a need to get past my feeling of self-directed disappointment, I said, "Today we are discussing conviction, correct? How does that relate to charisma?"

He answered, "Your question underscores your eagerness to learn. Good."

The restaurant was busy, so he had to speak louder to overcome the background murmur of many conversations.

"Today, we will cover the fourth of the outcome traits, conviction. This particular leadership trait sustains the energy like the bumpers that keep the pinball in motion. It too is a powerful pinball that creates solid wins. Conviction works to keep the four outer leader traits in play in a big way."

"What do you mean?" I asked.

"Let's start with the **14th Natural Law of Leadership**."

> **Above all else, a leader must have conviction.**

"I assume you will explain this."

To pull my chain he grabbed my notebook and wrote 'ASS U ME.' When I saw this, I laughed so hard I believe I scared the man behind me. *Ron really knows what it takes to lift my mood.*

Gibbs's Rules

After finishing off his iced tea, he adopted his patient teaching manner. "One of my favorite TV programs is *NCIS*. The main character of the show is a retired Marine by the name of Leroy Jethro Gibbs. 'Gibbs,' as he likes to be called, is a man of conviction. In this highly rated drama of murder, detection, and high-tech forensics, Special Agent Gibbs leads a team of investigators, and he constantly reminds the team of his 'rules.' These rules are how Gibbs manages his life and team. He says it's 'a code to live by.' This might seem like a running joke to people who do not understand leadership and conviction, but these rules are a way the show's writers communicate the Gibbs character's intense conviction. He believes everyone needs a personal code. I do, too."

"That is Harold's favorite show. I watch it with him occasionally."

He asked, "Who wants to follow an indecisive or wishy-washy leader?"

I almost giggled but held it in and responded, "No one."

"That's very true and that question leads to the **15th Natural Law of Leadership**."

People follow a leader with conviction.

He continued the lesson. "Conviction is based on the word *convinced*. A leader is convinced of certain beliefs or principles or even a specific path to take. It is the state of being convinced. Conviction is a deep urging that something is right and must be done, an unshakable belief or opinion in something that is held firmly without the need for proof or evidence. Its deepness and power come from the acceptance by your mind that something is true or real, often underpinned by an emotional or spiritual sense of certainty."

I looked out the window and then turned back.

"Conviction is a passion for those things you believe in. They represent the principles and guidelines that you use to manage your life. Conviction gives you guidance and serves to define what is good or to identify what is bad. For instance, Gibbs has not had very good dealings with attorneys throughout his professional career, so he has three separate rules about dealing with them. If you are a lawyer, you may not like Gibbs' conviction regarding your profession. However, these rules provide Gibbs' specific guidance about how to deal with the attorneys he has to interact with."

> **Principle**
> A principle is the primary source of something or the basic way in which something works. A principle is an important underlying law or assumption in a person's system of thought. A body of principles is the range or extent of somebody's ability to see something.

I took several sips of my lemonade, finishing it off. *Is theirs the best, or is it just the atmosphere?*

Ron cleared his throat and said, "Conviction can be a double-edged sword, though. Since it is your opinion or judgment on something, the person with conviction can have beliefs that are extreme, hurtful, or destructive. This usually occurs when the person's zeal surpasses their common sense and understanding of right and wrong. Some power-hungry people somehow convince themselves that they are right, so they seek to destroy others in the process of carrying out their ruinous beliefs. Some can even inspire others, through the power of conviction, to take leave of their senses and commit crimes or suicide. Hitler, for example, had the conviction (was convinced) that anyone without Aryan blood was inferior. He later turned that conviction into a self-justification to conquer and pillage and later slaughter millions of people without cause."

I flinched when he mentioned Hitler. I willed myself to listen, recalling what he taught me about compassion. *Make no judgments.*

We paused as a very noisy group walked by, heading for a table. Thankfully, it was quite a ways from our table.

When it was quiet again, Ron continued. "High Road leaders outnumber destructive leaders. How do I know this? Because far more leaders build businesses, create charities, donate organs, mentor young people, and care for the sick because it is right. It is something they must do. An inspirational leader is convinced that an idea or course of action must be pursued. This conviction in a leader drives decision, promotes action, allows for the acceptance of risk, serves to overcome doubt, and draws others into the endeavor. A person with conviction will remove any obstacle in her path. A High Road leader with conviction has the confidence that somebody or something is good or will be effective. This leader uses her conviction often as a standard of morals or ethics in decision-making."

He paused again as the waiter refilled our water glasses and brought another round of cold drinks.

Sources of Conviction

Slipping back into his teaching style, he said, "Your convictions are derived from your values and what you hold as dear. Your convictions come through your experiences and occasionally the lack of them. Conviction can be sparked when you see someone else take a stand, like the sole Chinese student who held his ground against the military's tanks in Tiananmen Square. Your conviction develops over time through seeing the successes and failings of others. Eventually, it seeps into your soul and you become persuaded that 'I must do this' or 'I need to hold my ground on that.'

"Conviction leads you to take a course of action. It feeds into your persistence, which drives you. It may be the path of most resistance and the road less travelled, but you know this (whatever the belief is) is a nonnegotiable position for you. Throughout history, High Road leaders with conviction have been 'driven' to do heroic or courageous things. Rarely was this done for fame or glory or the desire to be seen as a hero. The person did what they felt they had to, based upon a deep conviction and a belief that inspired them to act."

He paused to see if I had a response.

I asked him, "What can happen when a leader does not have strong convictions?"

"I can answer your astute question with the **16th Natural Law of Leadership**."

> **Conviction does not guarantee success.**
> **However, a lack of it almost guarantees failure.**

Ron caught my eyes and asked, "If I asked you to make a list of your convictions or your rules, would you be able to?"

I took several seconds before replying, "I could probably think of a few things."

He nodded then continued, "Unfortunately, most reluctant leaders cannot. Yet the best leaders do have in their minds a set of guiding principles or tenets that they follow, such as: be kind, always do your best, care for the people you lead, and remember the customer in your decisions."

"Really? Do you think Reese has deep convictions?"

"Yes, he does. So does Stephen. In fact, because they share many common ones, that could be the reason Stephen nominated Reese for your board."

I had nothing to add so he continued.

"Believe it or not, you have a set of convictions or guidelines as to how you run your life, both personal and professional. However, you, like most leaders at all levels, have never taken the time to stop and think about what those are."

I said, "I make a bet that you want me to uncover my deep convictions regarding leading the company and managing people."

"Are you willing to do that?" he asked while holding my gaze.

I promised that I would and wanted to do it right then but I knew he had more to teach me.

Leader's Global View

We then shifted gears to what Ron described as the fourth factor of charisma—how I viewed my leadership role in general.

He said, "One important thing a CEO must always do is to seek the bigger picture."

I nodded and kept taking notes.

He reached into his briefcase and took out a colorful box. In it was a round, wooden figure which he placed in front of me. I'd seen one of these before.

He explained the gift. "This is a matryoshka, a set of nesting dolls where you start with the large doll and inside of it is a smaller doll, which contains an even smaller doll, which contains an even smaller doll. You know what I am talking about?" He pulled it apart, and I watched as he placed all eight on the table.

"Yes, I do," I said as I picked up the smallest one. "I had one of these as a child, and my Dad, of course, explained how it was engineered, which took the magic out of it for me. I still treasured it since it was a gift from my partly Russian grandmother. Let's see. She told me *matryoshka* is Russian for mother."

He nodded in agreement, and then said, "Let's look at this nesting doll from the other angle, meaning that you focus on it by starting with the smallest doll and working up to the largest one."

I held it up for reference.

Pointing to it he explained, "In this point of view you can see that there is always something larger than it. Now imagine that doll is a point of view. As a CEO and leader, there will always be a bigger picture that you must seek out."

"Does that mean that I would never run out of dolls?"

"In effect, yes. As you put the top on the sixth doll, you would look for the seventh doll. Once you put the top on that one, you look for the next larger one. This is what is meant by your obligation to always seek out the bigger picture. Your view, since being promoted to CEO, has always remained at a lower level—sales and profit—while the board wants a CEO who sees the big picture."

Even though I was writing, I nodded that I understood.

He spread his arms out wide and said, "I'll use this Space Needle's structure as an example of what I am talking about. When local leaders wanted to put Seattle on the map and world stage back as early as 1950, they decided to host a modern World's Fair. Early on, a small group of dedicated leaders pondered how to attract visitors to this region, which then was considered remote and hard to reach. They decided that an audacious, almost preposterous fair was the answer. They chose the Space Age theme because of everyone's concern with Russia's launching of Sputnik in 1957. Later, they shared the conviction that this showcase required an icon that was big and unexpected, such as the Eiffel Tower created for the 1889 Exposition Universelle held in Paris and the first Ferris Wheel uniquely created for the World's Fair held in Chicago back in 1893. Dwelling on the 'wow factor,' Fair chairman Edward E. Carlson drew a rough sketch of a building that resembled a rocket ship to show what he had in mind. The Century 21—the name given to Seattle's world fair—planning committee agreed that it was exactly what was needed to attract attention and draw crowds."[25]

I responded, "The stories about this structure always amaze me."

"Me, too, and this is why I am telling its history. The means to create this unique structure didn't exist at the time of their decision, yet these leaders proved that it could be done! And instead of trying to obtain taxpayer money to finance this extremely expensive and risky undertaking, they chose to finance it privately because they knew the public-money choice would take years, with almost no guarantees of success. They had less than two years to design and build it, all while simultaneously creating the World's Fair."

He paused to let me catch up. Then he quizzed me, "What does the story of the Needle tell you about seeking out the bigger picture?"

I answered, "Daddy likes talking about this structure endlessly because he's fascinated with the engineering required, but he never mentioned what you just told me. To answer, I would say that the leaders who created this fantastic structure were looking far into Seattle's future rather than letting their vision and plans get bogged down with details. They played with...I

---

[25] Knute Berger, *Space Needle: The Spirit of Seattle*, Documentary Media ©2012 The Space Needle, LLC

mean, focused on the first three or larger dolls before getting to the smaller ones by looking at the why rather than the how."

He responded, "I notice that you used the doll analogy to explain."

"Thanks. You're rubbing off on me."

He took several sips of his drink before speaking again. "Now, on to your dilemma. What bigger-picture items have you been neglecting?"

I finished off my glass of water in order to remain calm. *I'm going to get upset with myself again.* "Oh, where do I start? The causes of our high employee turnover and the negative costs associated with it. Building and empowering a strong management team that can lead in case I leave. The loss of talented employees like Kelly and Dino. Placing attention on growing this company by means other than just pure sales growth." I sighed. *This hurts.*

He smiled. "That's enough of a list. You do see the bigger picture."

He lifted his glass of iced tea as a salute to me so I responded similarly with an empty glass. Our server took this to mean I wanted more. *Oops.*

By this time we had ordered dessert to satisfy my sweet tooth. As we began digging into it, he asked, "Would you like to tell me what you see as the bigger picture for your stewardship of Neoteric for the next three to five years?"

He listened as I talked about the marketplace, our product lines, and our current customers and prospects. I tried to be very fact-based and give a no-nonsense description so that he understood I knew what was going on.

The server brought us coffee to go with the dessert.

We talked further about other areas that needed my high-level attention, and he suggested ways that I could find the time to work on them.

At a lull he said, "I've noticed that your strategic plans are based on the assumption you would continue to work for Neoteric. This tells me that you still define yourself as the CEO and have not given up. This attitude could hold sway with Stephen as he makes his decision."

I felt a chill in my heart and shivered inadvertently.

Ron noticed and gave me a generous smile and let me finish off the last piece of decadent chocolate cake.

Ron said, "You mentioned earlier that you still have a few concerns. Shall we go over them now?"

As I shared my thoughts, his calming nature helped me relax enough to recognize that I was still doubting the progress I had made so far. He explained that my concern was normal in reluctant leaders and offered two ongoing actions that would help me overcome any backsliding. The first was to use trusted members of my team as my sounding board and be open with them. The second was to keep up my daily journaling. *Boy, he likes to remind me about that stupid journal!*

"My journaling has been hit and miss, so I promise to make it a daily habit." I offered that because I realized I had mentally blamed the messenger. *I can backslide easily!*

He said, as if reading my mind, "Many great leaders keep private journals."

I felt better and thanked him by saying, "You are so good at ramping up my enthusiasm."

He tipped his glass to me again.

I confessed, "I know that I have less than three weeks before Stephen makes his decision, and I am very hopeful that I will keep my job. However, at the same time I'm worried because while I grasp the things we've covered—such as strategic planning, our place in the market, and our company's long-term path to success—I have this nagging feeling that I am not doing everything that the CEO needs to be doing. I cannot rely entirely on your coaching, as much as I would like to. I guess what I'm saying is that very soon—if I stay—I need to stand on my own two feet. I guess that is what worries me the most."

As we chatted, or rather as he talked and I took notes, he seemed to sense that my anxiety had grown. He could tell I'd lost enthusiasm and that something was clouding my thoughts.

"Something is bothering you. Joslyn, what's on your mind?"

It's like he knows my thoughts before I do. Scary at times.

Backsliding

I gulped hard before I said, "I fear...I'm afraid I might fall down again. You use the word 'backslide.' How will I know if I do? And if I do fall, what should I do." I felt a pang of ice inside of me.

Ron explained this naturally occurring phenomenon this way: "When people and organizations experience change, they have natural periods of regression due to the pull of equilibrium. This is known as the Plateau Effect. Another reason for the plateau effect is the human X Factor of change. As in any arduous journey, once things get really difficult, it is easy for you to take the nearest exit off the mountain and give up. Quitting then becomes the path of least resistance.

"When you know there will be natural regression or backsliding, you can plan for it. Each major movement forward is followed by a small or large regression. As you climb the big mountain of an individual transformation, at each small hill of change expect to take four steps forward and then one step backward. Each step is a shift. The numbers are not exact; they only represent the normal ratio of progress to regression."

Ron stopped to draw this diagram.

THE PLATEAU EFFECT

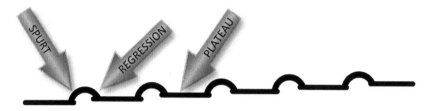

"The goal of making progress requires that each backslide ends up on a growth level that is higher than the last regression. If you fall lower than before, it means you might need more coaching. You also need feedback from people whom you trust to be honest about what they see going on with you."

"That is good to know. I am working on the trusted sounding board you suggested. I can use them to watch for my backsliding, is that correct?"

"Yes," he said.

Oh, gawd, I have another thing to worry about.

"Joslyn, I have every confidence that you can carry out the full spectrum of the CEO's role while meeting Stephen and the board's gauntlet of expectations. I foresee two supporting structures that would reinforce your continued growth, and they are first, more coaching, and second, having an experienced mentor. These structures also help whenever you regress to old patterns and habits."

I wrote his suggestions then finished my coffee. I noticed I was out of lemonade.

A Surprise Visitor

Just as if it were part of a sitcom script (which this wasn't), a man was suddenly standing at our table. Thinking it was a manager since he was not dressed in a server's uniform, we ignored his presence at first, then I looked at the man and it was Reese! I did a double take. I tapped Ron's hand since he was looking over his notes. I pointed at the man. Ron looked up in surprise and recovered quicker than I did. As I abruptly stood to shake his hand, I bumped the table with my hip, rattling the glassware.

Ron said while greeting Reese with a handshake, "Reese, it is a pleasure to see you again. Are you dining here today?" which echoed my unuttered question.

Reese looked at Ron, then at me and asked, "May I join you?"

We both nodded yes.

I was stunned by his pleasant interruption. He took the empty chair on my left.

"I apologize for the intrusion." Reese turned toward me and said, "A few hours ago I met with Ron and he brought me up to speed on your situation. I understand what you are going through right now because I have experienced it myself and of course coached executives and managers through their difficult times. Ron did not invite me…but he did mention where you were meeting."

My eyes sought Ron's to verify what he said, and he nodded. He made a sign that showed he was surprised, too.

Reese continued, "Ron asked if I was willing to be your mentor. At first I hesitated and said I would think about it, but then I recalled the sense of desperation that you might be feeling right now. Personally, I'd like to see you retain your job as CEO of our great company. An hour after Ron left, I realized that I had already decided. That is, if you want me to be your mentor."

In my stunned state, I imagined that I was a cartoon character whose chin fell to the floor. I didn't have a response; all I felt was gratitude for these two amazing men.

I guess attempting to cover for me, Ron spoke up. "I have a feeling you startled the 'yes' right out of her mouth, Reese!"

We all laughed at my embarrassment.

"It is not that you need someone to rescue or save you," Reese said directly to me. "It is just that you have done a great job at Neoteric in terms of building up market share and acquiring new customers. The market Neoteric lives in is shifting. We need to quickly adapt for what's coming next, and changing horses in the midst of a transformation is a bad idea. For that reason and based on what Ron described regarding your personal growth, I believe that now is a critical moment in your development as a CEO, and that maybe I could be an element of your support system."

I finally found my composure, saying, "I do not know what to say other than thank you. I would be honored to have you as my mentor, Reese. In fact, we were just talking about what I admire about you and your charisma. I told Ron that I envy this quality of yours and wish I had it."

> **Servant Leadership**
>
> Servant Leadership is a very popular leadership model developed by Robert K. Greenleaf in 1970. The servant-leader serves those they lead, which implies that employees are an end in themselves rather than a means to an organizational purpose or bottom line. Servant leadership is meant to replace command-and-control models of leadership, to be more focused on the needs of others.
>
> Leaders devote themselves to serving the needs of the organization's members, focuses on meeting the needs of those they lead, develops employees to bring out the best in them, coaches others and encourages their self-expression, facilitates the personal growth of all followers, and listens well. They strive to build a sense of community and joint ownership.
>
> Servant-leaders are believed to be effective because the needs of followers are so looked after that they reach their full potential, hence perform at their best. One positive of looking at leadership this way is that it forces the person away from using self-serving, domineering leadership and makes those up in front think harder about how to respect, value, and inspire those they lead.

Servant Leadership - *cont*

A leader should have a servant-leader attitude, meaning they need to have the capacity to lead through service. The leader needs to get out of their own way while removing any impediments to the people's ability to provide service. Specifically, a servant-leader must demonstrate the traits of humility, integrity (beyond honesty into congruence and wholeness), empathy (the capacity to discern who the stakeholders are, what they need, and the ability to read the room), and the capacity to absorb pain (take unfair criticism without responding negatively).

Servant Leadership is a way of viewing life that will forever alter the way you lead. It is a process of opening one's self to new and deeper awareness of everyday issues, like power and human dignity. Looking through this lens of servant leadership and using what you see as a guide can forever transform your life, your relationships, and the world. Robert Greenleaf explains, "The best test [of a servant-leader], and difficult to administer, is: Do those served grow as persons; do they, while being led, become healthier, wiser, freer, more autonomous, more likely themselves to become servants? And what is the effect on the least privileged in society; will he benefit, or, at least, will he not be further deprived?"

Reese laughed and thanked the waiter who brought him a menu and water. He declined to order anything except a hot tea.

After the server left, Reese continued speaking. "I believe you are very likeable, Joslyn. If I have any sort of unique charisma, I'd say it comes from my convictions about the CEO as a Servant Leader."

As Ron and I enjoyed another round of coffee. Reese shared his view of Servant Leadership.[26]

When Reese finished the summary he spoke directly to me again. "Based on my understanding of this leadership model, I believe that you have some strong and uplifting convictions as a leader, and I'd like to see you turn them into ideals that make your management team stronger. It's another area where I believe I could be of service to you as a mentor. There is just one thing that I ask of you, Joslyn, and it is that you commit to focusing on areas where you have not fully owned your strengths. By now you

---

[26] Robert K. Greenleaf, *Servant Leadership: A Journey into the Nature of Legitimate Power and Greatness* November 2002 and Center for Servant Leader website https://greenleaf.org

know what those are based on your work with Ron and your self-assessments. Will you promise me to work diligently on improving those things?"

"Yes, I promise." My voice probably sounded as giddy as I felt.

"Then I will email you a questionnaire that I use with those I mentor. It'll let me know where to guide you. I leave for Europe tonight and will be unavailable for two weeks. Therefore I'll send it to you via email before I leave. Will that be okay?"

I said it would.

He continued, "After I return and go over your responses, we can talk by phone. My personal assistant will call you to set the appointment. See you at the next board meeting."

Right after he finished off his tea, Reese rose from the table gracefully, shook our hands and exited.

"Wow!" I exclaimed. "I cannot think of anything better happening to me...except maybe Stephen extending my contract. Between the work that you have done with me, Karen's kind words, and now Reese's willingness to be my mentor, I know that I will be able to prove to Stephen beyond a doubt that I am the CEO he needs me to be!"

I felt as if I were a 16-year-old getting my first driver's license. I just knew I was grinning ear-to-ear.

Ron let me revel in my good feelings. Then he said, "You are in such a good mood that I think a brief story will help you transition to the hard work that is ahead in the next three weeks."

The Trusted Advisor and Egoless Leader

Whenever I meet a leader that I sense is a High Road leader, I ask to interview them to discover how they define themselves. Many of these are reluctant leaders, like you, yet to those around them, they are shining examples of how to lead. I met Maxwell in 2002 and I was immediately impressed.

From my perspective, Maxwell has four outstanding traits as a leader: 1) He has a natural charisma and people feel very comfortable and at ease with him, 2) he is a take-charge type of person who rises to the occasion, 3) he has the ability to see the big picture quickly and think strategically, and finally 4) he is trusted deeply by his employees and by the owner of his organization.

In addition to his role as the CFO and acting operations manager, Maxwell sits on the Board of Directors of a regional publicly traded bank, and he noticed that on occasion, the bank's management communicates in a very technical sense. This underscores for him the importance of being a good communicator and listener as a leader.

I view Maxwell as a preeminent person who leads from the High Road. Interestingly, despite his visible and influential role in the organization, Max does not define himself as a leader, yet he is perceived by those around him as a great leader.

Maxwell told me, 'I would say leadership is something about your own personal characteristics. For example, I challenge myself by growing my abilities, yet I tend to overextend myself at times. I continue to learn. I did not set out to be a leader, but I saw the need and opportunity to become one. I am glad I did, because as a leader it is those personal characteristics that need to be highly regarded by those you lead. People have more respect for you when you are their leader. All leaders are expected and obligated to have the highest standards of objectivity, morals, character, ethics and values. I was amazed that even though he said plainly 'I became a leader' Max still is uncomfortable wearing the leader label. This is a trait common to Reluctant Leaders.'

When he finished, I thought about this for the time it took the server to refill our water glasses and my lemonade.

I told Ron, "It's my turn to tell a story, only this one is probably an example of how not to lead, and it's about a person I worked for at a prior company."

The Untrustworthy, Ego-driven Non-leader

The only skill Joan was competent at was tooting her own horn. She was not a planner, nor was she good at managing her time effectively or learning from example. However, being at the right place at the right time, stretching the truth about what she had accomplished previously, and her boastful way of presenting herself landed her in a middle management position at an emerging technology company.

Our company was launching a new product, and according to Joan, she claimed to have led a very successful product launch at her previous employer. Since the other members of the newly formed management team did not have this direct experience, we planned to rely on her experience to guide us. Demonstrating the new product to prospective buyers required a small Tiger Team to travel and present the new product at dinner meetings designed to solicit feedback from key end-users.

Joan was appointed to lead our team and make sure everything was perfect so we could sell with confidence. A dinner presentation is quite complex and each detail matters.

Planning required booking a private room at a location convenient for the guests, organizing the audio/visuals needed for the presentation, booking hotel rooms for our guests and ourselves, and most importantly, developing a working draft of the presentation which the rest of us would analyze and perfect.

But Joan wasn't up to the task and it showed at the first presentation. She never sent out a final meeting agenda with logistics, using as an excuse: 'I am so busy, I've been drinking from a fire hose.'

As the date of the first dinner presentation drew near, there were many opportunities for Joan to ask for help or to double-check with us if she had missed any of the myriad details, but she failed to ask for help.

When members of the presentation team arrived at the airport near where the first dog-and-pony show would be, I noticed Joan was frantically calling local hotels. 'Joan, do we not have hotel rooms?' I asked.

'Oh, I always book last-minute; I've never had a problem,' she claimed.

As it turns out, that was the tip of the iceberg. The private dining room was 30 miles from our invited guests' office, and they ended up arriving late to dinner after being stuck in traffic and not having sufficient directions. Joan had not reserved an LCD projector for the dinner presentation (the restaurant's sole LCD was in use by another party). Joan desperately purchased a projector minutes before dinner started, wasting company money.

Even though she remained a member of our presentations team, everyone found ways around having Joan lead anything. She not only let her team down due to her lack of attention to detail, none of us ever again trusted her ability to lead.

Leadership Lesson

"Good story," Ron told me. "What new perspective do you have regarding this incident?"

Ever the coach…always teaching even with my stories.

I answered, "The first thing that comes to mind is that maybe how I felt about Joan is how the board feels about me. When Stephen offered me the CEO position, I implied that I could lead and yet I've demonstrated otherwise. I hope it's not too late in the game for me, now that I recognize where I went wrong and where I need to improve."

He said, "That is very astute, Joslyn, and your answer proves how much you have grown. In leadership it is never too late. I suggest you focus on getting people such as Angela, Brian, and Isaiah to trust in you again. That is the hard work that has urgency written all over it. Even if you do not remain at

Neoteric, those same lessons will apply at your next leadership position."

We were the only two diners left as far as I could tell, and the staff was setting up for dinner.

My Assignment

"I guess that is the cue for my assignment. What should I work on next, Coach?" I was teasing him because I knew what he would do.

He shook his head at me and covered his eyes, while trying not to laugh, and asked, "What work do you assign yourself?"

I responded with confidence, "First, I commit to following up with Reese and completing his questionnaire. Second, it is time to make amends with all members of our management team. So far, I focused on the executives, but the rest of middle managers and supervisors need to trust me. I commit to meeting individually with all of them."

Ron cut in. "May I make a suggestion that will help you help them?"

"Please do."

"Start these conversations by asking how they have been negatively impacted by your reluctance to be a true leader. Then ask what you can do to gain their trust again. See where the conversation goes from there."

"Can you give me an example of how this might look?" *I am stalling because this sounds intimidating.*

He said gently, "Pindar told us you don't trust him to write marketing copy. Decide how you can best show that you do trust his judgment because once he senses that you trust him, you will become worthy of his trust. Once you decide what needs to change, make it happen."

His example eased my mind.

He added, "I can foresee that you may encounter some difficulties doing this, so I ask you to see it through, no matter what. See this as setting up a win-win game. Rely on your compassion because this is some of the hardest work you've assigned yourself. If you need to bounce ideas off of me or have me role play with you, I will make myself available."

The mind reader is at it again. How does he do that?

I got excited again and remembered something I needed to tell him.

"Oh! Let me tell you about what happened with Jayna over the last two weeks!" I related what I had done to improve our relationship and how she was responding. "I feel very optimistic about our relationship now."

That led to further conversations about my personal life and changes I was making to it as we rode down the swift elevator to the Plaza, where we said our goodbyes. I wanted to hug him as a sign of gratitude, but wasn't sure I should. *He's my coach, not my friend.*

I showed my ticket to the parking valet and gave him $20. Waiting for my car, I took a business card from my purse and studied it. *I AM a good CEO. I AM a good leader.* I breathed deeply three times. For just a second, I felt like Dorothy in the Wizard of Oz as she chanted, "There's no place like home. There's no place like home."

*****

Ron's Assessment of Joslyn's Progress

I made a mental note on my drive back to the office to call Jackson, Latisha, Kendra, and Marlene. I would ask for their assessment of Joslyn's progress before speaking with Stephen. I did not want to state that she was ready when she might not be.

Upon returning to my quiet office, I dictated my thoughts for Joslyn's file.

I believe that Joslyn has found her resolve. She has shed her hesitancy and is willing to stand strong and deliver as a leader should. It was good to see her focused and at the same time happy.

I also believe that Reese's desire to mentor her will weigh heavily in Stephen's decision.

Whatever Stephen decides, I believe that Joslyn is well on her way to becoming a great leader and a strong CEO.

*****

The Bottom Line of Leadership

In 2009, employee turnover cost U.S. businesses an estimated $300 billion. The staggering cost of employee turnover can be viewed as simply the cost of doing business; however, additional damage occurs when turnover is compounded by poor hiring and management practices. Fortunately, the number of employees who are fired or leave on their own accord can be managed. Some of the most common reasons employees give for voluntary separation include boredom, weak or toxic supervisor relationships, wrong cultural fit, and job descriptions that don't match the reality of the position.

Less-than-optimal leadership practices cost the typical organization an amount equal to as much as 7 percent of their total annual sales.

At least 9 percent and possibly as much as 32 percent of an organization's voluntary turnover can be avoided through improved leadership at all levels.

Better leadership can generate a 3 to 4 percent improvement in customer satisfaction scores, and a corresponding 1.5 percent increase in revenue growth.

Most organizations are operating with a 5 to 10 percent productivity drag that improved leadership practices could eliminate[27].

The emotional state of leaders and their employees plays a significant role in the behaviors both groups display at work. The actions of employees and the people who lead them impact how customers perceive the organization, and ultimately affects the organization's bottom line.

The climate or culture of an organization as a whole is impacted by the emotions of the leaders because the leader's emotional state impacts what employees feel, how satisfied employees are with their work and the company (which impacts your brand or reputation), how loyal employees are in their willingness to give extra effort, and employee productivity and efficiency[28].

To be successful in your career and with your employer, show your convictions that demonstrate you lead fairly and wisely. Soon you will see that employees are responding to you in more constructive ways.

---

[27] *Putting the Service-Profit Chain to Work*, by James L. Heskett, Thomas O. Jones, Gary W. Loveman, W. Earl Sasser, Jr., Leonard A. Schlesinger July 2008 ©Harvard Business Review https://hbr.org/2008/07/putting-the-service-profit-chain-to-work/ar/1
[28] *Bottom Line Impact of Succession Planning* whitepaper ©2011 CEB Corporate Leadership Council   https://clc.executiveboard.com/Public/PublicOverview.aspx

Chapter 10
Moving Forward

*"You have shown me that you
are worth taking the risk for."*

Month 6: Time's Up!

It was 10 minutes before Joslyn's scheduled arrival. Stephen was sitting directly to my right on the settee that fit nicely in the corner of his upscale office.

He was deep in thought about a question I had just asked him. During the pause, I resisted the temptation to stand up and peek out of the windows. The views from the 58th floor are magnificent and each time I visit Stephen, I sneak time to gaze out his windows.

We had just concluded his personal coaching session and I had inquired, "Have you made your decision about Joslyn?"

I glanced over at the tall man dressed in a charcoal gray suit, cut exactly to his athletic body. His tie practically lit up the room with its bright colors.

Stephen's large office carried the scent of cedar because somehow a small three-foot bonsai Japanese cedar tree lived happily and prosperously in his office. It was an unusual office plant, but Stephen has unique and expensive taste. I glanced over at a display case filled with tin toys from the 1930s and 40s. Stephen is a man who knows what he wants and goes after it, something I admire about him. *Why hasn't he decided on Joslyn's fate? He's usually decisive.*

I heard metallic thumping and grinding, and Stephen explained, "The floor below is being remodeled, and the sound radiates loudly."

The clock was winding down toward Joslyn's appearance. Suddenly, Stephen rose off the black leather settee and walked over to his uncluttered dark walnut desk where he grabbed two sheets of paper lying on top. He looked them over, crumpled up one and lobbed it into the wastebasket. Looking at me directly he explained, "This morning I wrote two letters. One terminating Joslyn's employment and the other extending it for another two years. Even this morning I was undecided…but no longer."

"Which letter got tossed?" I asked. "Good shot, by the way."

He smirked and ignored my quip. "The termination letter, because based on what you and Reese suggested to me and from what I have witnessed regarding Joslyn's improvements in her demeanor, I think it's worth retaining her as CEO."

"But," I said, waiting for more.

He pointed a finger at me. "You know me so well it's scary! But she has to continue to grow and show me that she is worthy of my confidence, and she has to continue with the coaching. There are a few other conditions that I'll lay out to her."

At that moment, we heard a knock on his office door. Stephen opened it and there stood Joslyn. To me she appeared somewhat subdued and maybe a little scared.

Today, Joslyn was dressed modestly, going against her normal flamboyant style, with a traditional navy blue business suit, consisting of a plain blazer and a matching pencil skirt. Her simple blouse, without any form of decoration or flash, was coral. She wore black flats, forgoing her normal high heels. Her recently styled hair was layered and highlighted.

Stephen greeted her then walked over to a small refrigerator and grabbed several bottles of Evian water, handed them off, and sat down behind his desk. I took that as the cue to move to one of the two chairs placed in front of his desk, choosing the chair on the right.

After walking to the second chair, Joslyn smiled at me and reached out her hand. "No matter what happens today, Ron, I want to thank you for helping me to see where I needed to improve myself." I felt her tension.

She turned and addressed Stephen. "Thank you, Stephen, for urging me to work with Ron."

I blinked. This was a side of her that I hadn't seen much. *Maybe Joslyn finally tamed her willfulness. The chip on her shoulder is apparently gone. She's accepting her fate with relative calmness.*

Stephen made small talk, seemingly not wanting to get to the point of this momentous meeting. Since he reveled in sharing his wisdom, I knew that Steven would want to teach her something BEFORE he offered his verdict.

*****

Stephen Speaks

Looking at Joslyn, I thought, *Why am I feeling nervous? I am not on the hot seat.*

After looking at Ron to ground myself and clearing my voice, I said slowly, "It's my turn, Joslyn, to provide you with a coaching lesson. This is something I've learned to apply."

I pulled a file from my desk, took a sheet from it, and turned it so Joslyn could read it. "This is something Ron taught me right after my first promotion to CEO. I realize now that I should have shared this when I promoted you."

I felt the need to apologize to her because in hindsight this was one of several actions I should have taken, which might have helped her from the get-go.

With her delicate hands folded in her lap, Joslyn sat perfectly still while I launched into a lesson regarding sustainable profits.

I said, "Nearly every business is concerned about staying alive, and the best way for any organization to achieve that intention is to generate profits—sustainable profits."

"The term *sustainable* means that the methods employed for generating those profits are steady, dependable, and consistent. This has been the Holy Grail for business organizations since caveman Og gladly gave up his extra hides to Gor in exchange for the knowledge on how to build a fire.

"In their zeal to find the 'magic' for generating sustainable profits, some executives believe that listening and paying attention to their customers, while delivering high-quality services and providing good products, are the MOST IMPORTANT activities to focus on. While I agree that those are crucial to a successful and profitable business, these activities are secondary in nature. There is something even more vital that must be in place first, which serves as the catalyst for both activating the repeatable formula for sustainable profits and guaranteeing it remains self-sustaining. That must-have component derives from the benefits of having a high-caliber leadership team.

"Please notice in this diagram that sustainable profits are at the bottom or base of the pyramid. When the base is strong and broad, it dramatically increases the odds that we will survive the ups and downs of the marketplace and changing fortunes of our customers. The level above the base shows another set of vital ingredients: our people and our intellectual capital. Above that level is another vital ingredient, Neoteric's business personality or culture.

LEADERSHIP AND SUSTAINABLE PROFITS

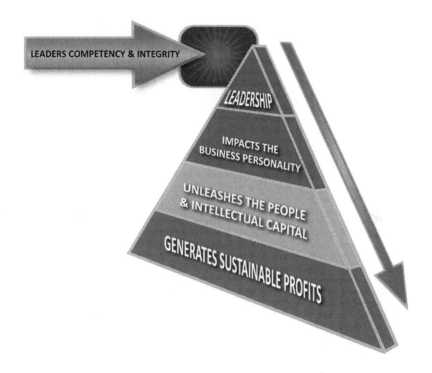

"The crowning cap of this pyramid is leadership because it is always our leaders at all levels who unleash the power of the business personality. It is this company's leadership body who must have a positive impact on their people and the firm's intellectual capital, turning these dynamic assets into something of lasting value that outsiders willingly and consistently pay for. This continual stream of ingredients renews and feeds Neoteric so that profits are innately sustainable and easily end up in a solid base. To make this formula and all its components work, there needs to be a source or capping piece that holds it all in place. That factor of the formula is our entire leadership group."

I paused to let her grasp the total picture before I went further.

Next I said, "I can use a metaphor. Imagine a constant flow of water running down the side of a sheer cliff and ending up in a crystal clear pool of icy water. It's a thing of beauty which exists only if the water is fed by a source from above that cliff; say, a snowcap or ice sheet. In a profitable organization, the flow's source is its leadership."

I finished off my bottle of water and cracked open a second. I noticed Joslyn had not touched hers. *I can feel her anxiety, but why am I so nervous? I know, I'm feeling guilty!*

Ignoring that feeling, I elaborated further. "In this diagram you will notice an arrow (coming from the left) that points to the pyramid's cap. It represents the everlasting spark or fire that generates the zeal or momentum needed for the consistent flow to commence. In a waterfall, gravity and warm temperatures are the catalysts for the water's flowing nature. In a business organization, leadership's competency and integrity are the catalysts for profits' flowing nature. The arrow pointing toward the pyramid represents the leadership energy that sparks the effectiveness of this simple yet irreplaceable formula, and from there everything else flows from the top down to the bottom. This flow infuses the entire organization with a limitless energy for success—sustainable success."

"Competency is self-explanatory, meaning that our leaders must know what they are doing and adopt a commitment to always improve. A leader's integrity is crucial because some leaders will always attempt to generate profits that are not sustainable. Their purpose for doing this may be to obtain a loan, attract a buyer, or impress an investor. Quite often the tactics employed are illegal or unethical and definitely unsustainable. Imagine you have a car that runs poorly and requires costly repairs. You detail the outside and interior to make it look attractive and then attempt to sell your flawed vehicle. All you need is one person to take this problem off your hands and you are temporarily successful (and maybe without a conscience). Through smoke and mirrors you 'made' the car or business appear successful. The methods that business leaders use to put lipstick on a pig are numerous, and new ones are invented every year."

"My board...I mean, our board, both wants and needs leaders who believe that their honor is on the line in each of their actions and therefore stick with the highest standards of conduct. We want to ensure that everything we do now—strategies and tactics—will help this organization succeed in the long run. This means that if you believe that selling products at a lower price will serve to generate sustainable profits and keep customers returning to buy, we want you to choose that course and forgo the short-term tactic of gouging the customer just so this quarter's profits wow Wall Street. The best organizations are those built by wise leaders who want their business to be around 100, even 200 years into the future."

"And we were...I mean, are depending on you, Joslyn, to MAKE THIS HAPPEN. This is why I and others felt it was worth investing money in your growth. Do you understand?"

"Yes, I do," was all she said, glancing at me and then looking away.

I cannot string this out any longer; it's unfair to her.

Stephen's Verdict and Conditions

Before speaking again, I drained another bottle of water. *I can't suppress this nervousness. Even after all this time, I fall into that darn reluctance again.*

"Joslyn, I believed in you from the beginning and I still do. You did disappoint me for a while when you decided to burn bridges with members of the board and with most of your management team. However, I can tell that you now recognize the error of your ways and have made great strides in rebuilding relationships. I recently spoke with Paula, Jackson, Marlene, Kendra, Aaron, Latisha, and Dawn, who each recognize improvements in your relationships with them. There are a few on your team, Curtiss and Isaiah in particular, who will need more of your time and attention."

"That being said, I convinced the board and they authorized me to offer you a two-year extension as our CEO."

I paused to let it sink in. I heard a nearly silent sigh of relief. I could see in her face a release of tension and also a resolve that I had not noticed before.

Ron turned to look at her, and she rewarded him with a very broad smile and a thumbs-up sign. Restraining her grin she turned her upper body back toward me and sat up a few inches taller.

"However, you are not getting a free pass!" *I need her to pay attention to this.*

I continued. "There are specific things that I expect from you. My first requirement is to mend fences with Angela. This was the most vital relationship you tarnished. When the board voted, she was clearly against extending the contract. She was not advocating for your termination, though, which I take as a sign that she has not written you off. However, she believed you should be demoted."

Ron had warned me that Joslyn viewed a demotion as the kiss of death, and as I expected, she flinched.

I said, "The second requirement is to quickly fill the open positions on your management team. Once you have narrowed the candidates to your top two or three, I expect you to discuss your choices and explain your recommendations. I recently met with Dino and Kelly, and they might consider returning to Neoteric. So you have a decision to make there."

News of their interest surprised her, as I thought it would.

"My third requirement is for you to make nice with every member of our board and win them over with your charm. My fourth requirement is that you continue to improve employee morale. Every three months, Ron's organization will conduct an employee survey, and I expect to see improvements in employee engagement. My last requirement is that you continue having Ron as your coach." I was grinning at this point because my nervousness was gone. *Whew. I'm glad that's over.*

She replied, "Thank you, Stephen. I sincerely appreciate your faith in me. I will exceed your expectations, the ones you just asked of me and all future ones."

I remembered something. "Speaking of expectations, there is another action I should have taken long ago, and that is admitting to you that without coaching, I probably wouldn't have this job! Ron has been my coach for more than six years."

She smiled and said, "That admission helps me understand why you urgently suggested that I have a coach to be accountable to…but knowing that wouldn't have made any difference, Stephen. I had to own my reluctance."

Nodding at her I added, "I recently read that in most organizations of our size, more than 60 percent of the people in a leadership position fail to own up to their leadership responsibilities. These are the Reluctant Leaders Ron talks about. The article also reports that this number keeps growing."

She remained composed and without response, so I continued.

"Joslyn, I will make the official announcement right after lunch. Be prepared for employee reactions."

In a subdued voice she replied, "I am ready."

To myself I thought, *Now I can put my pent-up energy to good use.*

"Please excuse me, Joslyn, because I have a press announcement to prepare about your renewed contract, and an all-employee email to write before the grapevine gets hold of our decision."

I nodded at Ron to communicate that he could take control of this meeting. I walked out the door.

*****

Ron Adds Perspective

Stephen nodded to me that it was my turn to take over this meeting, and he left the room.

I turned toward her and said, "Joslyn, now that you know your immediate future, I will take this opportunity to place the final colors on the figurative leadership 'picture' you and I began to paint seven months ago."

Joslyn grabbed a notepad from her attaché and got ready to write.

"Today we turn to my third metaphor about leadership traits, and that is the atomic bomb. I know—it has such a negative connotation—but the part of the image I use is the tremendous burst of energy that a simple configuration of atoms can have."

I reached into my trusty briefcase and pulled out a folder, then removed a sheet of paper, which I placed in front of her.

As she glanced at it I said, "In our first session you asked if I had a visual image of the eight traits and how they work together. I waited until now to show this to prevent confusion. On paper here now are the skills or traits we worked on."

I let her study it for several minutes

NEED OR DESIRE TO LEAD

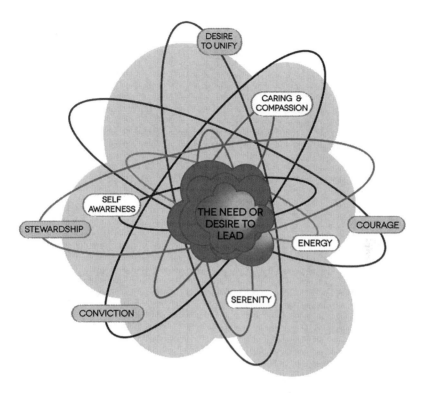

She said, "It looks like an atom or series of them. I can sense the motion."

"That is my intent. I had to use three different metaphors to describe the details, but now in one image you can see how the pieces fit together. The Need or Desire to Lead is in the center of this image. Its energy activates the eight circling atoms, represented by ovals. The passion to lead sets in motion your leadership Energy, which in turn bursts and activates your Desire to Unify, your Courage, and a deep Self-Awareness. The energy released by the four inner traits or atoms create more energy and, importantly, momentum. They produce specific effects within you that soon show up on the outside. These leadership outcomes are Good Stewardship, Caring and Compassion, knowing and sharing your Convictions, and finding Serenity.

"Notice that the eight atoms are in motion already, and this tremendous release of energy of all eight then produces an evergreen energy that turns into true leadership. When I say 'evergreen,' I mean that it is a renewing energy that never goes away. I can explain that in the **17th Natural Law of Leadership**."

> **Good leaders renew themselves from within. They use their passion, vision, and intention to overcome any and every obstacle they face.**

She continued to pay close attention.

"In this image, notice that there is a bright glow surrounding all these objects. This is the positive impact that an inspirational leader will have on nearly every situation they may encounter. Now that you understand leadership better, what do you think this area represents for you?"

Joslyn thought deeply before she spoke. "I recall how many times you explained courage and the energy I needed to maintain it. When I was scared, I felt hollow, but when I felt courageous, I didn't. In this image, I can see how a leader's energy fills the spaces. Maybe that hollow feeling came from not knowing what leadership was about. I had a title of leader but lacked the understanding of what that meant."

She added further, "That natural law reminds me that I need to hold onto that passion in good times and bad times, because it will sustain me so I can share the energy with my employees."

I responded with obvious pride, "That is a powerful insight. You truly have shifted your thinking about leading others!" I clapped for her.

Then she said, "I placed those Ping-Pong and silver balls into a glass case that sits on my desk so I can see them and think about what they mean."

"What a great idea," I said, feeling very proud.

Joslyn asked a few questions, and then I quizzed her to see if she could recall specific incidents over the last seven months and connect them to the traits in the diagram. From her answers I could tell she needed time to analyze this, which would become one of her next growth steps.

Inspirational Leaders Always Move Forward

"Because we will continue this coaching relationship, together we will define additional growth steps. I suggest that your first assignment will be to review this diagram early in your day and decide which trait you will work on that day. Instead of focusing on skills, I want you to bring out those traits you already own and enhance them. For example: maybe tomorrow, a day filled with meetings, work on showing compassion and caring in all that you do. Or if the day turns stressful, practice feeling serene."

She replied, "That sounds easy."

"It is and it isn't. Just looking at this is not enough. You could and probably will fall into old patterns unless you stay hyper-aware of your words, actions, and thoughts. This image is designed to enhance that awareness."

"Right. Right. It will help me if I memorize this image and all its components."

I nodded my approval.

"I know you have at least one more assignment," she said.

Joslyn smiled and so did I.

"What do you assign yourself in terms of further winning over each member of your entire leadership group?"

She must have already thought of something because she responded quickly. "I plan to meet one-on-one with each member of my team within the next week, doing what I need to regain their trust. I will ask 'What can I do to make your job easier?' and 'How can I best serve you?' As Jackson said to us, I must 'mend fences.'"

I nodded, saying, "That is a good strategy to gain their trust by asking them what they need from you. Use these sessions to really listen to them. Get to know them as individuals and human beings. Most important of all, follow through on what they ask for. When they see that you are genuinely concerned, that you believe in and support them, you will earn their trust and gain respect. Over time, you can enter into a dialog about what you need from them but refrain from making these requests seem like a swap or 'I'll do this for you if you do this for me.'"

She nodded several times as I described this work.

I had to ask, "Are you willing to do that?"

Very boldly and without hesitation, Joslyn replied, "Yes, I am. I am ready to and look forward to doing it."

We had another 20 minutes before we adjourned, so I continued with another lesson.

I stood up and walked to a window to peek at the snow-capped Cascade Mountains. Speaking to the window, I said, "Not too long ago, when speaking on leadership at a national conference, a young emerging leader asked this unusual question: *What is right with leaders today?*

"I gave this answer: Leaders are the moral center of the group or organization they lead. What we hear about most often are the unethical leaders who don't have a moral center or who prefer the low road. Thankfully, there are numerous people serving as leaders who take the High Road.

"Another participant asked: *How do you identify a High Road leader?*

"I answered this way: At HRI, we isolated 21 traits that are common among leaders committed to taking the High Road in all that they do. You can identify the preeminent High Road leader because he or she does those things that are shown on this chart. They also refrain from the behaviors that employees dislike." I handed her a document. "Add this to your leader tool kit that you've been creating."

HOLISTIC EVALUATION OF THE LEADER

1. Has a high moral code that is embedded in their personal DNA. They take the High Road because it is the right thing to do and not because someone tells them to.

2. Establishes high personal expectations out of the desire to set an example for others and to challenge their abilities.

3. Sets the bar high for others because people always rise to the level of their own expectations.

4. Has a vision for something they want to accomplish which benefits the greater good.

5. Has the energy to turn their vision into reality.

6. Has their own unique 'charisma' that naturally attracts people to their cause.

7. Shares a passion and/or drive to make a difference, which is usually part of their vision.

8. Expresses a sense of urgency to see the fruits of their hard work while realizing that their hard work and efforts will impact the world long after they are gone.

9. Finds it difficult to accept "no" or "can't" for an answer because they have great faith in their team's abilities.

10. Has the ability to see possibilities in every obstacle and gets frustrated with people who see only obstacles.

1

1.

18

19.

20.

21. R
   te
   and grow.

...s willing to
....u use the information to improve

11. Recognizes that they cannot achieve their vision alone, and accepts that other people's contributions are vital to reaching the final destination.

12. Has an inner drive to succeed; however, this can lead to problems when they focus on the goal instead of the journey. They adopt high ethical standards to guide them.

13. Has an attitude of caring, compassion, and empathy.

14. Has an attitude of gratitude for those around them and for what they receive from them.

15. Strives to remain courageous in their ability to quickly assess the risks, weigh the odds, and take wise chances.

16. Holds himself/herself accountable for their own results.

17. Knows they are accountable for their team's results.

18. Asks for honest feedback from each person on their team and uses that information to improve.

19. Recognizes their humanness and, knowing they are fallible, never covers up a mistake. When they make one, they apologize and work to make things right.

20. Knows when to lead and when to let others show what they are capable of.

21. Relies on the counsel of a trusted advisor who is willing to tell them the truth and use the information to improve and grow.

5.

6.

7.

8.

9. F
   b

10. Ha   ...s abilities.
    ..., to see possibilities in every obstacle and gets frustrated with people who see only obstacles.

She laughed, probably at the intensity with which I described it. Then she responded, "To my ears, that sort of leader sounds like Stephen…and you."

I said, "Thank you."

She laughed at my obvious embarrassment for the praise. I returned to my chair to regain my poise.

A Leadership Tool to Hold Leaders Accountable

I said to her, "I am telling you this because all too often, the CEO's primary obligation is to make the business profitable, and this leads to unreasonable CEO salaries, inflated share prices, questionable business practices, outright fraud, and other unsavory practices. This list of 21 traits needs to be used by Boards of Directors to ensure that their CEO is well rounded and looks at the business in ways that contribute to a sustainable business, as Stephen shared with you.

"We ask Boards of Directors to use this list as a performance evaluation tool for their CEO and senior leaders. Those clients who have followed our suggestions are among the most profitable and successful and, according to my knowledge, have never experienced a breach of ethics by a senior leader."

"Wow." She meant what she said. "Can I assume that Stephen has been using this tool on me?"

I grinned and said in a serious way, "Yes. He probably didn't tell you. I'll assume he had his reasons. I will recommend to him that the two of you go over it regularly to evaluate each other's performance."

"That sounds reasonable."

High Road Leaders Never Stop Growing

Before we could continue the conversation, Stephen reentered the room and sat behind his desk. Since our attention was on him, he seized the opportunity. He looked at Joslyn and said, "There is one more condition, and it is simple: Do not stop growing as a leader. You have a lot to learn. As Ron has probably told you, a leader must be curious and continue to seek out new information. A preeminent leader will always have someone he or she trusts, guiding him or her in the right direction."

Joslyn grew quiet, put fingers to her forehead as she gently rubbed her brow in thought. I could almost sense the wheels of her brain churning through the catalog of things she learned from this experience.

Stephen took a deep audible breath before saying, "I can admit now that I really had deep empathy for your situation. I once faced the same challenge you did. During that awful meeting when the board was suggesting that I fire you, I recalled a lot of my old characteristics and bad patterns. Years ago, I was willful yet unwilling to get feedback. My employees were afraid of me, and I trashed important relationships that I needed to maintain.

"Based on my own experiences as the scared, timid, and ineffective leader, I knew two things for sure. The first was that I needed to fight for and believe in you. The second was that coaching you myself wouldn't work."

Joslyn cocked her head at his comment.

Smiling at her reaction, he continued, "Intervening as a coach or mentor would be the worst thing I could have done and is why I brought Ron in. In my reluctant years, I had supervisors and managers who tried to coach me on the things I needed to know. I always rejected what they said because I thought that their advice was self-serving. It was when I took my blinders off and looked at myself truthfully that I recognized my unflattering characteristics and inability to lead effectively. At that moment I realized I needed to improve."

Joslyn was clearly surprised by his honesty but at a loss for words.

Stephen said, "I really appreciate that you were willing to make the effort because I made a bet with myself that you would stop working with Ron after one session!"

I responded, "Whoa, Stephen! Great vote of confidence!" It was my turn to add to the jocularity of the moment.

Stephen chose to ignore the ribbing, but he couldn't hide his winning smile.

He again addressed her directly. "It is never too late to learn. Please keep that in mind as you go forward. It is never too late to learn. I still am learning how to be a good leader."

She replied, "Thanks for that advice, Stephen. Seven months ago I didn't understand that; now I do."

They were speaking to one another as if I weren't in the room.

Stephen walked over to Joslyn and placed a hand on her shoulder. "You have shown me that you are worth taking the risk for. Since I had to arm-twist a few board members to accept the risk, do not make me regret this decision."

After taking two deep breaths, she looked up at his face and said quietly, "Thank you, Stephen. I won't let you down."

She stood to shake his hand, which then turned into a warm hug. Then she walked away from Stephen's desk in deep thought.

*****

Joslyn Asserts Herself

I needed to ease my tension I felt so I walked over to the window, taking in the beautiful azure sky.

I turned to face them and announced, "I have been reading the leadership books Ron recommends, watching TED talks, and writing in my leadership journal. A few days ago I found an allegory you may be familiar with. I believe it sums up what you and I went through, Stephen. It is called *Burn the Ships*."

Overcoming Reluctance

This is what I told them.

The phrase 'Burn the Ships' comes from a historic conquest of history when, in 1519, Spanish Conquistador Hernando Cortez landed in Mexico on the shores of the Yucatan, with only one objective: to seize the great treasures known to be there, hoarded by the Aztecs. Cortez was committed to his mission and his quest for riches is legendary. Cortez was an excellent motivator; he convinced more than 500 soldiers and 100 sailors to set sail from Spain to Mexico, commanding 11 ships, to take the world's richest treasure. The historic question is 'How did a small band of Spanish soldiers arrive in a strange country and swiftly bring about the overthrow of a large and powerful empire that was in power for more than six centuries?'

For Cortez, the answer was easy. It was all or nothing, a complete and total commitment. Here's how Cortez got the buy-in from the rest of his men: He took away the option of failure. It was conquer and be heroes and enjoy the spoils of victory...or die. When Cortez and his men arrived on the shores of the Yucatan, he rallied the men for one final pep talk before leading his men into battle, and uttered these three words that changed the course of history: 'Burn the ships.'

As the story goes, when the ships were safely anchored in a harbor, he had his men transfer from the ships to their campsite all the supplies, provisions, and anything of use to protect themselves. After this was accomplished and his tough-minded sailors were setting up camp, he ordered that the ships they had arrived in be burned. He announced to his stunned men, 'As long as you have the desire to return to the ships as we face hardships ahead, you will be tempted to do so. You will not feel an urgency to do the exploring we have been asked to do. I burn our ships as a way to remove this desire. Without our ships, there is no turning back.'

He met with resistance from his men. 'Burn the ships,' he repeated. With that, Cortez and his men did it, and by burning their own ships, the commitment level of the men was raised to a whole new level. A level much higher than any of the men, including Cortez, could have ever imagined.[29]

Ron replied, "Cool story."

"I recall that tale," was Stephen's response.

Leadership Lesson

As an explanation, I said, "This is a story about a leader who traveled to distant and unexplored land. His two ships were filled with brave sailors who preferred the sea to land. This leader was afraid that his men would only explore for a short while and that their desire to return to the sea—i.e., their comfort zone—would be too great to resist. He wanted and needed his men to fully explore this strange land and to tap into some of the resources that it offered.

"I believe that I experienced what Cortez's men must have felt like. My livelihood and professional reputations were at risk if I failed. It is not a pleasant experience, but sometimes, or maybe rather often, a high-level executive like me needs a demand like that from her commander in order to find the leader within. Thankfully I am that person."

Ron moved over to me and shook my hand. He told me, "That story sums up what you went through to learn how to stop being reluctant. I am proud of you."

Turning toward Stephen, Ron repeated his praise. "And I am proud of you, Stephen."

---

[29] Wikipedia, *Seven Myths of the Spanish Conquest* by Matthew Restall, Oxford University Press (2003), www.pbs.org/conquistadors/cortes/cortes_d00.html, and other sources

Joslyn Solicits Lesson Learned

Before we ended this meeting, I decided to prove to Stephen that he made a good decision by supporting me, giving me the time and room to grow. I walked back to my chair but didn't sit.

I asked him, "Will you tell me one thing you learned about yourself relating to leading that you would pass on to a future leader?"

After thinking about my question, Stephen looked up at me and responded, "I learned a lot of things, but the one that comes to mind is this: Leadership is a discipline as well as a mindset and a calling. As in any profession, a calling by itself isn't enough. You must put in the time and effort to gain the discipline required to lead others well. I can now recognize when other CEOs and executives fail to understand this about leadership. They seem to think of leadership as a trait or simply a title. Imagine what would have happened if Michael Jordan or LeBron James never practiced."

I said, "I agree."

From his position by the window, Ron commented, "I agree also. With so many reluctant leaders out there, it means that I have a steady source of potential clients!" He grinned at his obvious brag.

I turned to look at Ron and said, "Okay, I'll be the coach for a moment. Of all the things that you've learned through your process, what is the gem that you gleaned from working with me? And I apologize for being difficult."

He didn't need time to think and replied immediately, "Each time I coach a leader—experienced or not—it's a fresh opportunity to discover who they are in terms of their capabilities. This keeps me fresh. My challenge with you was to determine where you were and then intuit the skills you needed for quick results." Laughing, he added, "And in the beginning you were an enigma!"

I laughed, too.

Ron continued. "You were not difficult, just willful. I knew that if I challenged you back with tough love and held up the unflattering feedback mirror repeatedly, you would tap into your courage and tenacity."

My cheeks burned. *I don't care that I'm embarrassed right now.* "I guess that's a lesson learned for both of us…and maybe a compliment for me? What do you think, Stephen?"

Although he chuckled, Stephen wouldn't respond to my bait.

I added, "I can sum up what I learned. First, I was what Ron calls the reluctant leader. Even though I was in a position of leadership, I was not leading. I had not walked through the leadership door purposefully. It was as if I had one foot outside the door and one foot in. Because of this I was having a mostly negative impact on my team and all our employees. I discovered that I was the instigator for many of the personnel and cultural problems here in Neoteric the minute I became CEO. I now own it and I am accountable for fixing it."

Aha! I need to share this. "This afternoon, I will meet with or call everyone on my team individually and tell them what I just told you after you make the announcement, Stephen."

Ron commented, "That's a wise idea."

Stephen nodded that he agreed. "Everyone will have received my email within an hour."

I don't care if this sounds mushy, it needs to be said. "Stephen, I want to thank you for your confidence in me as well as your concern, patience, and support. There are still many repairs I need to make to this great organization, and I am willing to do it because I created them."

I had one more thing to say. "Ron, do you recall when we first met? I think I shouted at you, *Why should I care about leadership. I have a business to run!*"

He smiled, walked over to me and gave me a hug. "I remember it well. You were testing me and also communicating that you didn't need help."

"I apologize for that and all the other excuses I gave and for the roadblocks I put in your way."

A little part of me wanted forgiveness, but I knew he allowed me to be who I was back then so I could become who I am now.

He just grinned and said nothing.

I added, "Now that I see things differently, I'll tell you another lesson I learned: You cannot run a business successfully if you are not a leader. I do care about leadership, and I want to be the best one I can be."

Stephen beamed as he said, "Nicely put."

It seemed like there was nothing more to say other than for me to announce, "Let's get lunch." As we walked out the door, feeling joyful and grateful, I announced, "Lunch is on me. Where do you want to go, Stephen?"

*****

Ron's Final Assessment of Joslyn's Situation

I just love it when someone finds the leader within and takes the time to bring it forth and let it shine. I am grateful to my coaches who showed me how to let the true leader inside of me show up.

Like Stephen and Joslyn, I too experienced a time when I was not acting like a leader. I had many experiences of failing those I led and worked for. It took many painful situations for me to realize I had to find the leader within me. At first I did not have a coach to help me recognize my self-inflicted wounds. Later, when I employed the services of a professional coach, I found that I recovered quicker, and the honest feedback helped remove the many blinders I wore. Maybe it was these embarrassing and sometimes humiliating lessons on how not to lead that became the fuel that fed my unquenchable desire to help people like Stephen and Joslyn become great leaders.

*****

The Bottom Line of Leadership

You may wonder why Stephen didn't fire Joslyn and find a replacement.

The cost of replacing an employee currently runs between 40 percent and 70 percent of the employee's annual salary, depending on the person's level and knowledge. The cost to locate and recruit a highly skilled executive or a technical expert (such as a scientist) would be at the 70 percent level.

If you assume Joslyn's compensation package is $600,000, finding someone to replace her would cost Neoteric approximately $300,000 or more, a figure that does not take into consideration the negative impact on employees, shareholders, and customers, who get very nervous whenever a CEO is terminated or quits unexpectedly. A void at the C-suite level causes a tremendous amount of instability and chaos.

It made economic sense for Stephen to pay for coaching in an attempt to get Joslyn to improve herself rather than to just give up on his investment in her. Plus the termination of a CEO or high-level executive is almost always public knowledge, while mandatory or voluntary coaching is not. Therefore, from a reputational standpoint, it works to Neoteric's advantage to hire a coach to help Joslyn find her way.

Organizations with top-tier leaders outperform their competitors. Buying leadership talent from the outside carries a significant premium when compared to building the leadership pipeline internally.

Organizations with bottom-tier leadership quality experience a 5.8 percent *decline* in total shareholder return relative to their peers over a three-year period.

Organizations with top-tier leadership quality experience a 9.6 percent *increase* in total shareholder return, relative to their peers over the same time[30].

The incremental costs to hire talent from outside of the organization can range from a low of $371,000 to a high of $1,271,000.

The average senior leader in a business holds an average managerial span of control of 112 reports, seven of which are direct and 105 indirect.

A leader truly makes a significant impact in any organization, and hopefully the results or manifestations are positive. As I stated before, the success and failure of any team, company, and nation are ultimately dependent on its leadership. So if the company you work for is great and produces positive results, congratulations! You have great leaders.

But if you are like a majority of organizations and you do not manifest great results, then you must examine the primary source of your problems and decide what to do about the situation.

I sincerely hope that you choose wisely and do the work that can turn every reluctant and ineffective leader into caring, committed people who lead from the High Road.

---

[30] *Navigating Your Way through Succession Planning whitepaper* © 2013 CEB Corporate Leadership Council

How to Use This Book

1. Write your own personal leadership action plan

Based upon what you have learned about yourself, write out a plan for what you will need to do to develop your leadership skills further. If you need assistance, look at suggestion 2.

2. Create a leadership support system

Most reluctant leaders feel the need for assistance to gain the courage and zeal to lead better. We suggest that you find a mentor, seek out a coach, or form a Master Mind group of leaders who are interested in supporting each other's growth.

3. Share *The Reluctant Leader: Own Your Responsibility with Courage* with others

Don't keep this information a secret. Loan the book to a friend, or buy some for colleagues and employees. We offer special pricing for large-quantity purchases. Call 425-898-8072 for details.

4. Provide feedback

We want your thoughts, comments, and ideas on leadership. If you have ideas for future books or publications, please share them by emailing us at Ron@HighRoadInstitute.com

5. Visit www.HighRoadInstitute.com

We offer leadership tools to assist you in growing into the best leader you can be. Sign up to receive Ron's leadership blog posts and video version of the blog.

6. Follow Ron and HRI on your favorite social media platform

You can find The High Road Institute and Ron Rael on Linked In and Facebook. Ron regularly provides insights on Twitter, Google+ and YouTube.

About the Author

Ron Rael is known as the Leadership Provocateur.

Ron is an author and executive coach who delivers state-of-the-art solutions and tools used for developing great leaders. Ron has trained and coached over 10,000 executives, managers, and supervisors throughout the United States and Canada. He has authored 17 leadership related books and more than 60 leadership articles.

Ron is known for his state-of-the-art training techniques and for adeptly facilitating people to immediately apply what they learn. Through his leadership keynotes, training, and written works, Ron inspires people to think, act, and improve.

Ron is CEO and founder of The High Road Institute (HRI) located in Seattle, Washington.

Through this Institute, Ron works with larger organizations and helps them develop effective leaders who are vital in getting people to work together for a common purpose. A leader can make the difference between a business lasting 100 years or failing after one year.

The vision of those working for HRI is that one day every organization will be led by high quality leaders and will prosper by numerous high road influencers who are willing to serve and make a difference.

Schedule Ron Rael,
the Leadership Provocateur
to speak at your next event

Since leadership is mostly an art, people need both insights and real-life experiences to grow into a true leader. Ron is able to develop those experiences for you, your team, and your employees. People will learn to use Ron's innovative tools and be able to apply them immediately. Everyone leaves with a personal commitment to improve, which translates into better results.

Whether your next event has 25 people or 5,000, Ron Rael will use his coaching skills that enable people to lead with courage and conviction. By customizing his materials to your message or purpose and unique culture, each event attendee will leave inspired to lead with his or her heart.

Ron will travel to wherever your next event is held in the United States and abroad.

Ron Rael's speaking style is described as enlightening, entertaining, and inspirational. Relying on his wealth of experiences as a leadership coach, members of his audience feel validated and heard while simultaneously owning the need to be accountable for their own development.

Ron@HighRoadInstitute.com
www.HighRoadInstitute.com

(425) 898-8072

Made in the USA
Columbia, SC
29 November 2017